Self-Directed Learning

George M. Piskurich

Self-Directed Learning

A Practical Guide to Design, Development, and Implementation

Jossey-Bass Publishers • San Francisco

Substantial discounts on bulk quantities of Jossey-Bass books are available to corporations, professional associations, and other organizations. For details and discount information, contact the special sales department at Jossey-Bass Inc., Publishers. (415) 433-1740; Fax (415) 433-0499.

For international orders, please contact your local Paramount Publishing International office.

Manufactured in the United States of America

The paper used in this book is acid-free and meets the State of California requirements for recycled paper (50 percent recycled waste, including 10 percent postconsumer waste), which are the strictest guidelines for recycled paper currently in use in the United States.

The ink in this book is either soy- or vegetable-based and during the printing process emits fewer than half the volatile organic compounds (VOCs) emitted by petroleum-based ink.

Library of Congress Cataloging-in-Publication Data

Piskurich, George M.
　Self-directed learning : a practical guide to design, development, and implementation / George M. Piskurich. — 1st ed.
　　p.　cm.—(The Jossey-Bass management series)
　Includes bibliographical references (p.　) and index.
　ISBN 1-55542-532-1
　1. Adult learning—United States.　2. Occupational training—United States.　I. Title.　II. Series.
LC5225.L42P57　　1993
374'.13943—dc20
　　　　　　　　　　　　　　　　　　　　　　　　93-12369
　　　　　　　　　　　　　　　　　　　　　　　　CIP

FIRST EDITION
HB Printing　10 9 8 7 6 5 4 3 2　　　　　　　　*Code 9334*

The Jossey-Bass
Management Series

Consulting Editors
Human Resources

Leonard Nadler
Zeace Nadler
College Park, Maryland

Contents

Preface

In the field of training and human resource development, particularly in technical and performance skills training, there are few tools as powerful, misunderstood, and misused as self-directed learning (SDL). Modern technology has dramatically increased our ability to provide SDL, but the technology itself often becomes a substitute for well-designed SDL materials and systems. As a result, training and educational programs can look impressive but still fail to help trainees effectively and efficiently learn what they need to know.

Purpose of the Book

Self-Directed Learning provides a practical approach for constructing good SDL programs. As a professional who is constantly seeking better training methods and the right way to employ them, you will find that the book provides the insight you need to perform a proper analysis of needs and abilities, effectively design and develop SDL materials, choose the "right" implementation strategy, and construct solid, useful evaluation tools. In addition, the book explores the reasons why some individuals have difficulty with SDL and the ways in which companies can promote and prepare for SDL. By following the system presented here, you will be able to create SDL packages in various media formats that will meet the needs of both your trainees and your organization—in other words, SDL that works!

My purpose in writing this book is not to convert you to the "religion" of SDL. Such an attempt would be self-defeating, since SDL is simply another training (learning) design. Rather, I hope to make you knowledgeable enough to consider SDL as a possible training design and proficient enough to use SDL when and where it is appropriate to your training needs.

Audience

Self-Directed Learning is written mainly for the training practitioner who has some experience in the field—namely, instructional designers or senior trainers who are familiar with material or program development and training managers or directors of training who understand the need to match training designs with a range of training situations. However, the book's extensive glossary and detailed references in the topic-specific Suggested Readings list make it useful to students of instructional design and to new practitioners. For instance, training novices who may not understand how to perform a needs analysis or exactly what interactive video is can consult the Suggested Readings list to learn enough about these and other concepts to apply them in SDL or to become expert at them if their roles demand it.

The key to this book is that the basics that are discussed here in detail are the basics of SDL. No matter which media format is used, whether it be computer-based training, interactive video, other newer technologies, or a simple print booklet, the system for creating good SDL remains much the same. When you've mastered the basics, you will be well on your way to mastering all formats of SDL.

Although *Self-Directed Learning* is written in and for a business environment and uses business terms for the sake of simplicity and consistency, it is also useful for any educational specialist who is considering SDL. As noted in the first chapter, if you substitute the terms *student* and *learning* for *trainee* and *training*, the concepts will, for the most part, be interchangeable across all learning and instructional environments.

As you read and use the book, you may notice some overlap in topics or areas that seem to be out of sequence. This is because SDL design and development is not a linear process, whereas a book, by its nature, presents things in a linear order. For example, facilitator roles are discussed in the analysis chapter (Chapter Two) and in the chapters that cover preparation of the company (Chapter Seven) and implementation strategies (Chapters Eight, Nine, and Eleven).

Overview of the Contents

Chapter One considers what is meant by the term *self-directed learning,* from both the academic and business points of view, develops a working definition of SDL, and examines SDL's strengths and weaknesses.

Part One covers the development of SDL materials. Chapter Two presents the process of training needs analysis and how it leads to a preliminary design decision, then looks at the various other decisions that must be made in the first stage of planning an SDL intervention.

Chapter Three illustrates how the tasks isolated by the job analysis are turned into objectives and then further refined into content for the SDL package. The chapter discusses the use of subject matter experts for content development as well as developmental shortcuts, such as off-the-shelf programs and consultants.

Chapter Four proposes the addition of media to the SDL package. The chapter considers the print format in detail and discusses other media formats—including audiotape, slide-tape, video, and various computer processes from CBT to multimedia—and explores advantages, disadvantages, and hints for better use.

Chapter Five focuses on trainee evaluation, examining in detail the development of criterion-referenced test questions and considering how performance evaluations can be developed and used in SDL.

Chapter Six discusses the process of reviewing and piloting the SDL package.

Part Two details SDL implementation. Chapter Seven considers the preparation of the company—including top management, supervisors, and, most critically, trainees—for SDL.

Chapter Eight is the first of two chapters concerned with distributed SDL implementation. The chapter outlines the process of implementation, considers the justification for using SDL, and looks at the special costs and design problems that are part of SDL's makeup.

Chapter Nine illustrates the actual implementation of a distributed SDL process. The chapter looks at methods for getting SDL packages to the training sites, provides examples of forms that can be used to maintain control of a distributed system, and discusses special evaluation techniques.

Chapter Ten presents the basics of the learning center implementation. The chapter explores the advantages and disadvantages, then offers information on how to decide to develop a center and how to sell this decision to upper management.

Chapter Eleven provides the "how to" for creating a learning center, discussing location, size, environment, furniture and equipment, hours of operation, internal policies and procedures, how to store and distribute the SDL packages, publicity, and how to evaluate the center's effectiveness.

Chapter Twelve provides a methodology for evaluating any SDL system. The chapter presents the five key criteria and how each can be evaluated, then looks at cost-benefit analysis as it relates to SDL, and finally, considers how to use evaluation data to revise SDL packages and systems.

To minimize confusion and facilitate usability, some material is covered in more than one chapter. This is not repetition or mere rewording but rather my attempt to consider the topic from multiple points of view. When you've completed the book, it should be apparent how all these angles come together to make the whole of SDL.

One of the concepts that both expert and novice alike may find confusing is the distinction between the two SDL strategies of learning center implementation and distributed implementation. The dichotomy affects everything from your decision to use SDL to how you evaluate the finished product. Basically, a learning center implementation occurs when you use a learning center to implement your SDL packages, and a distributed implementation occurs when you do not have a learning center. To put it another way, when your trainees come to a centralized, designated facility to use your SDL packages, you have a *learning center implementation*. If your trainees receive their packages on a job site that has no central

Figure P.1. A Model for SDL.

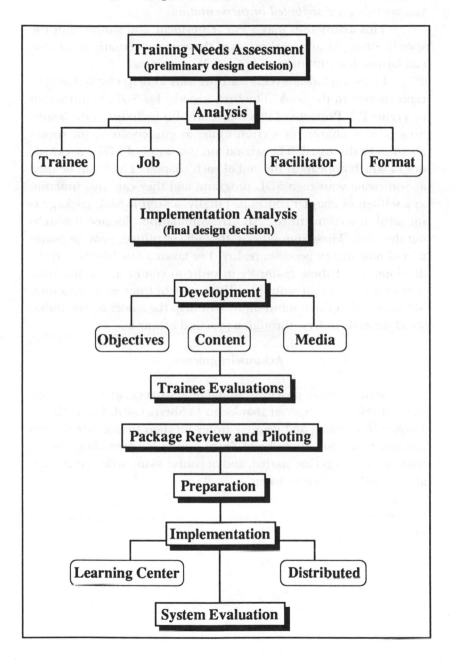

facility, and they are expected to complete the packages on the job, you are using a *distributed implementation.*

This distinction may seem self-evident and simple, but the specific strengths and weaknesses of these implementations are crucial factors that can make or break SDL programs.

I have included several learning aids to help clarify the concepts covered in the book. The first, a model for SDL, is illustrated by Figure P.1. Portions of this figure are also included at the beginning of each chapter or section to act as guideposts to the topics about to be discussed. The second aid is a series of SDL checklists, one of which appears at the end of each chapter. These can be used as you create your own SDL program, and they can also function as a self-test of chapter concepts. Finally, a sample SDL package is included in sections titled "An SDL Simulation" located throughout the book. These simulations, though simplified, provide examples of how theory becomes reality. I've taken a few liberties in the development of these examples in order to compress the information into a form that would be illustrative but not overwhelming. My hope is that these simulations will help the reader better understand the SDL process through a practical example.

Acknowledgments

Many people provided valuable assistance in the development of this book. Special thanks go to Sherri Gaul, Lynn Huler, Jacquie Nekawdzic, and Peggy Painley for their invaluable reviews and assistance, to Leonard and Zeace Nadler for providing the encouragement to get me started, and of course to my wife, Janet, who always finds the time to listen.

Cleveland, Ohio   GEORGE M. PISKURICH
February 1993

The Author

GEORGE M. PISKURICH is director of training and development for Revco Drug Stores, headquartered in Twinsburg, Ohio. He received his B.S. degree (1972) from Pennsylvania State University in biology, his M.Ed. degree (1978) from the University of Pittsburgh, and his Ph.D. degree (1985) from the University of Pittsburgh in curriculum and supervision.

Piskurich has been involved in almost every phase of instructional technology during his career. He has worked as a public school teacher, a media director, a producer of slide and videotape programs, an instructional designer, and a director of training and education in private industry. His special areas of interest include self-directed learning (SDL) and the development of training functions, and he has presented papers before national and international conferences on these topics.

The American Society for Training and Development named Piskurich Instructional Technologist of the Year in 1986 and gave his SDL system an award for best use of instructional technology in business in 1992. He is editor of *The Best of Instructional Technology* (1987) and *The Handbook of Instructional Technology* (1992) and is author of numerous journal articles on SDL, instructional design, customer service, and other topics.

Piskurich is presently exploring the use of self-directed learning centers for choice-directed management/employee development and for retraining the diverse and changing workforce.

Self-Directed Learning

1

Why Self-Directed Learning?

The term *self-directed learning* (SDL) conjures up disparate images: babies in Skinner boxes, or children in a classroom motivated to learn because they are exploring interesting topics in ways that match their personal learning styles; rows of automatons endlessly sitting before teaching machines, rewarded with bits of candy dispensed from a slot in the device, or computer-mediated training programs that are time and cost effective for training one employee or one thousand; self-actuated adult learners taking responsibility for the education that moves them from where they are to the place they want to be, or the anarchy on campuses during the late 1960s, when self-direction seemed to mean that students did only what they wanted; teachers who have lost their status as purveyors of knowledge, or managers who have found the ability to train their staff when the need and the time coincide rather than when the training department says they must attend a class. All these images and more have come under the label of self-directed learning.

Even the terminology of SDL is confusing. *Individualized instruction, prescriptive learning, self-instructional packages, programmed learning, computer-mediated instruction, contract learning, computer-based training, interactive video,* and a dozen other terms are used interchangeably with *self-directed learning.*

Purpose of This Book

This book cannot resolve all the discrepancies in terminology, but it will provide you with a practical method of creating a different type of training or instruction. In the right situations, this

1

method will be more efficient and more effective than classrooms, mentoring, or any of the other instructional designs available to you. For those of you who are training managers or directors, it will be more cost effective, saving you both time and real dollars in your program design and implementation. Simply stated, you are about to learn when, why, and how to use SDL.

You will learn how to assess your need for SDL, design an SDL system, develop SDL materials, and implement and evaluate SDL in your business or educational environment. To help you understand these concepts, I have provided examples of how SDL is being used in the field of human resource development. *By the end of this book, you will be able to decide if SDL is the correct design for a particular training need and will be able to develop an appropriate SDL package or system to meet the need if the decision is yes.*

What Is SDL?

With this as our goal, we'll start by considering SDL from both the training and academic points of view in order to develop a foundation from which to proceed. To begin with, a few comments on the background of SDL may be useful.

History

The first systematic attempts at SDL occurred in the mid to late 1950s, with the advent of programmed instruction and the famous (some say infamous) teaching machines. Like almost every other technological innovation that has hit the fields of training and education, teaching machines and programmed instruction were touted as tools that would revolutionize the way all forms of teaching were done. Unfortunately, like most other technological innovations, they could not achieve this goal and so lost their appeal.

The death knell for programmed instruction sounded in the late 1960s with the push toward more "humanized" education. It's interesting to observe that SDL, which is extremely humanistic since it encompasses concepts such as learner readiness and individual learning differences, has its roots in systems that were considered dehumanizing to the educational process.

In the 1970s, SDL branched out along two different pathways. In the humanized education environment, designs such as individualized learning, learning contracts, and prescriptive learning began to exemplify the concept of learner choice. Meanwhile, in the training setting, self-teaching audiotape programs that soon became filmstrip or slide-tape programs began to appear. While some of these were no more than a lecture with pictures, many were highly creative. They often incorporated sound effects, multiple voices, and live photography in place of the first rudimentary line drawings. The best actually began to employ a learning methodology with objectives, activities, and evaluations. This format reached its peak in the mid 1970s with the process of audiotutorial instruction, a true SDL methodology—but one that was decimated by a still newer technology, the videotape.

Video set SDL back thirty years. It made it possible to take the same boring lecture technique that had been putting students to sleep for generations and distribute it for use at any time, to hundreds of training sites simultaneously. This was the new SDL: world-renowned subject matter experts that trainees could listen to when they had time and as often as they needed to "truly understand." No good design methodology, just convenience, and when these "talking heads" turned out to be as ineffective on tape as they were in person, SDL once again slipped toward oblivion.

SDL was resurrected in the 1980s by still another form of technology, the personal computer. A few individuals were concerned about the term *computer program* because it reminded them of another programmed idea that had already been discarded. However, once again everyone was assured that computer-based instruction was the wave of the future and would soon replace all the other education and training designs. And once again, the prophets were wrong. Trainees and students simply turned off thousands of boring computer-based training (CBT) programs that were poorly designed and poorly executed. Of course, interactive video was extolled as the design panacea in the late 1980s. In the early 1990s, the fad became multimedia.

A Definition of SDL

By now, you may see a pattern. The reality is that no matter how SDL is dressed up with technology or touted by "true believers," it is simply another design methodology. As such, it will work well for some educational and training needs and not well for others. This brings to light an important aspect of SDL as the term is used in this book: SDL is a training design. Or, to be more specific, *SDL is a training design in which trainees master packages of predetermined material, at their own pace, without the aid of an instructor.* This is not the only possible definition of SDL, nor is it all-inclusive for any one learning environment. But it is the one we'll rely on in this book. In the next few pages, we'll compare it to other interpretations of SDL. The point is not so much to familiarize you with these other concepts as to help you understand the dimensions of the definition we are using. From time to time, we will go beyond it to explore how SDL can meet specific human resource development (HRD) needs, but for the most part we will confine the discussion in this book to the boundaries of the definition just given.

A Training Design . . . We'll begin by analyzing our definition of SDL. We've noted that it is a *training design*. This means that it is one of a number of possible methodologies that you might choose to solve a training problem or need. Alternatives might be classroom processes, mentoring, or on-the-job training. Your choice will depend on the nature of your problem, your environment, your resources or lack of them, and the strengths and weaknesses of the various designs. This is what is termed a *design decision;* it is usually made after you have completed your analysis of the performance problem that caused you to think about training in the first place. Chapter Two discusses the process of choosing (or not choosing) SDL as your training design in detail.

In Which Trainees Master . . . The term *master* specifies the evaluation criterion for SDL. Simply stated, it is what the trainees must do to complete the program. The term indicates that the trainees must exhibit a certain level of expertise through the process of criterion-referenced evaluation. There is no curve, no relative or comparative measure, not even a grade. There is simply a preset goal to achieve. Trainees who do not reach this level, no matter how close they come, are not considered to have completed the material. Chapter Five will give you a more complete description of this process.

Packages . . . *Packages* means that SDL divides content into parts. These parts are further subdivided and divided yet again until you get down to pieces that are small enough for a trainee to absorb easily. The trainee masters each of these small pieces in sequence, which leads to mastery of the complete package—and beyond this, the program. The largest pieces are the basically self-contained SDL "packages" that the trainee is given or obtains to begin the training process. When we talk about SDL throughout this book, what we will be discussing is the development, distribution, evaluation, and so on of these packages in their various formats. The package is the *basic* (do not read *smallest*) working unit of SDL.

Of Predetermined Material . . . *Predetermined material* is where this particular definition of SDL diverges from many other SDL paradigms. This phrase signifies that the trainees are, for the most part, not able to choose what they want to learn. Academic definitions often consider learner choice to be one of the major factors that differentiate SDL from other instructional formats. However, in business—which is the basic environment for this definition—certain essentials govern what is and isn't possible in a training design. Decisions such as what material needs to be learned or when the training will take place are often made by others. These decision makers include subject matter experts, supervisors, managers, and executives. The previous concepts of an SDL "package" and "mastery" indicate that there is certain information that the trainee must learn.

These "demands" of business don't prevent features such as learner choice from being characteristics of SDL in other circumstances. There are even times when choice becomes possible in a business environment. For example, an international electronics firm headquartered in the eastern United States uses a series of computer-based SDL packages to train over 30,000 assembly-line employees in the basics of their various positions. After mastering the basic packages, the employees may *choose* to work on packages that deal with advanced assembly techniques to prepare themselves for higher-level jobs.

Choice can also be a factor in a developmental learning center, where packages are available on a number of topics and the users decide which will help them reach various developmental goals.

However, in most training situations—particularly technical and skills training—SDL requires a more structured, less trainee choice–centered approach if it is to meet the needs of the organization. Even the electronics firm just mentioned expects trainees to finish what is needed by the company before they can choose other training topics.

At Their Own Pace . . . The phrase *trainees work at their own pace* is self-explanatory, though in the business environment, this is also achieved within certain limits that are set by the day-to-day needs of the company and by the time it can afford to devote to training. This concept is difficult for supervisors to come to terms with when SDL is introduced to them. They picture trainees spending hours doing one SDL package and not doing any work. Or they see them completing the training on their own time so that no work hours are lost. This is fine for some development processes but will cause wage and hour problems if used for basic training programs. Dealing with this and other management qualms concerning SDL is explored in Chapters Eight through Eleven.

Without the Aid of an Instructor. Finally, the phrase *without the aid of an instructor* can be taken verbatim. SDL packages are self-instructional. An instructor, as disseminator of knowledge, is neither needed nor desirable for a well-done SDL package to be effective. As you will see, there is often the need for a facilitator or a site implementor, and at times a special evaluator, but the instructor is not in the cast of SDL. This tends to make some people—particularly stand-up training specialists—a bit wary of SDL. But, as we've seen, SDL is a *design* and as such does not negate the need for classroom instruction. It simply gives you another alternative in certain cases.

Other Definitions of SDL

SDL has been described as a research thesis, a how-to-do-it handbook, or a single individual in a classroom whose mind suddenly takes that quantum jump beyond what the teacher is teaching. It comes in the guise of open curricula, teleseminars, and adult education classes at the local "Y."

So how does all of this compare with other SDL definitions? Earlier it was noted that one prerequisite of many definitions for SDL is that some type of student choice be involved. This may be as limited as choosing the time during which the learning will occur, may be expanded to include choosing the method by which "predetermined material" will be learned, or can go as far as student determination of the material itself. Conceptually, SDL has been defined as:

- A process of mutual inquiry between the teacher and the student (Hiemstra and Sisco, 1990)
- Complete independence from a teacher (Long, 1990)
- A personality characteristic of learners (Long, 1990)
- The selection and/or modification of course materials to illuminate particular objectives, structured in a way to allow the students to carry out the learning (Rowntree, 1986)
- A process in which learners take the initiative for analysis and diagnosis of their learning needs, formulation of personally relevant learning goals, identification of how to achieve them, and reflection on their achievement (Knowles, 1975)

As *contract learning*, SDL has been defined as a belief that everyone is capable of self-directed involvement and should assume the responsibility for making material, technique, and evaluative choices as part of their writing of a performance-based contract with the instructor (Gagne, Briggs, and Wagner, 1988).

As *self-instructional packages*, SDL involves learning the material without instructor mediation.

As *individualized instruction*, SDL may include individualization of pace, materials, objectives, content, or methods at the behest of the student, the teacher, the instructional system, or any combination thereof (Romiszowski, 1986).

As *audiotutorial instruction*, SDL is a procedure in which the learner must carry out all learning activities in an active study mode using slide-tape programs complete with diagrams, performance practices, and written workbooks (Mentzer, 1974).

As *distance instruction,* SDL involves learners learning without regular face-to-face contact with teachers (Rowntree, 1986).

As computer-based training, SDL utilizes a computer program designed to support instruction by providing a learner with display prompts, instructions, information, and interactive exercises on a specific subject.

As *interactive video or multimedia,* SDL is a process in which trainee contact with content experts and other trainees is minimized in favor of explicitly specified and approved content scripted for exact visualization and wording, presented through the use of computers and computer video machines, and evaluated through quantifiable scores and other performance measures.

Training Versus Instruction

In short, much of what went into our working definition of SDL is contained in these other definitions, and much is not. Some consider these differences to exemplify the disparity between the concepts of education and training, or between HRD and academic approaches. My reason for presenting them to you is not to get involved in this controversy, but simply to acknowledge that there are many forms of SDL and to reemphasize that this book is only considering one of them, as it relates to training and HRD.

To further reinforce this point, the use of the terms *instruction, teacher,* and *learner* will be curtailed in the rest of the book. In their place, the more HRD-related terms of *training, trainer,* and *trainee* will be used. However, this should not be construed to mean that the rest of the book is not useful in other instructional environments. These sets of terms are basically interchangeable and can be easily substituted for each other or even combined, depending on your particular circumstance. In reality, terms such as *learning,* as in *learning organization,* and *education,* as in an *Education and Training Department,* are so prevalent in industry that the distinction is disappearing. The choice of one particular set is partly for simplicity's sake and partly to remind the reader of the environment from which the information in this book comes.

Advantages and Disadvantages of SDL

With our definition firmly in mind, let's look at the pros and cons of this training design.

Advantages

I've tried many times to categorize the major strengths of SDL in such a way as to make valid comparisons to other designs. I've divided them into time and cost considerations, listed them by effectiveness and efficiency measures, and developed point-to-point lists. However, the method I always seem to return to is to compare how each design solves the basic training problems of my training situation.

Every training design has advantages and disadvantages that become more or less important depending on the training situation. How these advantages and disadvantages match up with your particular training needs is one of the basic pieces of data you use in deciding which training design is best.

Classroom training has the advantage of being able to handle large numbers of trainees simultaneously. Of course, a major disadvantage of this approach is that it does not allow for individual differences in learning style to any great degree. If individualization is important in your training scheme, classroom training may not be your best choice.

On-the-job training, on the other hand, is an excellent design for performance training and can be very individualized. However, it has the disadvantage of being basically a one-to-one process, and so it is inefficient if you have large numbers to train.

As these examples suggest, the trick is to compare the basic strengths and weaknesses of each design in relation to your needs, and then to choose the one that looks like it will work best.

For instance, suppose you face a training situation where you have a large number of trainees (let's say 10,000) spread around a large number of training sites (maybe 500 or so). You need to train them on the basic policies and procedures that are necessary to do their relatively nontechnical but skills-based jobs within a week or two of their being hired. And we'll throw in one more kicker: your turnover is approximately 50 percent per year!

One of your basic problems is how to get to all those individuals in a reasonably short period. A classroom design would require the hiring of hundreds of trainers, who will wear out quickly from being on the road all the time and will cost lots of money to keep on the road. You'll spend even more money for training sites like hotel rooms. And a hotel room may not be the right place to train at all, since you almost certainly need to do some skills training. Another consideration is whether all these trainers will be consistent enough for policy and procedures training.

While you'll solve the problem of too many expensive trainers if you choose an on-the-job training design, you'll be left with the same consistency question. Other concerns include whether you have the right people out there to be trainers, whether they have the time, how to train them, and how to evaluate their part in the training.

If SDL is a training design, it works best where the training problems relate directly to its strengths. These include the following:

- *Availability when the training is needed,* not when a class is being held
- *Nonreliance on an instructor,* which not only increases availability but decreases cost, since you don't have trainers on the road gobbling up budget dollars in travel costs and wearing themselves out doing the same thing time after time
- *On-site implementation,* so the trainees don't waste time and money traveling either; also, if there are skills to be learned, they can be learned and practiced in the same environment in which they will be performed
- *Consistency of presentation,* because you have your SDL packages presenting the same information exactly as *you* want it done instead of a partly trained on-the-job training instructor doing it who thinks he or she knows a better way

Other advantages include *trainee readiness* and *individualization.*

In case you're thinking, "But I don't have 500 training sites or 10,000 trainees," let's look at a different basic training problem.

Suppose you have only one training site, perhaps a corporate head-quarters or a manufacturing plant. You're handling technical training through classes and on-the-job training and even have time to run a supervisory skills class or two.

But what about those supervisors who are working second and third shift, or who can't fit the classes in when they are offered? What about the clerical staff, or that new computer software program that everyone wants to learn how to use? What about management development? Well, there are always off-site seminars—those excellent, expensive, uncontrolled, "we can only afford to send one of you to it" seminars.

Your answer could be a self-directed learning center. In it, SDL packages on supervision can be available to any supervisor when he or she has the time to use them. Clerical programs ranging from policies and procedures to speed typing can be on the shelves. A tutorial on that new computer software might be found there. As for management development, how about video programs on everything from motivation to strategic planning? Add to these perhaps a simple assessment process to determine individual development needs and prescribe various programs from those available. (The price of a good video program is usually less than the fee for a seminar, and it can be seen by hundreds instead of one.) Even some of your classroom technical skills material could end up in the center, thus freeing your trainers to do more development instead of continuous teaching.

The reason I picked these two training scenarios to illuminate SDL advantages and not others just as relevant is that they illustrate the two most basic strengths of SDL: *efficient multiple-site instruction* and *high individual flexibility*. These strengths coincide with the two implementation scenarios of SDL, the learning center and distributed implementation.

Individual Flexibility. The latter scenario describes the real-life situation of a petroleum refining and distribution company in Pennsylvania whose learning center provides individual flexibility for their management development program. An assessment of the 350 management and supervisory positions at this company found a large variation in the skill level of incumbents and in the types of skills that were needed at the various management levels. Instead of following the usual corporate route of running a series of classes that covered the most obvious needs or that presented the skills most common to all levels, the company developed a learning center. In this center, it placed SDL programs that encompassed *all* of the skills that were determined as needs by the assessment. Most of these programs were purchased, which proved to be a time-effective approach, since the information was fairly generic. A few others were developed in-house to meet specialized needs of the company. Supervisors and managers use the center programs to remediate their own individual weaknesses and to develop new skills for higher-level positions.

Multiple-Site Instruction. The first scenario, which dealt with multiple-site instruction, came from my own experience working in a large retail environment. My staff and I used a distributed SDL system in which simple print SDL packages that dealt with every task a retail clerk had to perform were sent to each of 2,000 stores. Distributed SDL will be discussed in more detail in later chapters, but for now, let's just say that you use distributed SDL when you have multiple training sites that don't contain designated learning centers.

With this approach, we were not only able to train all 20,000 current employees simultaneously, but we had a system that dealt effectively and efficiently with a 70 percent turnover rate among full-time employees. The number of trainers needed to do this by a classroom design would have been cost prohibitive, and some type of mentoring or "buddy" system would have been too inconsistent for policies and procedures training. SDL was not only the best way but the only way to train under these circumstances.

Cost Reduction. These scenarios also exemplify some of the other advantages of SDL. One is the reduction of the administrative costs of doing training, particularly travel and possibly salary costs for field trainers. A more direct instance of this cost reduction can be found in the insurance industry. A large Northeastern underwriter was bringing its ninety sales representatives to the main office for product knowledge training on an average of three times a year. The cost of this process when travel, hotel, and lost productive time were added together was approximately $4,700 a year per sales representative.

The company changed to a video-based SDL approach where each representative received three to five tapes a year. Each dealt with a new product or better way to do the job. Each tape came with a trainee guide. The guides included a series of written simulations for the employee to complete after finishing the video. These simulations were sent back to the main office for review. If weaknesses were noted, the district manager was notified to initiate remedial training on an individual basis.

The training director's guesstimate was that this program was saving the company close to $500,000 a year. This figure took into account the cost of developing, reproducing, and mailing the videos. Part of this cost savings was used to bring the sales representatives together once a year for training on material that didn't fit the SDL mode, such as interactive sales training techniques. This was done at a fancy resort instead of at the corporate offices! The rest of the savings went right into the corporate bottom line.

A computer software firm located in Texas used a different SDL approach to save both travel time and administrative costs. It had the problem of needing to send trainers to its many distributors each time it put a new or upgraded product on the market.

As you might expect, the SDL packages it now sends to its distributors instead of trainers involve CBT. Not only is the company saving on travel costs, but it has reduced its need for trainers. Valuable developers, who once spent time on the road training, have been reassigned to software development activities. The decrease in "on-the-road" time, with its associated wear and tear, has also made the permanent trainers more productive and a lot happier.

Time Effectiveness. Yet another SDL advantage is in its relationship to downtime and crisis time. A major medical center near San Francisco has instituted a learning center where both technical knowledge and self-improvement programs are available for its 900-person nursing staff. The technical programs are developed by a hospital SDL designer in concert with nursing subject matter experts. Much of the self-improvement and continuing education programming is bought "off the shelf." When the patient load is light or staffing is high, what might be referred to as "downtime" is created. During these intervals, a few of the nurses can leave their assigned floors and go to the center to take advantage of the programs.

Using the center instead of classes for technical and continuing education programs also gives the head nurse a choice when the hospital is full or staffing is down because of illness, vacations, and so on. This might be termed "crisis time." During these periods, instead of leaving her floor shorthanded to send people to a scheduled class or ignoring the class and hoping it will be rescheduled, she can put off training until the next occurrence of downtime. The training department becomes more efficient as well, because it doesn't spend time giving half-full classes where even those in attendance may be called out for emergencies at any time.

To further augment this downtime training system, the center prepares mobile carts with a number of programs on them that are left on the patient floors for the night shift. Since night shifts are often short staffed, nurses usually can't leave the floor. However, since the patients are normally asleep and require less care, there is often time for training using SDL programs available at the nursing stations on the mobile carts.

This SDL advantage of making it possible to put off the training until next week because this week happens to have more than its share of crises is tremendously useful in erratic workflow environments like the health care setting. The same is true of "just-in-time" manufacturing environments.

"Just-in-Time" Training. "Just in time" as a training process is another strength of SDL, and one that takes full advantage of trainee readiness. It is exemplified at a specialty machining company located in Silicon Valley. The workforce here is small, less than sixty full-time employees, but there are a number of different complex machines in use on the shop floor. Thus there is minimal overlap of expertise among operators.

Each machine has been equipped with its own SDL video package that explains the basics of how to use it. If someone without previous experience has to run a particular machine, the would-be operator completes the specific SDL package first. Each package includes several practice exercises and a final performance test evaluated by the shop manager. The trainee is motivated to learn because he or she will immediately be using the machine. The immediate use also reinforces the learning, and so it increases confidence and proficiency. This method allows the company to quickly have someone ready to take the place of the missing operator.

The company also uses its SDLs for cross training and review. Employees are trained during slow periods on machines they may not be using immediately. The package is then available as a quick review and reference tool when the cross-trained employee needs to operate the machine. This reduces the learning time even further when a crisis develops and gives the employees a sense of advancement as they learn new skills.

Dealing with Individual Learning Differences. An entire class of SDL advantages is related to its ability to take into account individual learning differences, particularly in that it allows trainees to proceed at their own pace toward mastery. To exemplify this, we can turn once again to a health care setting.

A Cleveland hospital's training department was given the task of training the institution's 750 nurses and aides—many of whom had never used a computer—on newly computerized admission and discharge techniques. The SDL program it developed employed the actual machines the staff was going to use to teach them the tasks they needed to master.

Ten of these machines were placed in a room with a trained facilitator, and informal classes were run every two hours for a few weeks. The classes were termed "informal" since the facilitator only introduced the topic and taught the trainees how to reach the main menu on the machine. From there on, the accompanying workbook guided each trainee individually through the learning.

Those with some computer experience or who took to the process easily finished quickly and were back to their duty stations long before a typical instructor-mediated class would have ended.

Trainees who had problems with either the material or the concept of computerization were identified and aided by the facilitator. Since in most classes there were only one or two trainees who had major difficulties, the facilitator could literally work one on one with these individuals. The other trainees completed the training and went back to work as their own individual abilities dictated.

Using this method, 98 percent of the trainees mastered the

material and were able to do the tasks competently back on the job. Further analysis found that the other 2 percent had reading disabilities that precluded their use of the computer completely. It's unlikely that this fact would have been discovered had the training been done using a classroom approach.

The whole approach was not only effective for the trainees' learning but efficient for the hospital as well. Taken from an aggregate point of view, SDL is one of the fastest methods of learning.

The following list summarizes the SDL advantages we've discussed and a few others as well.

Trainee

Available when trainee is ready
Trainee works at own pace
Individual choice of material
No surprises
Immediate feedback
Provides review and reference

Trainer/Developer

No constantly repeated classes
Less time on road
More time to develop

Corporation

Multiple-site training
Reduced meeting-room cost
Capture knowledge of subject matter experts
Requires fewer trainers
Reduced trainer travel cost
Eliminates trainee travel costs
Just-in-time training
Downtime training
No training classes when busy
Easier shift training
Cross training possible
Training consistency (quality)

Development programming
Less aggregate time spent

I'm sure that other SDL designs can add to the list, but this should be enough to get you thinking. The important thing to remember is that whether you want to use it because it frees trainers from travel or frees them up at home to do more course development, reduces costs or increases efficiency through use of downtime training, provides for individualization or takes into account trainee readiness, SDL is a training design. It is cost effective whether you are a small company or a large one or are training at one site or many—but only if you use it where it works. Take advantage of its strengths when they will do you the most good and don't try to force it into situations where it won't be effective.

Disadvantages

Even though SDL is a highly advantageous design in many training situations, it has, as you might expect, some disadvantages as well. These weaknesses have to be considered as carefully as the advantages when deciding to use it or not.

Logistics Problems. One possible disadvantage was noted in the example of the insurance company and was even more acute in my retail scenario, though I didn't remark on it. For large distributed systems, there are significant reproduction and distribution cost and logistics problems, particularly if you use more complex media such as video.

Each time you add a training site to your system, you increase the costs of material and reproduction. Large distributed systems will also create problems when you need to revise your material. This is a particular problem if you have many packages in the field or if you use more exotic forms of media that are not easily revised. Cost, time, and logistics all work against you when revisions are needed. Unlike the situation illustrated by the insurance company, you are seldom lucky enough to be able to prove that the extra costs are outweighed by the costs associated with the previous training methods. Often there are no previous training methods to compare it with.

At a large bank not long ago, I ran across one video-based distributed SDL system in use that had fallen out of favor with those that mattered most—the supervisors of the trainees. The reason was that the tapes were out of date. The training department simply did not have the staff to revise the tapes or the budget to keep duplicating and sending out new copies as policies and procedures changed. The supervisors found the old tapes worse than useless because the tellers were expected to follow the new procedures. The whole system had basically fallen apart, with training being conducted on a one-to-one basis as it had been before the video process was installed.

Development Obstacles. A second disadvantage is that the actual development costs of SDL are very high, simply because development time is much greater than usual. SDL packages must stand on their own, because no instructor will be available for filling in the gaps. In a class, the instructor can sew up the loose edges or clarify points the developer did not explain in enough detail. With SDL, your analysis, development, and review processes must be much more extensive than in a classroom lesson plan.

This added development time creates another disadvantage: if your situation demands quick solutions, you may not have the time to develop your SDL packages properly, with strong analysis, good objectives, proper media, and so on. And for SDL, more than any other training intervention, your motto must be *"If you can't do it right, don't do it at all."* No matter what advantages an SDL approach will give you, if for one reason or another your deadlines for getting the training out are tight, you should consider other designs.

I saw a perfect example of this problem occur on a consulting assignment. We were asked to develop an SDL package for a new computerized cash register system at a retail clothing outlet. The problem was that the software for the computer system wasn't quite developed yet. Unfortunately, organizational demands made it imperative that the implementation begin on the first day of the new fiscal year. We should have turned down the assignment, but we were assured that all of the "training aspects" had been decided on and wouldn't change. They weren't, and they did, and one month before the implementation date, we were still changing objectives in the package. Needless to say, SDL was not the design that was finally used to do the training. We did develop the packages later, and they worked just fine for training new employees, but we had the time to *do it right* then.

Loss of the Synergism of Group Learning. Yet another disadvantage is that in SDL, trainees are usually working alone. There are times when you need a group—for example, if the material demands role plays or person-to-person interactions. Modern technologies such as interactive video and multimedia CBT can simulate some of these processes, but development costs often skyrocket when complex simulations are needed. And no technology can duplicate the synergism that occurs when groups of learners work together. If this is what your material demands, SDL may not be a wise choice.

SDL is Unfamiliar. The fact that SDL is not a well-recognized form of instruction, unlike, for example, the classroom approach. This means that you will need to define and in all probability sell the concept to your company, starting with the CEO or at least the COO and working your way down.

In other words, you will need to prepare everyone in your company for this new and different form of training. You won't have to contend with varying definitions as you might if you were dealing with other trainers or educators. However, you'll probably have the problem that no one understands what you're talking about at all when you say *SDL*. So be prepared to define your conceptualization in detail, but in terms that the uninitiated will understand.

This preparation of the company does not stop at higher levels, as often occurs with other training designs, but must continue all the way to your first-line supervisors. These individuals will make the final decision on how effective your program is, simply by allowing their employees time to use your SDL packages or go to your learning center or by refusing to do so. Such multilevel preparation will take you more time in more meetings, with a lot more planning, but will be worth it.

Fortunately, selling and preparation can be a simple process if you have a quality training package that solves the problem and looks impressive—which you will have if you follow the steps of good SDL development discussed in this book. Some of your audience, particularly those first-line supervisors, will be sold by your thoroughness and the efficiency of your packages. Others will buy in because of how good they look. Both reasons are acceptable. Your top management will be impressed when you show them how SDL can be cost effective by reducing travel and classroom costs and how it is time effective for the trainees.

The point isn't how you impress management but that they are impressed, at all levels. This helps get you the support you need to control the process of implementing SDL in your company.

SDL and Control. The idea of control is critical to SDL, and lack of control can be a major—in fact, an almost insurmountable—disadvantage. In one of the health care examples described earlier, we found that the ability to put off training until next week if this week is too busy is an advantage of SDL. It can also be a disadvantage, because in some companies, next week never seems to come.

Control measures like completion records, management monitoring, and honest evaluation are necessary to ensure success, and these only work if there is plenty of commitment to the process from the top on down. There are many examples of marvelous SDL packages that were never used simply because the trainees' supervisors didn't believe in them. Most of these processes didn't have enough control measures built in to recognize and remedy this situation. You can avert such disasters in your own SDL system by carefully preparing everyone at every level for SDL. This preparation gathers the support that leads to the control you'll need to make your SDL work.

Trainee Fears. Preparing everyone also means preparing the trainees. A few theorists have stated that the personal responsibility engendered by SDL is a natural and preferred way for people to learn (Dewey, 1938; Penland, 1979; Knowles, 1980). This is probably true, but by the time they have made it through our school system, few people are comfortable with true SDL. Thus, trainees who have not been prepared for and introduced to SDL can easily become a major impediment to the success of your SDL.

You need to prepare the trainees to be responsible for learning on their own and for having no instructor to fall back on. Most important, you have to convince them that the objectives they find in your SDL packages are truly all they need to know. They need to be assured that there aren't any hidden meanings, trick test questions, or war stories full of useless information.

This requires a lot of discussion and then completion of a package or two where they find that what you promised is true. However, if you do your trainee preparation well and prepare the rest of the company so the trainees are given the chance to use them, SDL packages will soon be the only way your trainees want to be trained. That in itself can be another problem.

I've actually seen letters addressed to the training director of one company that instituted an SDL system asking for the rest of the classes to be dropped in favor of more SDL packages. It seems that the instructors were not following the objectives as closely as the trainees thought they should. They felt that they could "learn better if allowed to do it ourselves." If you don't understand why I consider this a problem, you need to remember our definition of SDL as a training design. As such, it is not correct in all circumstances. Following is a summary of the disadvantages we've discussed, together with a few additions.

Trainee

Not used to being a self-directed learner
Lack of an instructor
Not comfortable relying on objectives
Needs synergism of group

Trainer/Developer

Difficult to develop material properly
Choice of media limited
Must revise more often
More trainee preparation needed
Development time greater
Selling concept harder
Control needs greater

Corporation

Production costs higher

Reproduction costs higher
Distribution costs higher
Revision costs higher
Possible logistics problems

SDL disadvantages and problems exist and need to be considered, but don't lose sight of the advantages we have discussed. And there are other advantages of self-directed learning that we didn't even explore here, such as SDL's usefulness in structuring OJT, its ability to make large-scale training highly consistent, which is a prerequisite to any total quality process, and its ability to take advantage of SME expertise, even if that expertise has physically left the company.

In a Houston-based high-tech research organization that I know of, it is mandatory that each technical expert describe on videotape what he is doing each year. They also get a more complete compilation of each expert's expertise before they retire or otherwise leave the company. These tapes are turned into video SDL packages by training developers so that even after the experts are gone, new researchers can learn from them.

How to take advantage of the strengths of SDL while eliminating or at least circumventing its weaknesses will be the focus of the rest of this book. By using what is presented in the following chapters, you will be able to add to your design toolkit a method for developing effective SDL packages—packages that will enhance your trainees' ability to learn and make the training process more efficient for your company.

Why use SDL? *Because it works!*

An SDL Simulation

To help illustrate the concepts we will be discussing, you'll find an ongoing narrative concerning the construction of an SDL package at various points throughout this book. In this simulation, we will develop an example SDL package and will hopefully make some of the theories more of a reality for you.

Part One

Developing
Effective Programs

2

When to Use
Self-Directed Learning (SDL)

Analyzing Training Needs
and Program Requirements

The first step in using SDL is to decide whether you *can* use it. This means you need to assess and analyze a number of factors ranging from your organizational environment to the trainees who will be using your programs. In some instructional design models, this is called the *analysis phase*. In others, it is considered part of the design process.

The process that will be used in this book for creating SDL is based on a model called Instructional Systems Design (ISD). Readers who are used to this model will notice some differences, but basically SDL is developed along the ISD phase approach. (New practitioners who have not dealt with ISD before should consult the Suggested Readings for background information on similarities and differences between the two models.)

The important point to grasp in this chapter is that the first step in SDL is good analysis. You will see your analysis data referred to again and again as we work our way through SDL development and implementation. It is the foundation on which proper SDL is built.

The Design Decision

By now you should have a pretty fair idea of what SDL is and how it has been used in other training settings. So the question you're probably asking is, "Is SDL right for me in my situation?"

That's a good question. In fact, it's the first question you should ask any time you consider using SDL. Remember, by our definition SDL is a training design, one of many possible designs that you can employ. You need to decide if it is the right design for your training need. Too often, trainers become enamored of a certain design and literally do not think before deciding to use it. A good example of this is what occurred in the early days of CBT.

When this form of training first became popular, many trainers decided they wanted to try it. But they often failed to consider its adaptability to their particular situation, which led to some ineffective programs. The designers developed them correctly, but the original decision to use a CBT design was not necessarily a wise one. In some companies, CBT never recovered from this first failure.

Another example of this lack of design consideration is some trainers' overdependence on classroom instruction. When a training program is needed, a classroom scenario is designed and developed, with no thought to other, possibly more effective or efficient designs. "Classes are what we do, so a class is what we'll have." It doesn't matter if a self-directed video might be more effective or a mentoring system more efficient; to some designers, training means classes.

To guard against becoming a "classroom addict," or an "SDL addict" for that matter, you need to take the time to consider the possibilities carefully. Then make an informed decision on which design to use. This is often termed a *design decision,* for obvious reasons.

Needs Assessment

A prerequisite to making a design decision is knowing what your training needs are and which ones are most critical. In Instructional Systems Design, which is a systematic process for developing training and a useful model for SDL development, this is termed the *analysis phase.* It begins with a training needs assessment (Figure 2.1).

A strong training needs assessment is important to any training design, but perhaps especially so to SDL. This is because so much of the time and energy spent on SDL occurs early in the

Figure 2.1. A Model for SDL.

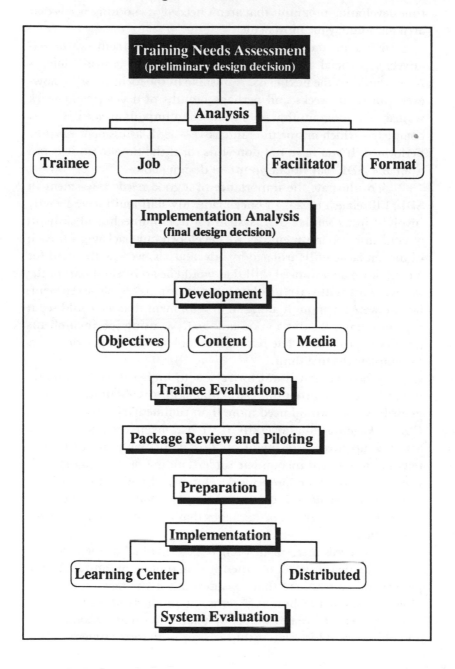

development process. You can't afford to waste large amounts of time developing programs that aren't needed or choosing needs that aren't absolutely the most acute.

For some training designs, the needs assessment can be relatively superficial. If a mistake is made, it can be adjusted later—for example, in the next class. A mistake in the focus of SDL, however, can mean weeks and perhaps months of development work wasted on a program that doesn't meet an important need. Thus a complete—which means time-intensive—needs assessment *must* be performed. If you have not done this, or if the time to do it is not available, SDL may not be your best design choice.

To illustrate the importance of a good needs assessment in SDL, I'll relate a mistake I once made. My staff and I were heavily involved in a complex SDL system for teaching technical skills in a retail store environment. As we developed our packages for each of the ten basic skills isolated by our analysis, we saw the need for a module on an advanced skill that would be an integral part of the system. This skill wasn't isolated in our original needs assessment, but we were far enough along in development that we could see it was important. We did a good task analysis using job incumbents and developed a complete package. It took about 500 person-hours to complete the first draft.

When we sent it out for review to higher-level administration, we found out that this particular skill was about to be downgraded. No one would need more than rudimentary training on it. Our package was total overkill. If we had taken a few hours to do a follow-up needs assessment on this particular topic instead of relying on our own incomplete understanding of the situation, we would have saved 500 precious development hours. This is what a needs assessment does. It protects you from spending time and money developing programs or packages that are not needed, or worse, not wanted.

The needs assessment itself is as individual as the company or designer that initiates it. Often it is part of an organizational or performance assessment that considers factors far beyond training. However, no matter how it is done, its product—in our case, the training needs it isolates—must be related to organizational goals and objectives. This relationship is your primary argument in sell-

---

An SDL Simulation

A corporate goal for this fiscal year is to develop incumbent first-line managers by making them more efficient at the tasks they need to perform. You perform a needs assessment in relation to this corporate goal by talking to the managers themselves and to their superiors. One of your findings is that a number of first-line managers are weak in time-management skills. You decide this problem can be solved through training.

---

ing the concept of SDL (or any training, for that matter) to top management. Without a clear relation to organizational needs, it will be difficult to get top management to "buy into" your training structure. And without their support, it will be impossible to create a training package, program, or system that works.

Examples of various needs assessment tools and products can be found in the books and articles listed under "Needs Assessment" in the Suggested Readings list. If you are new to this concept, you will probably want to browse through at least one or two of these sources before you continue with your study of SDL.

Making a Design Decision for or Against Using SDL

With solid information on your training needs in hand, you now have to make a design decision to use (or not use) SDL. This should be based on factors that represent the strengths and weaknesses of SDL, as discussed earlier. One problem is that they come in no particular order or progression. Many of the factors are so interrelated that at times it's difficult to say where one begins and the other ends. To simplify the situation, I've found it is sometimes best to start by considering the negatives—that is, reasons why you would not want to use SDL.

Time as a Negative Factor. The first and probably most important of these is time—development time, to be exact. There are plenty of estimates and guesstimates concerning development time. On average, you can assume that it will take you at least two to three times as long to develop an SDL package as it does to develop a good classroom program. If you are going to get into more exotic forms of medialike computers or interactive video, you can double and even quadruple that number. And this does not take into account the much longer and more complicated review process for SDL, which will be discussed in Chapter Six.

Basically, if you have either internal or, as is often the case, external pressure to get a program out by a short, absolute deadline, SDL is probably not the design to use—unless, of course, no other design will do. This is where it starts to get complicated.

In one case that I am familiar with, a trainer was asked to develop a training system for a large retail company that had no training to speak of. At first glance, time might not seem to be a major factor here. The company had been going along without training for years and could probably continue for a while longer. In actuality, the company was near bankruptcy. While lack of training was an unlikely cause, it was assumed to be a contributing factor, particularly by top management (those external pressures I just mentioned). Thus, time constraints would dictate not using SDL.

On the other hand, the company had almost 2,000 training sites in twenty-six states but only twenty trainers in the field. Add to this a turnover of the training population that was approaching 120 percent and you will probably come up with the same answer as the training director did. The firm developed an SDL system as quickly as it could.

Dealing effectively with such complications requires a careful consideration of both your needs and the possible alternatives. When everything has been analyzed, make the best possible design decision under the circumstances. Then work at selling it to those external pressure makers. *Remember, design decisions are usually a compromise between what is best and what is possible.*

Other Negative Factors. You may decide against an SDL design for other reasons, including the following:

- The *content* is either so affective or performance oriented that it makes SDL difficult to develop, and more important, evaluate.

- The *environment* is so dynamic that the material is constantly changing.
- *Subject matter experts* are not available to the extent you need them to develop and review the material.
- *Publishing* the packages will be difficult, since you don't have the necessary facilities or expertise.
- *Learners* will be unable to learn without verbal instruction (literacy problems).
- *Facilitators* are not available or cannot provide feedback where necessary.
- *Commitment* from management to support the development time and implementation plan is lacking.
- *Capital* is not available for a learning center or the necessary machinery.

Positive Factors. On the positive side, your analysis might cause you to decide in favor of SDL. This would occur if you encountered conditions such as the following:

- *High turnover* exists, which means that training must be given often.
- There are *multiple training sites,* which create the need for more instructors than you can afford.
- *Travel costs* are high for instructors and don't even account for their personal wear and tear.
- The organization has a *small staff* whose time could be better spent developing than running from place to place.
- A need for *standardization of instruction* exists to ensure that everyone is doing the job in a consistent manner. This is a prerequisite for producing a quality product.
- There is a critical need for each individual to achieve *mastery* of the material.
- Major *time constraints* exist, since—though these are a disadvantage as far as development is concerned—they can be an important strength in implementation. An SDL design can be implemented almost simultaneously in all areas and facilities of the company, no matter where they are located.
- *Money constraints* occur because there are situations where the

total development, implementation, and long-term continuation of an SDL design make it cheaper than any other system.
- *Individualization* is critical, because of multiple training or development needs of the target population.

This list is not exhaustive, but it does give you a good idea of the questions you need to ask. It also suggests some of the interrelation-

Exhibit 2.1. Twenty Questions to Ask Before Using SDL.

If you answer no to Questions 1 through 12, you may want to reconsider the appropriateness of SDL in your training situation.

1. Is the content cognitive or performance oriented, rather than attitudinal?
2. Can the material be understood without immediate verbal feedback from an instructor?
3. Is the content fairly stable?
4. Has a job task analysis been done, or is it possible to do one?
5. Are subject matter experts available and willing to help write content, and will they be given the time to both write and review?
6. Can the material be easily facilitated?
7. Does the material follow some sort of linear progression?
8. Is demonstrated mastery possible?
9. Are facilitators available?
10. Do you have a way to conveniently format and publish your materials?
11. Are the learners capable of reading and understanding written content?
12. Do you have commitment from management to support the development process in terms of time (yours and subject matter experts') and the implementation strategy in terms of dollars?

If you answer yes to Questions 13 through 20, SDL is appropriate for your organization.

13. Is it important that the learner work at his or her own pace?
14. Are the learners starting with the same experience levels?
15. Is standardization (consistency) of learning important?
16. Are your training sites dispersed?
17. Do you have large numbers to be trained or high turnover?
18. Do you have a limited number of trainers?
19. Is it important to train the trainee in a specific period of time?
20. Will the cost (both money and time) of SDL development be cheaper than the long-term cost of implementing a classroom program?

An SDL Simulation

As you consider possible training designs, you find that one of your biggest problems is that your target population of forty-five first-line managers works different shifts at different times in three widely separated locations. A classroom-based training program would necessitate holding the class at least nine times to cover all trainee schedules, and this doesn't include vacations or emergencies. You are a one-person department, so this means taking up a lot of your time and some travel budget. Mentoring is out, because the second-level managers aren't well informed about time management either, and on-the-job training doesn't seem the right approach. You have the time to develop the program, and the content is stable enough. Mastery isn't terribly important, nor is standardization a real issue, but there are enough indicators to make a preliminary design decision to use an SDL approach.

---

ships that can occur when considering the usefulness of an SDL design to meet your training need.

There are situations where some of the factors—time and money are good examples—can be simultaneously positive and negative. Your problem is to make the correct decision by weighing all the factors you can find. Your charge is to do it right, not to take the easy way out by choosing the design you know best or the one you always wanted to try. To give you some help, I've provided a checklist in Exhibit 2.1. Use it when considering SDL for your training design.

Job Analysis

So you've considered all the advantages and disadvantages, and your decision is to use an SDL design. Now what? To begin, you need to study your job analysis (Figure 2.2). If you ask "What job analysis?" you've got a problem.

Figure 2.2. A Model for SDL.

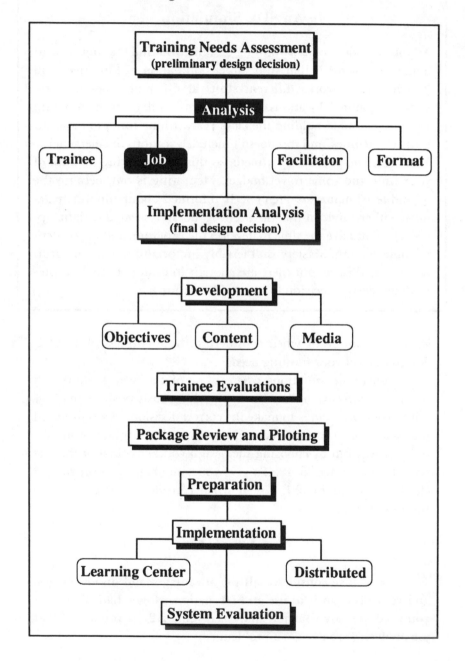

First Cornerstone of SDL

The first cornerstone of SDL is that no effective SDL package can be written without a good job analysis. Let me repeat that another way. If you can't or don't have the resources to do a proper job analysis, go back and make a different design decision. As you go through this book, you will find other statements like this, and they are made for a reason. They indicate the cornerstones of an effective SDL package. Complying with these requirements will not necessarily ensure a perfect package, since there are other factors to consider. However, skimping on or ignoring them will ensure an SDL package that is not effective.

If you don't know what a job analysis is, I once again refer you to the Suggested Readings. We will consider one type of job analysis here, but there are many other forms, and you may want to know a little about the concept itself before you proceed.

Need for a Job Analysis

Why is a proper job analysis necessary? Simply stated, the analysis is the basis for everything that goes into, or—just as important—everything that doesn't go into, your package. It is the foundation on which you build your instruction. You've probably heard this before in relation to most forms of instruction, and a good designer knows that a job analysis is always important. In SDL, it's more than just important; it's a mandatory part of the development process.

By way of explanation, let's look at classroom instruction. Often your instructors are subject matter experts. As such, they have a good to excellent grasp of what the trainee needs to know and can make sure that everything is, at the very least, presented. If important tasks were missed or minimized in the lesson plan, instructors can draw on experience to present the concepts that the designer overlooked. They also have the priceless benefit of instantaneous feedback, if they care to use it. With these advantages, a poor or incomplete job analysis can be overcome by a competent instructor.

However, in an SDL package there is no subject matter expert to embellish concepts and no instructor observing the trainees for points that need clarification. If the developer misses it, nothing can be done about it, at least until a supervisor notices the gap in performance. This "lack of immediate support" is the main reason for doing as complete a job analysis as possible before beginning development of your SDL package. The tasks your job analysis tells you should be taught will be what you develop your package to teach—no more, no less. And your package will be considered successful or not based on how closely you adhere to this relationship.

Job Analysis Versus Task Analysis

You may have noticed that I've been referring to a job analysis and not a task analysis. Hopefully this hasn't confused you. A full-blown task analysis is a good idea whenever you develop instructional materials, particularly SDL. It has been my experience in private industry that few companies are going to give you the time or the human resources to do a proper task analysis.

If you have that luxury, you should certainly take advantage of it, because it will make your SDL package easier to write and probably better. But if you are like most of us and have trouble convincing top management of the need for development time already, a job analysis will suffice. If you are confused over the terminology of job analysis and task analysis or aren't sure how to distinguish between them, I refer you to the topic of "Job and Task Analysis" in the Suggested Readings list.

One Type of Job Analysis

The type of job analysis you need to do is up to you. There are many good books and articles on the subject, all of which divide and subdivide methods of job analysis according to the authors' preferences. I prefer to use a "sit-down, brainstorming" method for SDL. In this approach, small groups of subject matter experts meet to analyze each particular job.

During these meetings, we literally write down every task the experts can think of that is part of the job we are analyzing. Then we categorize and classify, recategorize and reclassify, throw out and add, until we have depleted all possibilities. The tentative groupings of tasks are typed up and sent back to the subject matter experts for review and revision. These revised tasks are then sent to anyone we can think of in the company who might have an idea to add or constructive criticism to offer. Their suggestions are considered, and a final list of task groups is prepared.

There are two extra benefits to this approach. The first is that you, or whoever else is going to be the developer, can sit in on these meetings. You'll come away with notebooks full of ideas and technical nuances that will make the writing of the actual material easier. Including these items in your package will also make the final product closer to reality and therefore better.

I've found that the person leading the analysis session does not really have time to jot down all these ideas. Thus, we've made it a practice to have the developer or developers attend the session, but only to observe and record and not to ask questions, since this disturbs the thought processes. By watching the participants, the developer will know who to contact later with questions. The analysis leader in this system is someone who has the skills to lead the session but is not necessarily involved directly in the development of the program being analyzed.

The second added benefit of the "sit-down, brainstorming" method is that the subject matter experts you use for the analysis can function later in the process as your reviewers. After spending an entire day going through an analysis, most subject matter experts develop an almost proprietary interest in the program. They have a good idea of what you're trying to do and will usually deliver reviews on time when asked. Since they have been in on the project from the start, their reviews are usually less general and more helpful than usual.

These experts also make good consultants if the developer runs into trouble while writing the material. It has been my experience that if you happen to see members of your job analysis group during the development phase, they will often ask, "How's *our* program coming along?" This type of commitment, particularly from busy subject matter experts, is difficult to achieve by almost any other method. It is invaluable to the developer and to the success of the package.

An SDL Simulation

To find out exactly what your training population needs in the way of time management skills, you convene a job analysis group consisting of three incumbent first-line managers and two second-line managers. From the meeting, a series of tasks that relate to time management are isolated. They include:

- Prioritizing things that need to be done
- Dealing with phone calls
- Delegating tasks to subordinates
- Holding meetings
- Reading reports, memos, technical updates, and so on

Job Analysis Product

The product that you want to obtain from this job analysis is a comprehensive, categorized task list detailing the job for which your package is being developed. Sometimes this list reflects an actual company position, and as you review the task categories you will decide that a specific number of SDL packages are called for. In other circumstances, the list may define a particular topic that several positions need training on. The task categories, if there are any, will become the sections of a single SDL package.

Remember that your SDL package, and therefore your reputation, will have to rest on its own merits. There will be no instructor to make up for important concepts that you slighted or tasks that you forgot. Help it stand on a strong foundation by doing a proper job analysis at the start.

Trainee Analysis

Since you're already in an analysis mode, your next step is to take some time to analyze the trainees for whom you're writing your SDL package (Figure 2.3). As in classroom instruction, your trainees have certain characteristics and experiences that will deter-

Figure 2.3. A Model for SDL.

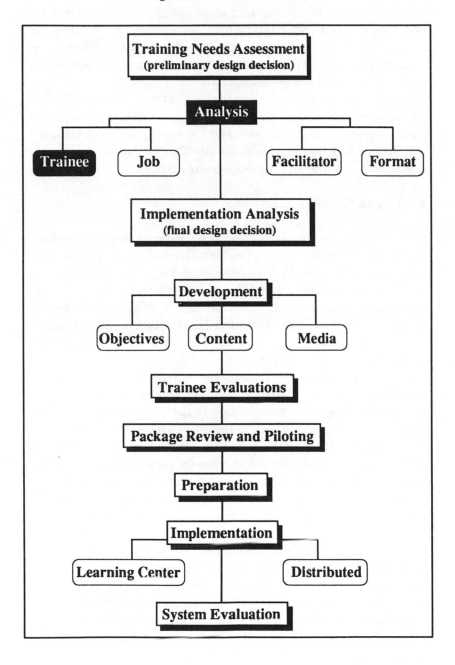

mine some of the parameters of your package. The problem is that you will not be able to ascertain these characteristics as you teach and thus to modify your lesson plan accordingly. By the time the trainee interacts with your program, modifications will be impossible, so you must be aware of these characteristics and experiences before you begin developing material.

I can't stress too often the importance of remembering throughout your design and development of SDL packages that there is no instructor at the other end to make up for the developer's mistakes or lack of attention to detail. This fact alone mandates a complete analysis of all important components.

Literacy and Reading Level

The most obvious trainee characteristic for any SDL package is literacy. If your trainees are unable to read, they are going to have a difficult time in almost any SDL setting. I have already mentioned the CBT program developed by a Cleveland hospital for a group of nurses and nurse aides. Completion of the program was demonstrated by a performance evaluation in which the trainee exhibited to a facilitator that she had mastered the four computerized functions the program had taught.

On the whole, the design was extremely successful. There were large savings in average learning time over classroom approaches and good job transfer due to the mastery approach. The only problem was a 2 percent nonmastery rate. Since the behaviors were relatively simple with no cognitive component to speak of, and on-line job aids were available during the performance demonstration, a 0 percent nonmastery rate was expected. Even with extra time in the training center, mastery for these trainees was not achievable. Since their numbers were small, they could be given individualized instruction.

What the instructors found was that the trainees were unable to read the directions on the computer screen. They were basically illiterate and learned to do their non-reading-intensive jobs by word of mouth and rote! This was back in the mid 1970s, before the extent of the literacy problem became common knowledge; I doubt if most trainers today would be surprised by this outcome. However, the point here is to remind you to make sure your trainee population can read before you start designing and developing a reading-intensive SDL package.

If absolute literacy is a significant consideration, then degree of literacy—commonly referred to as reading level—is also important, perhaps more so. This is because it affects more of your trainee population. There are plenty of studies done on reading levels, and plenty of tools available for checking the level of newly created material, so I won't go into this subject in detail.

Once again, your responsibility is to analyze your trainees and then decide on the appropriate reading level for yourself. My own guidelines are simple. I write SDLs to a sixth-grade reading level, unless I have a good reason to do otherwise. For example, if the subject is a bit technical, I'll let it slide to an eighth- or even ninth-grade level. This takes into account the fact that the instruments tend to skew a bit when technical jargon is introduced.

Since most of us do development work on word processors now, I'd suggest that you have two or even three reading-level instruments on your computer. They are all easy to use, and an average of them can give you a pretty good indication of the level you're writing at.

Don't wait until you've finished your development to check the reading level, unless you enjoy extensive revisions. Make level checks at the end of each section or module, just to keep yourself on course. If you don't have a computer, this is a lot more difficult; my advice is to get a computer. There are reading-level instruments available (Fog, Flesch, and so on) that you can do by hand, but it is much simpler and probably more accurate to use a computer readability tool. Most good grammar-checking programs have one or more that come bundled with the software.

Other Trainee Considerations

While reading skills are important, there are other trainee considerations that should be part of your analysis.

Computer Literacy. If you have been thinking about CBT as a media format, you'll need to estimate your trainees' computer skills. Even small problems such as the inability of a trainee to understand what you mean by a DOS command can negate your entire program. Menus might be necessary, with automatic boots, particularly if you are going into a highly distributed environment with no facilitator available. Are you sure your trainees know how to use a mouse, or even a keyboard with enter keys and cursor arrows? This level of information, which can only be gained by extensive analysis, can dictate how you need to begin your program. It might even help you decide if you can use a particular media format at all.

Trainee Experience. From a material development perspective, you need to consider the trainees' experience. As in any training design, the experience a trainee brings to the training tells you where to start and how deep you need to go. Once again, you can't adjust your perceptions later when trainees begin giving you confused looks, so you must analyze correctly now. You want to strike a balance between making sure each trainee can understand all of the information in your package and wasting everyone's time detailing things that are already known. A poorly done analysis of this factor may lead you to develop a package that is not based on a foundation of information that *every* trainee has already mastered.

Fortunately, one of the advantages of SDL is that the trainees don't have to sit and listen to you or some other instructor tell them what they already know. Because SDL is self-paced, highly experienced trainees can move quickly through areas that have been previously mastered. Inexperienced individuals can start from the beginning and take it slowly.

Your analysis should try to find the lowest common denominator—that is, the knowledge that you are sure every trainee will bring to the training. This is the point at which you start writing. Trainees can proceed faster or more slowly through the rest of the materials, as their personal needs dictate. If you're not sure, err on the side of too much information. The self-paced aspect will handle small errors in judgment.

Trainee Comfort with SDL. Finally, in relation to any first SDL program, you should analyze the trainees' familiarity with SDL materials. For individuals used to the comfort of an instructor who leads them through the learning, an SDL package can be intimidating. Trainees who react to smiles, nods, and words of

---

An SDL Simulation

You analyze your trainees to look for problems they may have with SDL. Basically, they are all high school or college graduates with no reading problems. Reading level should stay around eighth grade to be safe, but it can slide up a little. The trainees are not accustomed to SDL, so you'll have to prepare them well. A few have probably had time management training, but for the most part, you'll have to start with the basics. There don't seem to be any special problems.

---

encouragement from instructors may be uncomfortable with the more mechanical feedback of SDL self-quizzes.

You can prepare your trainees through either live discussions of the methodology and advantages of SDL or through expanded introductions in primary modules. Chapter Seven details the importance and procedures of preparing trainees for SDL.

There are other trainee characteristics to consider, depending on particular situations and specific material, but those we've already discussed are the most common and most critical for SDL. The important thing to remember is to do an analysis of your trainees. Go out and research them, talk to them, give them pretests, and talk to their supervisors. Now sit down and think, then use the data and analysis in your design and development decisions.

Facilitator Analysis

We turn to a different type of analysis next.

Facilitators Versus Instructors

A good designer always includes an instructor analysis as part of the analysis and design process (Figure 2.4). Understanding the instructor's strengths and limitations helps to set the tone for and the boundaries of the lesson plan. It also provides a guide for

Figure 2.4. A Model for SDL.

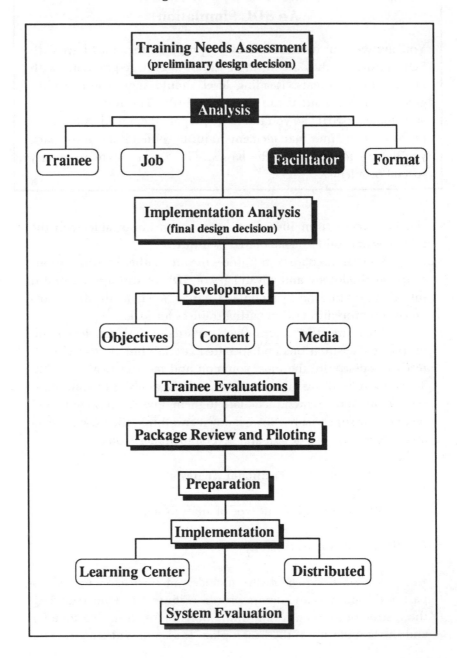

the intricacy level of any activities. In SDL, we do not have an instructor (that's part of the definition, remember), but more often than not there is the need for a facilitator.

A facilitator may perform any of a number of roles in SDL. Basically, a facilitator helps the trainee where necessary but is not responsible for providing information or answering questions. An analysis of whether you have a need for a facilitator, and what the strengths and limitations are of people who might be available to take on this role, is an important part of your design planning. (Facilitators are discussed in detail in the implementation chapters—Chapters Eight through Eleven—since what you may need a facilitator for is closely related to your implementation strategy.)

The critical thing to remember about facilitators is that they are exactly that—facilitators—and not instructors. If you design a program that requires a live presenter to deliver some of the material or to lead the trainee through the training on a continuing basis, you are not doing SDL.

On the other hand, if you realize during the material development phase that the training won't work without a highly involved individual, you probably made a mistake in deciding on an SDL design in the first place. I've seen designers who have come to this conclusion and then tried to salvage what they could by mixing SDL with instructor-led training. The results of the amalgamation have usually failed because of the increased complexity of the program and the confusion in implementation that this complexity causes.

In most cases, your best course in this situation is simply to change the design. This isn't all that terrible; since most of what you've done for SDL will be useful in another design, you won't have wasted all your effort. What you never want to do is to continue with a design decision like SDL after you've realized it isn't what you—and more importantly, your trainees—can use most effectively.

Facilitator Roles

So what exactly does a facilitator do if not instruct or lead? As with most aspects of SDL, that will depend on what you, as the designer, decide. There is no cut-and-dried part for a facilitator to play; sometimes there is no part at all. As you do an analysis of this factor, you can look for four possible roles: those of introducer, performance observer, package/program evaluator, and trainee evaluator.

The Facilitator as Introducer. The first facilitator role is what I call the *introducer* role—that is, orienting the trainee to the SDL package. This role is often filled by facilitators in a learning center. In its most basic aspect, this role requires the facilitator to simply hand the SDL package to the trainee and then get out of the way. You can augment this by making the facilitator responsible for finding a good place for the trainee to work on the package if the training is not taking place in a learning center.

The introducer may also have to gather needed supplies and schedule machines or other special equipment. Often an introducer will take a few minutes to explain what SDL is and how the trainee is expected to work with the materials. Don't discount the importance of this. I've learned through sad experience that when confronted with an SDL package, most people have little idea what to do with it. Even if you've gone to great lengths to write marvelous directions, just remember when the last time was that *you* read the directions first. SDL is not a common training practice (at least not yet), and often trainees need the assurance and direction of a live person to get them started.

At a higher level of complexity, you may need to make facilitators responsible for introducing an entire SDL system to the trainees who will be using it. This is a lot different from introducing a single package and will almost certainly require some type of facilitator training. Your facilitators will need an in-depth understanding of what SDL is and how it works. They will also be required to have a good grasp of your particular system and how the trainees will work within it. In one system I was responsible for, we accomplished this by designing an SDL package on self-directed learning. It taught facilitators what SDL was, and their responsibilities in the system, by having them experience self-directed learning. Chapter Seven describes this process in more detail.

The Facilitator as Performance Observer. The second facilitator role is that of *performance observer.* If tasks that include a performance component show up in your job analysis, you'll probably include some type of performance practice or demonstration in your package. A facilitator may be needed to observe the practice or demonstration and possibly to provide feedback. This is the point at which you need to consider not only the role but also who you have available to fill it.

Feedback, even with a good performance checklist, requires some subject matter expertise. If you need a performance observer, will you have people at your training sites qualified to fulfill this function? Do they have the time and motivation to do it right? In the extremely disseminated system that we already discussed (2,000 stores, so 2,000 training sites), I had the store managers act as performance observers. You can see the obvious advantages here, both in subject matter expertise and in motivation, but it took us a while to convince them that they could afford the time.

If you are using a learning center approach for implementation, you already have a built-in observer, though he or she may need some specialized training in what to look for. I once saw a system being used in a learning center at a power generation facility in South Carolina that made up for the lack of trained performance observers by using a video camera to tape the performance. The facilitator acted as cameraperson. The tape was sent back to corporate headquarters, where an expert observer critiqued it and returned it to the trainee for review. This was a little cumbersome, but it seemed to work. It was certainly an efficient use of the expertise of qualified observers, which was a scarce resource.

It might even be possible to do a variation of this and have videotapes showing the proper performance sent to nonexpert facilitators at each training site. The tape could then be compared to what they observe the trainee doing, and feedback could be generated from this comparison.

If your analysis does not isolate available performance observers and you can't use a technical trick to substitute for them, you need to reconsider the importance of the performance component. If it is critical, your design decision itself may require further review.

The Facilitator as Package/Program Evaluator. The third role for a facilitator is as *package/program evaluator.* This is basically a mechanical role and can usually be accomplished by anyone who has the time. Most often, it means handing out and monitoring some type of opinionnaire evaluation instrument and then collecting and forwarding or perhaps filing it. Keeping track of completion records, particularly in a multipackage system, is also a responsibility of this role, as are any other purely record-keeping or reporting functions. Once again, in a learning center process this is a normal role of the facilitator. In a distributed system, it may be a bit more difficult to find someone to fill it.

The Facilitator as Trainee Evaluator. The fourth facilitator role is as *trainee evaluator.* This role goes well beyond the behavioral observer or package evaluator role by having the facilitator certify package mastery by each trainee. Once again, the expertise of the facilitator is critical and can be the limiting factor in the use of this role in the design. If an evaluated performance demonstration is important (a good example of this is technician training in the nuclear industry), an expert facilitator/evaluator must be available. If material mastery requires analyzing each trainee's answers and retesting where needed, the facilitator must be able to perform these functions as well.

Even if the certification is more informal but is tied to promotion or raises, the facilitator must be a cut above the individual that was needed for the other roles. In the latter case, where the facilitator's decision affects job classification or pay, I've found it preferable to use the direct supervisor or even the next-level manager as facilitator/evaluator. This not only puts the burden of the decision where it belongs, but it ties in nicely with any coaching or performance appraisal mechanisms the company might have.

The Learning Center Facilitator

Using a learning center–type facilitator or even a nonsupervisory subject matter expert to make evaluations that have such direct effects can be controversial. I've learned to be careful about where my designs end up placing personnel decisions. I find that the use of a learning center facilitator in this role of trainee evaluator is risky and should be avoided if possible.

An SDL Simulation

Your preliminary analysis indicates that there should be no critical, specialized role in your SDL that a facilitator will be needed for. You may need someone to introduce the packages to the trainees and possibly to do an observed performance. You don't feel that you'll need a trainee evaluator, but a package evaluator to help you learn if the training is working would be a good idea. These tasks can be handled easily by the second-level managers, and you earmark them for this role. Your facilitator analysis indicates no major hurdles to using SDL.

On the other hand, a true learning center facilitator can fulfill all other aspects of each facilitator role quite adequately. This person will also be responsible for the general functioning of the center and, in some cases, even for the development of SDL packages. For analysis purposes, if you are designing packages for use in a center that has a well-trained facilitator, design to use this invaluable resource in all the roles that he or she is capable of fulfilling. (The hiring, training, and job responsibilities of facilitators are discussed in Chapter Eleven.)

To distinguish between the formal facilitator position and the role that a field person plays in administering or evaluating packages in a distributed implementation, we will refer to the latter as a *site implementor* rather than as a facilitator. The differences will be explored in detail in Chapters Eight and Nine.

In the meantime, no matter what you call them, the important point is that facilitators of SDL packages *do not* take the place of instructors. A good facilitator analysis will tell you what role they will play in your design. It will also determine if you have proper facilitators available or, if not, that you have chosen the wrong design.

Format Analysis

Format analysis raises still other concerns.

Media Formats as Instructional Settings

Though you've analyzed the job, the trainee, and the facilitator, you still have more to do for your SDL design. If this was a simple instructor-mediated approach, you might now decide what setting would be best to use: classroom, laboratory, on-the-job training location, and so on. In SDL, there are settings as well, though they are related more to how your trainees will use your SDL packages than to where. These settings are called *media formats,* and to decide on which format to use, you need to do a format analysis *before developing any material* (Figure 2.5). As in an instructor-mediated design, the environment will shape the material development.

What Is Format Analysis?

In its most basic form, format analysis is nothing more than making a considered decision on what media format your SDL will be developed in. That is, will your package be a simple printed document or will you add diagrams to it, or possibly slides, or maybe video, computers, laser discs, or . . . Once you start to consider the possibilities, it's not as simple as it first seems.

The importance of this analysis is that it forces you to take a hard look at your capabilities and to recognize what you can and can't do. It also demands that you consider the material itself and how it is best presented to the learner.

For example, if your program is going to be used to introduce the learner to a new machine or even an entire new work environment, diagrams may not do the trick. Slides could at least show what the new environment will look like, and video could make it even more realistic. Perhaps an interactive video program, where the trainee simulates the actual running of the machine, would be appropriate.

Before your imagination runs away with you, don't forget to consider the *keep it simple* rule as well, or at least the SDL corollary of it, which goes something like this: *What is the least complicated*

Figure 2.5. A Model for SDL.

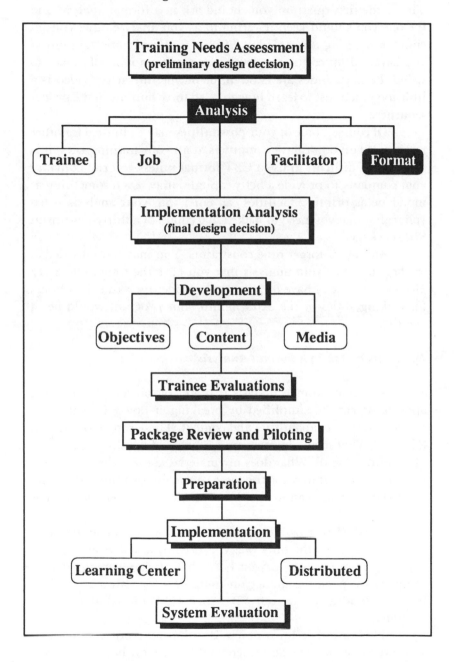

media format I can use and still produce the most effective package?
This is the first question you should ask in a format analysis and
the one you should keep referring to as you analyze other considerations. *Keeping it simple but effective* is always important unless
you have unlimited time to develop and vast amounts of money to
spend. Perhaps slides are enough, or maybe interactive video is a
little too much just to learn how to push three buttons in the proper
sequence.

Of course, some of your possibilities may be limited for other
reasons. If you don't have computers at all your training sites, it is
going to be difficult to use a CBT format unless you can convince
your company to provide a hefty capital outlay. Even something as
mundane as printing facilities can enter into your analysis when
you realize that you need to make 1,200 copies of a thirty-page print
SDL package.

And don't forget time constraints. You may have decided at
the beginning of your analysis that you have the time to do SDL.
However, you may have forgotten to consider the extra sixty hours
for making slides or the extra month your program would be in
printing.

Questions to Ask in a Format Analysis

As I said, format analysis is more complicated than it first
appears. It can be simplified by breaking it down into the two
considerations of capabilities and content. These can be phrased as
follows: "What media formats am I capable of developing and implementing?" and "What does my material content demand that I
use?" It is difficult to prioritize these considerations, since they tend
to overlap, but you can utilize three questions to make the analysis
easier.

What Must I Do? This might seem like a strange question,
but sometimes it's the only one you need to ask. For example, if
you—or, more important, your boss—has already convinced your
company to spend big money on computers for training, it might
be a smart idea to do your SDL in a CBT format if humanly
possible.

This rationale for a design decision may not go over well
with everyone, but I've been there and I've seen it happen. I know

of one company that now does *all* its training with video. This is because several years ago it spent a lot of money on video production equipment and sold the CEO on its effectiveness. If I were to design an SDL package for that company, I'd try very hard to do it in a video format.

What Should I Do? This is the question to ask if the first one turned up nothing critical. It's the question that looks at the relation of the material to the media. Most of the considerations here are the same as for a media decision in any design. They are discussed in detail in other books, such as Anderson and Reynolds's *Selecting and Developing Media for Instruction* (1992), so I won't go into them in detail. However, some important points to consider for SDL specifically include:

- The need for diagrams if your media is to be print
- The need to show your subject in real life, which suggests photographs or slides, or possibly video
- The material's readability, which if low might suggest the use of audiotape
- The need to depict action, which may mean video is called for
- The need for the trainee to interact with the material, which can best be met by CBT or interactive video

What Can I Do? This is the question you ask when you consider your actual capabilities. Time is a major consideration: Do you have the time to produce a video or even find one from an off-the-shelf source? Can you afford the hundreds of hours needed to do CBT? Do you have the time to get your print material printed? A common mistake that new SDL developers make is to assume that when the program is written and ready, it's done. Your program isn't done until it's in the hands of your trainees. The time you need for the print shop to print your program and to mail it out will need to be factored in as well.

"What can I do?" requires you to look at your production capabilities. This comes in two parts: "What can I do myself?" and "How much can I buy?" Desktop publishing and laser printers have made quality print materials fairly accessible to almost everyone, but if you need a thousand copies, you still have to use a printing facility.

Audiotape and even slides are relatively simple to produce

with minimal equipment and expertise, but they can be expensive if you need to go outside for production.

In-house video is not cheap when you consider the salaries and time of those involved, and professional productions cost a great deal, though the quality is worth it.

If you don't have CBT expertise, it takes a long time and a lot of frustration to acquire it, while interactive video is no place for amateurs.

A good hard look at exactly what you, your staff, and your company are capable of doing or buying in terms of media production can save you a lot of aggravation later.

Finally, "What can I do?" means you also need to look at your distribution capability. For their first attempt at centralized training, a national fast food chain I interviewed got involved in a big way with filmstrips as an SDL media format for its 4,000 stores. It bought high-speed tape duplicators, fancy cameras and copy stands, and the talent to develop the programs. Then it bought enough filmstrip viewers for only about one-fifth of its training sites. The idea was that the viewers could be shared. If you remember, one of the advantages of SDL is that it is there when the trainee needs it. Well, it wasn't. It got to the point where no one knew exactly where the machines were, so they just ignored them. The programs were good and some were great, but the distribution made them worthless.

So consider carefully what you have out there and how convenient it is for the trainees to use it. An interactive video program that's locked in a room in another building isn't worth much to a manager who can't get too far from the factory floor. It's worth even less to workers who are afraid of computers.

Technology and the Format Decision

One final thought on format analysis may be useful. Remember that the need, the trainees, and the material should govern media selection and not vice versa. I once saw a tremendous interactive video program at a nuclear plant in North Carolina that led trainees on a plant tour. Some of these areas could not be seen otherwise, since they were off limits due to security regulations. As

An SDL Simulation

Your format analysis indicates that there are no political reasons for using one form of media over another. The material you are planning on presenting seems to have no particular media needs associated with it. There will probably be some charts and lists, but these can be done in any format. Video or even computer simulations might help but they are not necessary, nor are live pictures in the form of slides or voices on audiotape. Your training sites do not have computers, and you do not have the expertise to develop CBT. They do have video machines, but your need for video is not crucial. You have the means to do a good paper-and-pencil program, and it seems to you that this will be the best format. Distribution and print costs should not be a problem, since you have only three sites and a limited number of trainees.

an orientation device it served well, and I was informed that it cost over $80,000 to produce.

But when I asked to see some of the learning programs it was used with, I was told there were none. Here was a technological marvel that had no purpose other than to make vicarious voyeurs out of orientees. No one had considered the ways it might be used before it was made. It was simply "something we wanted to try."

As another example, I observed an entire SDL system in a medical supply company headquartered in Pennsylvania that was based on a microfiche machine as the media format. When asked why they chose this technology, I was told it was because all the training sites had these machines—this was their method of keeping product information up to date. Unfortunately, the machine they had was being used by someone about half the time, on a random basis.

Even without this barrier, the pages of material contained on the training cards were no different from what could have been done in a print format. The machines themselves were cumbersome to use, and no one ever trained the trainees on how to work them. The result? A nice program that no one ever used.

These two examples of technology making the decisions instead of the other way around are good illustrations of the need for, and importance of, a strong format analysis. There are times when a format decision is out of your hands, but let that be someone else's mistake and not yours. When it is your decision, use a format analysis to make sure the right type of media is being used for the right reasons.

Implementation Analysis

Believe it or not, there is still one more analysis to do. Actually, you've been considering this aspect from the time you first contemplated whether or not to attempt SDL, but we've never really addressed it formally.

Implementation analysis concerns itself with where and how you will deliver your SDL packages after they have been developed (Figure 2.6). However, you can't wait until development is completed to consider this factor. Like the format decision, it has a great effect on how you do the actual material development.

Performing an Implementation Analysis

To perform an implementation analysis, you need to pull together everything you've analyzed and decided on so far, and then to see if it all makes sense in relation to how your packages will be used by the trainees. From the job analysis, consider the type of material and its performance demands. From the trainee analysis, consider who and where your trainees are and what they are and are not capable of. From the facilitator analysis, consider what need you have for facilitators and the availability of people who can fill this need. From format analysis, consider what you have at your training sites or in your learning center to present the material. The sum total of all these decisions will indicate if you can implement the SDL packages the way you planned, or what you will have to change to do the implementation effectively.

Figure 2.6. A Model for SDL.

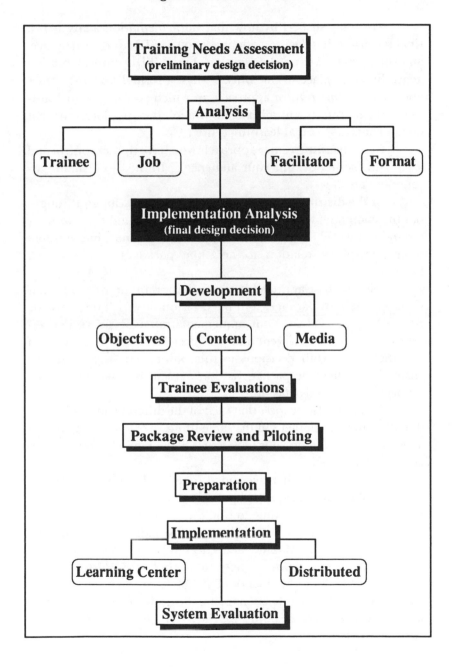

Learning Center Versus Distributed Implementation

You may suspect by now that implementation analysis is a final review of that decision you made to use SDL in the first place, and you're right. Stripped down to its basics, SDL implementation generally takes place in one of two ways: a formal *learning center* approach or a *distributed* approach, in which you send your learning packages out to a number of on-the-job training locations that do not contain a formal learning center.

In the learning center approach, you have tighter control and a built-in facilitator, but your audience is limited to a small surrounding area.

In the distributed approach, your packages can go throughout the company, whether your locations are around the nation or around the world. You can literally teach thousands, but you lose some control in relation to how the packages are used and facilitated.

Each of these approaches creates important needs and limitations within your packages, but the decision of which one to use is normally quite evident. Your implementation analysis, as an overview of everything that went into your decision to use SDL, will tell you that all of your decisions to this point were logical. It will ensure that when the package is done, it can be presented to the trainees in an effective fashion.

You may also suspect that each of the different analyses we've discussed in this chapter did the same thing—that is, they gave you a go/no go decision on your plan to use SDL. You'd be right in that assumption as well.

SDL is a time-intensive and at times highly involved design. In certain circumstances, it will provide you with uniquely effective training programs. The time to find out if those circumstances are favorable for your situation is before you spend time developing the packages, not after. Making and checking your design decision through this series of what I refer to as *analysis factors* will help ensure that the design will work. This can save you a lot of wasted effort. As we will see in later chapters, the decisions related to these factors are also reference points for the developer to use as the packages are written.

For those of us who are used to ISD or some other more formalized instructional design approach, the interrelated structure (some might say nonstructure) of this SDL analysis/design process may seem a bit uncomfortable. However, it works for SDL and prepares you well for the next step in your SDL procedure—material development.

An SDL Simulation

You do not have a learning center at any of your sites, nor are you planning on developing such facilities, so you'll need to use a distributed implementation. All of your previous analyses indicate that a distributed implementation will work for this training need and in your corporate environment. Your final design decision is to develop an SDL package on time management that will be distributed to your trainees at their work sites.

Exhibit 2.2. A Checklist for SDL.

Analysis

☐ A needs assessment has been performed.
  • Training needs that match organizational needs have been isolated.
  • A preliminary design decision to use SDL has been reached.
  • You have the time to properly develop an SDL process.
  • You have listed and considered the reasons you would not want to use an SDL approach and find they are not valid.
  • You have listed the reasons for using SDL and find that some of them apply in your situation.
  • You have sold your top management on the concept of SDL.

☐ A job analysis has been completed.
  • You have a categorized series of tasks that need to be trained to for the particular training need you isolated.

☐ A trainee analysis has been completed.
  • You talked to trainees and their supervisors.
  • You know what the reading and experience levels of your trainees are.
  • You realize the need to prepare your trainees for SDL.

☐ A facilitator analysis has been completed.
  • You know the four roles of a facilitator and which of them will be necessary in your SDL process.
  • You have individuals who can fill these roles.

☐ A format analysis has been completed.
  • You have isolated the least complicated format.
  • You know if there is anything you must do.
  • You know what you should do.
  • You know what you can do.

☐ An implementation analysis has been completed.
  • You have reconsidered the data from all your other analyses.
  • You have made a decision as to which implementation strategy to use.
  • You have reconfirmed your decision to use SDL.

3

Creating an SDL Package

How to Develop Trainee Objectives
and Organize Your Material

The heart of an SDL package is the content. However, before you can develop good SDL content, you must develop good objectives. We'll consider why objectives are important and briefly look at one method for writing them. Then we'll discuss how objectives become content and how "chunking" makes the content usable for SDL.

Objectives

Objectives are another crucial element of the SDL design process (Figure 3.1).

Second Cornerstone of SDL

You've done all the various types of analysis suggested in the previous chapter, you've decided on SDL as the design you want to use, and you know basically how you are going to use it, where you are going to use it, and what you are going to use it for, and so what's next? Now you write objectives.

Did I hear a groan out there? A whispered mutter of "Oh no, not that?" I doubt if there is an instructional designer alive who likes to write objectives. There is not one of us who hasn't at one time or another cursed Mager and the others who came up with the idea of behavioral objectives. Yet, without objectives, there can be no SDL. Let me paraphrase that in a way that you've already heard: If you won't or can't write objectives, go back to where you decided

Figure 3.1. A Model for SDL.

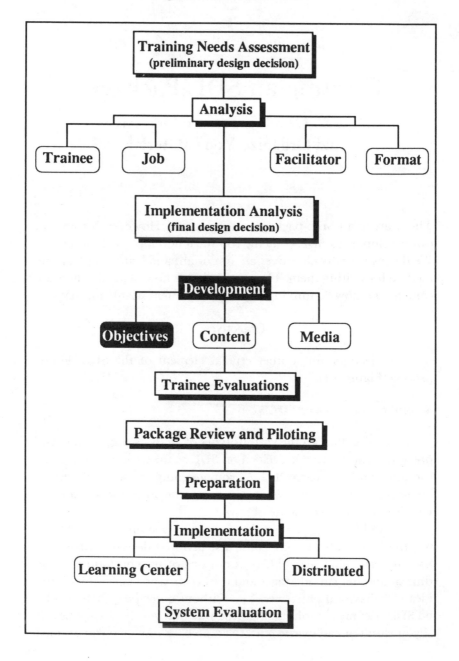

to do SDL and make another decision. *Properly conceived, properly written, and properly utilized objectives are the second cornerstone of SDL.* This is a process that many otherwise good SDL practitioners overlook, sometimes on purpose.

An Example of Why You Need Objectives

I once hired a well-known consulting group that specialized in SDL to do a package for me. I didn't have the time or personnel to do it myself. It was a dicey situation. The analysis was weak because the subject matter was still changing, and the subject included a computer system that was still not complete.

I left them on their own to deal with the subject matter people (there were no experts) and to come up with a first draft. Some managers might fault me for not keeping close enough control. However, I hired these folks because I didn't have the time to work on this program in the first place. I was dealing with other priorities and had to let them work on their own.

Their first draft was well organized and contained graphics of the computer screens that were superb. It was simply a fine piece of work, except for one problem. In the entire sixty-page package, there were only five "course" objectives. These were the objectives that I developed as part of my preliminary discussions with them.

When I asked them where the trainee objectives were, they showed me these course objectives. When I queried how the trainees were suppose to know what was most important in the material, they retorted that everything was important. When I asked how the trainees could know what they were to be evaluated on, they told me that since everything was important, everything was fair game. When I wondered how the evaluations were to be developed, they said in a rather perturbed manner, "From the material." It was obvious I knew nothing about SDL. So there it was, an excellent example of a well-analyzed, well-developed, very nice looking SDL package, with only one problem. It was written for the developer, not for the trainee!

Uses of Objectives in SDL

This scenario should give you a good idea of why you need objectives in your SDL package.

- They give your trainees guidelines as to what they have to learn.
- They tell the trainees what is important and what is just commentary.
- They single out those things that will be tested on.

In short, they make the package trainee oriented instead of developer oriented. And that's what you must strive for. There will be no instructor to explain, no expert to talk to. If your SDL package is to be a success, it must train the user on its own. It must be trainee oriented, and objectives make it so.

Objectives are important in other ways as well. I've already alluded to the fact that they are useful in evaluation. This is true not only from the trainee's viewpoint but also from the developer's. Good objectives make writing evaluation questions easier and make the questions more valid. This is discussed in detail in Chapter Five.

Good objectives can also be a check on the validity of your job analysis, particularly if you send them to the subject matter experts for review before proceeding to the next development step. After development, objectives play a key role in package reviews and in effectiveness evaluations. In short, objectives are used throughout the SDL process and are truly a cornerstone of the entire process.

You might better understand the importance of objectives for SDL if you have ever been asked to teach a topic that you really didn't know much about. Hopefully you had a lesson plan, and if you were lucky the lesson plan had objectives. With guidance from the objectives, you had a good idea of what the designer wanted you to teach—that is, what the trainees needed to learn. Without this guidance, you could spend days or weeks doing wonderful teaching that had no relevance to the trainee or, just as bad, to the test the trainees must take to pass the course.

For SDL, which is self-instructional, the trainees take your place in the scenario. They must figure out what is important, what needs to be learned, and what will be tested on. The objectives are their guide for doing this.

Rules for Writing Objectives

I'm not going to go too deeply here into the *correct* way to write objectives. There are plenty of books on the subject, and in all honesty, I don't think there is one correct way. Recently someone pointed out at a talk I gave that my nomenclature of *terminal* and *enabling objectives* was a bit passé, not to mention confusing. I'd used these terms throughout my career, but looking at it rationally, I had to agree. So now I use terms that fit each particular program or program piece, as you can see in this book.

The same is true of objectives as a whole. Write them to fit the program. If you like the three-step approach of *action, condition, criterion,* use it. If you call the steps something else, use that. If you skip that part or rearrange it so it works better, do that. The important thing is that you do it. However, there are three rules for the writing of objectives for SDL materials that I think are inviolable.

Rule 1: Write Objectives for the Trainees. The first rule is that the objectives must be written for the trainees. They tell the trainees what they must do, what they must learn, what they must master. They don't talk about what's in the course, or what the instructor must do (there isn't any instructor, remember), or how the course is evaluated.

Once upon a time, such objectives were termed *learner-centered objectives.* Somehow, this idea seems to have gotten lost in a lot of materials I now see. The objectives are written for everybody but the learner. In SDL, such an oversight invites disaster. When you write your objectives, write them for the trainee.

The best way I have found to do this is to start each objective with "The trainee will be able to . . . " You don't have to literally include this phrase at the beginning of each objective, but when you read the objective to yourself, put those words in front of it. If the objective makes sense with this beginning, the objective is probably trainee centered. If not, rewrite it so it does make sense.

Rule 2: Use Performance-Based Verbs. The second rule is closely related to this. It involves the use of action or performance-based verbs. The objectives must have proper verbs that help "tell the trainees what they must do." And these verbs must do exactly that. If you expect the trainees to be able to physically "do" something, that's what the verb must tell them they will have to do. If they must memorize a list, or recognize a part, the objective must say that through the verb.

This is the most important and hardest part of writing objectives for SDL. I keep my own modified version of Bloom's performance verb taxonomy, as well as other taxonomies I've picked up over the years for the affective and psychomotor domains, at hand whenever I write objectives. The following list contains some of these verbs in all three domains.

Cognitive	*Affective*	*Psychomotor*
Define	Set apart	Run
Identify	Share	Walk
List	Select	Raise
Name	Accept	Lower
Recognize	Respond to	Execute
Recall	Listen to	Perform
State	Control	Operate
Compare	Comply with	Set up
Distinguish	Follow	Portray
Associate	Approve	Exhibit
Estimate	Volunteer	Communicate
Describe	Play	Assemble
Predict	Applaud	Operate
Discuss	Acclaim	Write
Contrast	Relinquish	Complete
Apply	Specify	Recite
Classify	Assist	Inform
Complete	Help	Advise
Demonstrate	Support	Speak
Employ	Deny	Simulate
Illustrate	Protest	Read
Relate	Debate	Check
Solve	Balance	Put
Use	Organize	Take
Group	Revise	Affix
Analyze	Change	Place
Explain	Require	Draw
Summarize	Rate high	Diagram
Design	Avoid	Color

Develop	Manage	Choose
Prepare	Resolve	Designate
Propose	Resist	Say
Assess	Prefer	Manipulate
Evaluate	Value	Dramatize
Rank	Enjoy	
Select	Designate	

When developing objectives, I ask myself the simple question, "What is it that the trainees should know, feel, or be able to do when they have finished my SDL package?" This question, the verb lists, and one other thing are all the tools I need to write objectives.

Rule 3: Use a Valid Job Analysis. That other prerequisite brings us to the third rule of objective writing for SDL: No objective can be considered valid unless it is written from a valid job analysis. We've stated that a proper job analysis is one of the cornerstones for developing good SDL and that objectives are another. This is how these two critical concepts interrelate. Objectives, which are the key to the "trainee centering" of SDL, come directly from the job analysis.

I once had a staff member ask me how she would know when she had enough objectives. Rolling my eyes to the ceiling and asking where I had gone wrong, I sat down with her and matched her objectives to the job analysis. I was prepared to explain once again the importance of matching objective to task. I never got the chance. Her objectives were perfectly matched to the tasks listed in the job analysis!

So I asked her why she asked the question in the first place. She told me there had to be more to it than that, that just matching objectives to tasks was too simple. There isn't more to it than that! It is simple, but it isn't easy! The person I was working with was an expert instructional designer who knew how to write objectives, and she was working with a good job analysis. Most practitioners don't have all those advantages, and so it is a struggle.

Matching Objectives to Job Tasks

But it isn't that difficult either! You write good objectives for SDL by matching the objective to the task or, in some cases, the skill or knowledge that relates to your job/task analysis. If the task says the worker will have to "unscrew the front plate to get at the machine," one of your objectives should state: "The trainee will be able to properly remove the front plate."

Unfortunately, it's not quite that straightforward all the time. You may have to go as deep as a task analysis to find the link with your objectives. In other circumstances, you'll have to decide that you won't go as deep as you could. This is usually because your program will not be more effective if each skill or bit of knowledge that goes into a task is "objectivized."

Even in the above example, you can see that the objective could read: "The trainee will be able to use a screwdriver to remove the front plate," or going deeper still, "The trainee will demonstrate the proper method for using a screwdriver." This objective would be valid long before the worker ever saw the plate.

These are decisions that are best made with experience, and early on, it's better to err on the side of depth. However, as long as you base your objectives on a good analysis, use proper verbs, and make the objectives trainee centered, you won't be too far wrong, no matter what else you do. Following are some examples of good and bad objectives.

1. List the advantages and disadvantages of SDL.
    This is a good objective with an easily comprehensible verb.

2. Know the information in Chapter Five.
    Know is not a good verb, since it is hard to measure knowing.

3. Provide each participant with the ability to apply the four keys for developing SDL.
    Apply and *develop* are good verbs, but this is a course objective, not a trainee-centered objective.

4. Apply their understanding of SDL to a specific training need.
    Apply is a good verb, but *understanding* makes the objective hard for the trainees to understand and even harder to measure.

5. Learn the material related to distributed SDL.
    This objective seems to be trainee centered, but measuring learning is hard. This is actually an instructor-centered objective restated to look like a trainee-centered one.

6. Develop trainee-centered objectives for an SDL training design. This is a good objective, written directly for the trainee and with a measurable performance verb.

Reviewing Your Objectives

After you have completed your objectives, you need to have them reviewed. Notice that I didn't say that *you* need to review them. If you followed a good approach to developing them, your own review isn't likely to catch any problems. What you need is to have a second designer look at your objectives, both by themselves and in relation to your job analysis.

Your reviewer will be analyzing whether your objectives cover the job analysis as needed and whether the objectives themselves are well written. This means they should be clear to an uninitiated individual (like a trainee) and should use verbs that ask for appropriate actions.

You'll almost certainly need to make modifications, particularly for clarity, since what is clear to you may not be clear at all to someone who hasn't been working with the subject. This usually causes some interesting debates. You will need to review your objectives again and will probably change them again as you write content as well as when you review test questions. This is not bad; in fact, it is good, because it will make your program more effective for your trainees. So get used to it, swallow your "pride of authorship," and listen carefully to your reviewer's comments.

As I have said, the process is not difficult. Yet many developers of SDL continue to make the critical mistake of not matching their objectives to the analysis, or of not writing objectives at all. Then they wonder why the trainees can't understand their material. Of course it can't be their fault; they "spent many hours writing this stuff." So they decide that SDL doesn't work. SDL does work, if you are using it in the right situation and if you've designed and developed it correctly. And part of that task means writing good, trainee-centered, analysis-based objectives.

For those to whom the concept of trainee-centered behavioral objectives is relatively new, I refer you to the "Objectives" section of the Suggested Readings list on the subject, particularly Mager's (1984) little book, which is the bible on the subject. For those of you

An SDL Simulation

As the first step in developing your SDL materials, you take the tasks you isolated in the job analysis and write objectives based on each of them.

Task: Prioritizing things that need to be done.
Objectives: The trainee will be able to:
> Employ a daily "to do" list with priority symbols to plan and carry out each day's task.
> Discuss the importance of prioritizing activities that help his or her boss succeed as a good time management tool.

Task: Dealing with phone calls.
Objectives: The trainee will be able to:
> List three methods for decreasing the number of interrupting phone calls.
> Implement his or her own technique for reducing wasted time in returning calls.

Task: Delegating to subordinates.
Objective: The trainee will be able to effectively utilize the five-step method of delegation.

Task: Holding meetings.
Objectives: The trainee will be able to:
> Describe the importance of having a prepublished agenda for all meetings.
> Discuss techniques for eliminating meetings.
> List ten ways to decrease the time wasted in meetings.

Task: Reading reports, memos, technical updates, and so on.
Objective: The trainee will be able to discuss the nine keys to improving reading skills.

who have not had much practice in creating objectives, the best way to learn is to write them. Have someone who knows the process review them, and then write or rewrite some more. I promise you'll learn to hate them, but your SDL packages and your trainees will be proportionally better off for the effort you spend in learning how to write objectives well.

Developing Content

The next step in developing an SDL package is to write the content (Figure 3.2). Writing the content sounds simple enough, and in some cases, particularly if you are a subject matter expert, it can be. However, this isn't always the case.

Third Cornerstone of SDL

The third cornerstone of SDL is that your written material or content must be based directly on your objectives. It doesn't matter whether you're using paper and pencil, scripts for video, or CBT screens. The way to make SDL work is to make sure that what you write relates back directly to the objectives.

We all make the mistake of not writing objectives before content from time to time, most often when we think we know the topic, but it is a particularly critical error in SDL. The way to avoid this mistake is, once again, simple: have good objectives based on a proper analysis, and write the content based on the objectives. This is in essence a restatement of the first three cornerstones of good SDL.

Aspects of Content Development

There are several processes in content development that you need to consider.

Preparing a Preliminary Outline. To ensure that you keep the third cornerstone in mind and base your content on objectives, I've found that the best approach is to develop a *preliminary outline*. In this outline, each roman numeral should be one of your major objectives or tasks, depending on how you structured your

Figure 3.2. A Model for SDL.

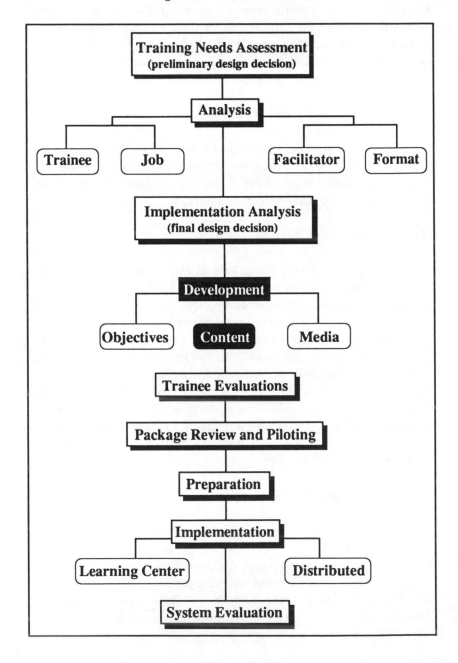

An SDL Simulation

From your objectives, you develop a preliminary outline for your content.

I. Prioritizing tasks that need to be done
   A. The "to do" list
   B. Helping your boss succeed
II. Dealing with phone calls
   A. Stopping phone interruptions
   B. Returning phone calls efficiently
III. The five-step method of delegation
IV. Meetings
   A. Agendas
   B. Eliminating meetings
   C. Meeting time wasters
V. Nine keys to improving reading skills

objectives. If you have multiple objectives for a task, or subobjectives, they are entered as capital letters under the roman numerals. When this outline is completed, you can check to see that all your objectives have been included. As you develop your content, you will be able to use this preliminary outline as a guide. If a concept does not fit under any of your outline headings, it may not be needed in your package. If you end up with an outline heading with no entries below it, you'll know you've missed something.

You can also use your preliminary outline to begin to arrange the flow of your material and to change things if necessary. If you find a concept that does not fit your outline but you realize it's important, you'll need to reconcile it with your job analysis, write an objective for it, and add that objective at the appropriate place in your preliminary outline. This may in turn necessitate revising the order and flow again to accommodate the new objective. However, it's much easier to do this when the material is in outline format than when you have it completely written out.

Creating an Expanded Outline. Your next step is to add

An SDL Simulation

By using various books, articles, and other reference material, you add content to your outline and create an expanded outline.

I. Prioritizing tasks that need to be done
    A. The "to do" list
        1. When to do it
            a. Before work
            b. End of day
        2. What to use
            a. "To do" sheet
            b. Blank paper
            c. Computer
        3. Priority symbols
            a. A, B, C lists
            b. Red, blue, green colored paper
    B. Helping your boss succeed
        1. What is superior performance
            a. A successful person
            b. A valuable person
        2. Who determines if you are valuable?
            a. Boss
        3. What makes you valuable to your boss?
            a. You help him or her succeed
        4. What tasks will help you help your boss?
            a. Make one a first priority every day
II. Dealing with phone calls
    A. Stopping phone interruptions
        1. Find a place away from the phone
            a. Leave a way to find if emergency
        2. Find an interceptor
            a. Secretary
            b. Co-worker
        3. Just don't answer
            a. What are the consequences?
    B. Returning phone calls efficiently
        1. Pick a time to return calls
            a. Except for emergencies

b.   When are people most likely to be in?
(1)   Before lunch, after lunch, end of day
c.   Let people know you do it this way

and so on

substance to your outline by including concepts, ideas, or whatever is necessary to cover your topic. I call this product the *expanded outline.*

The expanded outline is basically what you want to say to the trainees, but in outline format. Everything that will go into your package in the way of content should be represented here. In fact, the best expanded outlines are just some good grammar and a few articles and prepositions away from being your completed content, script, or whatever it is that the trainees will read, view, or listen to.

Since your expanded outline is based on your preliminary outline, which in turn is based on your objectives, everything that is in the expanded outline should be directly related to what the trainee needs to know. Concepts that are not in your expanded outline are probably unnecessary to the completion of the tasks (objectives) that the trainee needs to perform. As you complete the development of your content by adding full sentence structure, examples, and so on, you should not add major items to the outline unless absolutely critical to the learning.

"Need to Know" Versus "Nice to Know." Another problem in SDL content development involves a continuing battle between "need-to-know" and "nice-to-know" considerations. Need-to-know information is based on the objectives. It is described in the expanded outline and makes up the majority of the content, thus allowing the trainee to master the objectives.

"Nice-to-know" information is content that does not relate directly to the completion of an objective. At its best, it is useful in helping to reinforce the need-to-know material. At its worst, it is wasted verbiage.

Good nice-to-know information can generate more interest in your package. It can add to the depth of the trainee's understanding or open up new paths that will help solidify the basic material you are trying to present.

However, it is important to remember that any nice-to-know material—that is, any material that does not relate directly to the completion of an objective—will mean more time spent in completing the package. And this is a major consideration in most SDL systems.

Knowing when to stop writing content is probably one of the most important skills of an SDL developer. Unfortunately, it is another of those skills that can't be taught but must be gained through experience. The best rule of thumb is that enough content is the amount of material it takes to master the objectives. Anything beyond this may be confusing to the trainee, will definitely slow down the learning, and should be considered carefully before being included as part of the content of your SDL package.

Working with Subject Matter Experts. Once your preliminary outline is finished and you're working on the expanded outline, you may find that you need to use a subject matter expert to help fill out the outline and possibly write your package content. Notice that I said to *help,* not to write it for you.

A problem with subject matter experts is that they may fall into the same trap as the developer who has too much knowledge: they tend to ignore or skirt around the objectives. If you leave them on their own to write, you may end up with great content that has nothing to do with the objectives.

Subject matter experts often delight in spending pages and pages delving into obscure corners or relating exasperatingly complex examples. Such things are what interest them the most. It's not the basics but the exceptions that they find fascinating. However, that is usually not what the audience for your SDL needs. Most often they need the boring basics.

So you must guide the subject matter experts. Use your preliminary outline to keep yourself and the experts on track. Prepare them for the task by discussing the objectives with them in advance. Give them examples of other packages that effectively show how to match content with objectives. Examine together what the package needs and where pitfalls might lie.

And work with them as they complete development of the expanded outline to relate the entries back to the objectives. Discuss why a particular piece of information or concept was included if it doesn't seem relevant.

Making Changes. And don't be afraid to change an objective or to add or delete one. One of the biggest mistakes an SDL developer can make is to view the objectives as sacrosanct. Remember where the objectives came from. They began as an analysis by a group of subject matter experts, one of whom may now be working with you on the content. No one ever said the analysis was perfect.

Pay attention to what the subject matter expert is saying and writing. Objectives may need rewriting; verbs and other details may need to be changed. What looked like cognitive knowledge may really be best considered a performance. The analysis may have missed something, or the objective may have gone too far. You don't need to change everything on the subject matter expert's recommendation alone, but consider the reasoning behind his or her observations. If it makes sense, make the change.

The final product of SDL content development will seldom be exactly what you had planned, but it must be a document that is directly related to the objectives as they now appear. It should provide the learner with enough information to master each of the objectives. Remember, if your content doesn't perform these functions, there is nothing else in an SDL system that will.

Chunking. Your next step is to ready your content for formatting by making it as easy for your trainees to use and comprehend as possible. A good "bad example" of what I mean by ease of usage is a book.

Most books can be considered at least a rudimentary form of SDL. Users (readers) sit down, usually alone, at a time of their own choosing, and learn from one. But books are seldom formatted to make learning easier. They usually consist of long chapters, with little guidance as to what is in them, what is most important to get from them, or any way to measure the "getting."

A good SDL package, on the other hand, breaks the material down into discrete, digestible "chunks" of various sizes depending

An SDL Simulation

From your expanded outline, you write the actual content:

One of the most effective concepts in time management is prioritizing the tasks you need to do. This can be done on a daily, weekly, monthly, or even on a project basis. Usually people begin with a daily priority list, often called a "to do" list.

The first thing to do in using a "to do" list is to decide when you will make it up. This is usually done at the end of the day or the first thing in the morning. Many time-organized individuals will also take a few minutes at lunchtime to review and revise their list. If you make your list the night before . . .

There are as many ways of making a "to do" list as there are individuals who use them. We've included with this package three different types of preprinted sheets that might work for you. The first is simply a series of lines . . .

Other time managers find that a simple blank sheet of paper works best for their "to do" list. It can be full sized or simply a notepad, depending on your personal . . .

A newer application of the "to do" list is the computerized calendar/organizer. These software programs . . .

One of the important things you need to do with your "to do" list is to find a way to prioritize the tasks on it. This can be as simple as listing the first priority first, the second, second, and so on. It might also be as complicated as three lists, one for first-priority tasks . . .

Another technique is color coding. For example, first-priority tasks can be in red ink or on red paper, second-priority green, third-priority blue. The advantage of this system is . . .

One way to help you to prioritize your tasks has been postulated by Henry Sipes in his book *Time Management: The Reality.* He states that the best time managers are those who realize that they must be superior performers if they wish to get ahead in their company. To be a superior performer, you must be seen as a successful person, and the individual who determines your success and value is your boss.

Thus, the good time manager finds out what it is that will help the boss succeed and treats tasks that perform this function as his or her first priority. Sipes states that every day, one of your first-priority tasks must be to do something to make the boss look good.

Approaching time management from the opposite direction, you need to find ways to eliminate time wasters. The telephone is one of the most common of these. The first thing you do to prevent the telephone from wasting your time is to stop it from interrupting you when you are in the middle of something. Everybody has had those times when . . .

There are three methods you can use to stop phone interruptions. The first is to simply work away from the phone. Now this may be a problem if . . .

The second method is to find a phone call interceptor. This is a person who can answer your phone and take messages. It doesn't have to be a secretary if you don't have one. Even a co-worker can . . .

Another method of controlling your phone is to return calls only at specified times. This might be at the end of the day, or each morning, or right after lunch. There are a number of advantages to this . . .

on the amount and type of material. These chunks may be called *units, modules, sections, parts,* or even *books,* and there are usually a couple of different sizes of these divisions in an SDL system.

Each chunk starts off with objectives that tell the trainees what is coming and what they will need to learn. It ends with some form of evaluation that allows the trainees to check their learning. Simply stated, what all this breaking down and "chunking" accomplishes is to make the trainee's job of learning and retention that much easier. Your preliminary and expanded outlines can be of great assistance in this process.

As far as I know, there are no specific rules for how to "chunk" your material. My basic rule is that I try to limit my smallest chunks to from three to five objectives. Some developers I know say that three to five pages of text make a good chunk. If you are dealing with a graphic format like video or slide-tape, the accepted theory is ten to fifteen minutes maximum per chunk. After this, have the trainee do a different activity.

This is what separates chunks: changing to a new activity. The change may be as simple as a self-test to check the trainee's knowledge of the material just completed, or it may be a performance practice or evaluation if the material is more performance based. It may be as complicated as a change in media format if you are using multiple media for your package.

Perfect examples of "chunking" are branched CBT and interactive programs, particularly those using HyperCard technology. These programs are basically made up of small packets of discrete information that the trainee accesses and learns as needed. The truly self-directed part of this technology is that the trainees pick the order in which they will receive the chunks and, at times, which chunks they will receive. It's no wonder that such technologies lend themselves so well to SDL.

With your content written and chunked, you are now ready to continue the development of your SDL package by formatting it with the proper media.

An SDL Simulation

Using your expanded outline and the content you wrote from it, you decide to chunk your material as follows:

Module: Time Management

Section 1: Time Savers

The "To Do" List
   One of the most effective concepts in time management is prioritizing the tasks you need to do. This can be done on a daily, weekly, monthly, or even on a project basis. Usually people begin with a daily priority list, often called a "to do" list.
   The first thing to do in using a "to do" list is to decide when you will make it up. This is usually done at the end of the day or the first thing in the morning. Many time-organized individuals will also take a few minutes at lunchtime to review and revise their list. If you make your list the night before . . .

There are as many ways of making a "to do" list as there are individuals who use them. We've included with this package three different types of preprinted sheets that might work for you. The first is simply a series of lines . . .

Other time managers find that a simple blank sheet of paper works best for their "to do" list. It can be full sized or simply a notepad, depending on your personal . . .

A newer applicaton of the "to do" list is the computerized calendar/organizer. These software programs . . .

One of the important things you need to do with your "to do" list is to find a way to prioritize the tasks on it. This can be as simple as listing the first priority first, the second, second, and so on. It might also be as complicated as three lists, one for first-priority tasks . . .

Another technique is color coding. For example, first-priority tasks can be in red ink or on red paper, second-priority green, third-priority blue. The advantage of this system is . . .

Prioritizing by Helping Your Boss Succeed

One way to help you to prioritize your tasks has been postulated by Henry Sipes in his book *Time Management: The Reality.* He states that the best time managers are those who realize that they must be superior performers if they wish to get ahead in their company. To be a superior performer, you must be seen as a successful person, and the individual who determines your success and value is your boss.

Thus, the good time manager finds out what it is that will help the boss succeed and treats tasks that perform this function as his or her first priority. Sipes states that every day, one of your first-priority tasks must be to do something to make the boss look good.

Delegation

Improving Reading Skills

Section 2: Time Wasters

The Telephone

Approaching time management from the opposite direction, you need to find ways to eliminate time wasters. The telephone is one of the most common of these. The first thing you can do to prevent the telephone from wasting your time is to stop it from interrupting you when you are in the middle of something. Everybody has had those times when . . .

There are three methods you can use to stop phone interruptions. The first is to simply work away from the phone. Now this may be a problem if . . .

The second method is to find a phone call interceptor. This is a person who can answer your phone and take messages. It doesn't have to be a secretary if you don't have one. Even a co-worker can . . .

Another method of controlling your phone is to only return calls at specified times. This might be at the end of the day, or each morning, or right after lunch. There are a number of advantages to this . . .

Meetings

You've departed from the order of your original outline, because you've found while doing your chunking that the content makes more sense, flows better, and is more cohesive in this manner.

Exhibit 3.1. A Checklist for SDL.

Developing Objectives and Content

☐ Objectives have been developed.
  - They have performance verbs.
  - They match the tasks from your job analysis.
  - They are written for the trainees.
  - They have been properly reviewed.

☐ Package content has been written.
  - It is based on your objectives.
  - Preliminary and expanded outlines were used.
  - All "need-to-know" information has been included.
  - Any appropriate "nice-to-know" information has been incorporated.
  - If subject matter experts were used, they stayed with the objectives.
  - Your material has been properly chunked.

4

Formatting Your Material

How to Choose the Right
Medium for Your Message

Media formatting is an important aspect of SDL package development. This chapter considers the various media choices available for SDL and provides a general overview and some hints on how to develop each of them for this particular design (Figure 4.1). This chapter is not intended to make you an expert on any one medium. There are books and articles referenced in the Suggested Readings section that will help you explore individual formats in greater detail if they are new to you or if you need more in-depth expertise.

The newer technologies such as CBT, interactive videodisc, and multimedia will also not be treated in detail. While these formats are excellent for SDL and are used in more and more situations every day, the design and material development aspects are basically the same as for any other format. The particulars that go into making your content computer based or multimedia can be found in the excellent books listed in the "Technology-Based Media" section of the Suggested Readings.

We also won't go into detail here on media selection as a formal process. The format analysis area of Chapter Two explained the basics of media selection for SDL; for a more systematic approach, consult Anderson and Reynolds (1992).

To help you with this, Table 4.1 provides further information on media formats from a strengths-and-weaknesses viewpoint. Use it as an organizer to compare the various formats as they are discussed.

Figure 4.1. A Model for SDL.

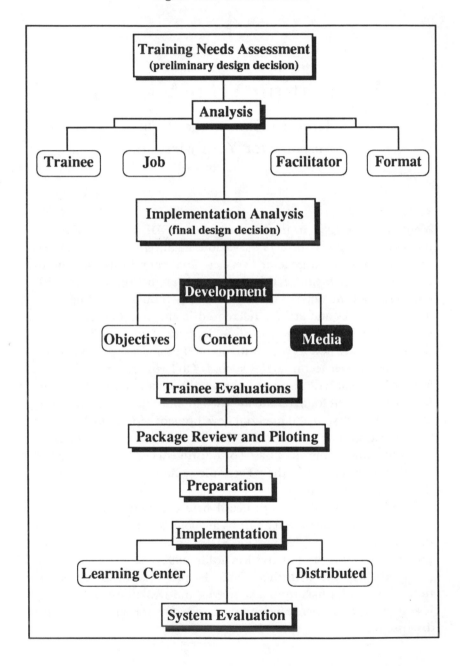

The Print Format

Now that you have completed your content, the next step is to finish the formatting of your material. Your format analysis began this process, but within the format you have chosen, there are usually other considerations.

Probably the most important format for SDL is print. In a number of training environments, particularly large distributed systems, print is the only feasible format. Even in slide or video formats, there are almost always ancillary print materials, and a lot of CBT and interactive video is basically print on a computer screen. This being the case, much of what is said concerning the print format in this section holds true for other formats as well.

Components of a Print SDL Package

If you've completed your chunking, it might seem that you should now move on to deciding how your completed package will look. However, you will need to consider some other factors, particularly in relation to that critical concept of making your package as user friendly as possible.

Trainee Instructions. One of the most important of these is trainee instructions. Since this is self-directed learning, which means that no instructor is available, the clarity of the directions you give the users will greatly affect your package's effectiveness. This includes both starting directions and those found internally throughout the package.

For the introductory directions, you might develop a boilerplate approach. This would include your general directions on how the trainee should proceed with the package, average completion time, what SDL is all about, and so on. Exhibit 4.1 gives you some examples of various types of directions for SDL packages.

Other boilerplate instructions usually occur at the beginning and end of each section, or whatever you call the smallest-sized chunk in your package. They basically tell the trainees how to proceed through the section and what to do when they have completed it. Section directions address quizzes, when to proceed to the

Exhibit 4.1. Sample Directions for SDL Packages.

Introductory Directions

Self-Directed Learning
   We call this a self-directed learning package because you will learn, on your own, how to correctly receive a weekly store order. There will be no instructor, just you and this workbook. However, you store manager will be available to help you get started, answer any questions and to help you comple the exercises you will be performing throughout this SDL package. If you follow the directions and complete all of the exercises until you are confident of your own abilities, you will know how to receive orders. Then all you will need is some practice.

Objectives
   To help guide your learning, this workbook begins with a series of objectives that list the specific things you will know or be able to do at the end of the SDL package.

   Each chapter also begins with a series of objectives that list exactly what you should know or do by the end of each chapter.

   Be sure to read the objectives so you know exactly what is expected of you. Complete each chapte by doing all of the short exercises that look like this as you go along. Then complete the quiz at the end of the chapter. You will write your answers to the quizzes and exercises on a separate answer sheet. *DO NOT WRITE IN THIS WORKBOOK.* If you miss no more than two questions, you may begin the next chapter.

   Turn to the supplies checklist on the next page and assemble yo SDL package.

Introduction

In conjunction with your distributor, _____ has developed this training program to give you some key skills that will help you sell more floor care.

The company you work for is investing a lot in your future success in the form of training time. Together our companies are committed to providing you the know-how critical to selling floor care.

If you are willing to invest the time now in learning this material, we have confidence that you will be a more successful salesperson.

OBJECTIVE

The purpose of this self-directed learning package is to give you the opportunity to learn enough information about _____ floor care so that you can build a solid foundation of business and expertise in this critical area.

Section Direction Examples

HOW TO USE THIS WORKBOOK

This workbook has been designed to help you learn floor care without the structured environment of a classroom. You are personally responsible for what you learn and can do so at whatever pace you choose. There are means within this workbook to measure your own progress.

_____ uses several different learning approaches to ensure that learning takes place:

1. Reading and written exercises provide the foundation.
2. Video exercises review products, proper procedures, and selling skills.
3. Group participation (when used in conjunction with a trainer) reinforces your learning.

Directions: Listen to the narration on the tape until you are directed to stop. Then write the correct response or circle the correct letter for the following objectives.

Directions: After you have responded to the objectives, re-listen to the narration on the tape to check the accuracy of your responses. Correct any wrong responses.

Introduction
   This activity assists you in learning about our four key product lines, the twelve other products presented in this course, and who to ask for help.

Training Aids
   • Four key product lines
   • Other products

Suggested Time
   Plan to spend approximately fifteen minutes completing this activity.

next section, and hints such as stopping for a break. These boiler-plate directions can seem a bit redundant at times, but the trainees get used to them quickly. They function as good reinforcers of the best way to do the SDL package. Exhibit 4.1 contains examples of section beginning and ending directions.

Supplies Checklist. Along with directions, another item that should normally be part of your SDL package is the supplies check-list. This list tells the trainees what resources will be needed to complete the package. It should include human as well as material resources, so that they can plan their learning time to occur when machines, supplies, and the right people are available.

Table of Contents. A feature of some packages is a table of contents. I've found this component useful at times and superfluous in other situations. I suggest that you include it if your package is complex enough to need it.

Objectives List. An absolutely necessary detail for any pack-age is an overall list of the objectives for the package. Such a list at the beginning of the package provides the trainees with an over-view of what they are going to have to accomplish. It also provides an advanced organizer of sorts to help them plan their learning.

I've also found that this list is a good spot for restating the importance of the objectives to the trainees. I usually remind them that the objectives are their guide and that when they are sure they have mastered the objectives, they have completed the package.

Trainee Evaluation. The final components of a print SDL package are the trainee evaluation pieces. These are discussed in more detail in Chapter Five, so I'll just note here that in your development you should plan quizzes for the end of each of your chunks. Often these are self-quizzes, with the answers on the reverse side of the page. Directions concerning mastery level, what to do when a question is missed, and possible remediation should be included as well.

You may choose to have final quizzes of either the self- or other-corrected variety at the end of larger chunks as well. This is the time when you make those decisions and plan how they will be implemented as an integral part of your package.

An SDL Simulation

You now add the directions and information that the trainees will need to complete your package.

Management Module 1: Time Management

Introduction

This is a self-directed learning package on time management. Its purpose is to help you learn to manage your time effectively. Since this is self-directed learning, there will be no instructor. You will be responsible for reading the material and showing that you have mastered it by completing the self-quizzes and the final test. You will be able to take all the time you need to achieve this goal. If job duties interrupt you, you may put the material away and return to it when you have time. The important thing is that you learn the material, not how fast you can do it in.

The objectives that you will find at the beginning of each section will help guide your learning. All the quizzes and the test will be based directly on these objectives.

Please do not write in this book. Answers to the self-quizzes should be noted on a separate piece of paper.

Supplies List

Paper
"To do" list pads (three types)
Videotapes: *Time Management: The Reality* (12 minutes)
            Five Steps to Better Delegation (15 minutes)

Package Outline

Section 1: Time Savers
        The "to do" list
        Prioritizing by helping your boss succeed
        Delegation
        Improving reading skills

Section 2: Time Wasters
    The telephone
    Meetings

Module Objectives

The trainee will be able to:

1. Employ a daily "to do" list with priority symbols to plan and carry out each day's task.
2. Discuss the importance—as a good time management tool—of prioritizing activities that help his or her boss succeed.
3. Effectively utilize the five-step method of delegation.
4. Discuss the nine keys to improving reading skills.
5. List three methods for decreasing the number of interrupting phone calls.
6. Implement his or her own technique for reducing wasted time in returning calls.
7. Describe the importance of having a prepublished agenda for all meetings.
8. Discuss techniques for eliminating meetings.
9. List ten ways to decrease time wasted in meetings.

Section 1: Time Savers

Directions: Using the section objectives as your guide, read the material contained in this section. You will also need to watch the videotapes *Time Management: The Reality* and *Five Steps to Better Delegation.* When you have finished, complete the self-quiz found at the end of this section.

Your learning time for this section should be approximately 60 minutes.

Section Objectives: The trainee will be able to:
    Employ a daily "to do" list with priority symbols to plan and carry out each day's task.
    Discuss the importance of prioritizing activities that help his or her boss succeed as a good time management tool.

Effectively utilize the five-step method of delegation. Discuss the nine keys to improving reading skills.

The "To Do" List

One of the most effective concepts in time management is prioritizing the tasks you need to do. This can be done on a daily, weekly, monthly, or even on a project basis. Usually people begin with a daily priority list, often called a "to do" list.

The first thing to do in using a "to do" list is to decide when you will make it up. This is usually done at the end of the day or the first thing in the morning. Many time-organized individuals will also take a few minutes at lunchtime to review and revise their list. If you make your list the night before . . .

There are as many ways of making a "to do" list as there are individuals who use them. We've included with this package three different types of preprinted sheets that might work for you. The first is simply a series of lines . . .

Other time managers find that a simple blank sheet of paper works best for their "to do" list. It can be full sized or simply a notepad, depending on your personal . . .

A newer application of the "to do" list is the computerized calendar/organizer. These software programs . . .

One of the important things you need to do with your "to do" list is to find a way to prioritize the tasks on it. This can be as simple as listing the first priority first, the second, second, and so on. It might also be as complicated as three lists, one for first-priority tasks . . .

Another technique is color coding. For example, first-priority tasks can be in red ink or on red paper, second-priority green, third-priority blue. The advantage of this system is . . .

Prioritizing by Helping Your Boss Succeed

One way to help you to prioritize your tasks has been postulated by Henry Sipes in his book *Time Management: The Reality.* He states that the best time managers are those who realize that they must be superior performers if they wish to get ahead in their company. To be a superior performer, you must be seen as a successful person, and the individual who determines your success and value is your boss.

Thus, the good time manager finds out what it is that will

help the boss succeed and treats tasks that perform this function as his or her first priority. Sipes states that every day, one of your first-priority tasks must be to do something to make the boss look good.

Delegation

Improving Reading Skills
Directions: When you are sure that you have completed all of the objectives in this section, go on to the self-quiz on the next page.

Section 2: Time Wasters

Directions: Using the section objectives as your guide, read the material contained in this section. When you have finished, complete the self-quiz found at the end of this section. Your learning time for this section should be approximately 30 minutes.

Section Objectives: The trainee will be able to:
List three methods for decreasing the number of interrupting phone calls.
Implement his or her own technique for reducing wasted time in returning calls.
Describe the importance of having a prepublished agenda for all meetings.
Discuss techniques for eliminating meetings.
List ten ways to decrease the time wasted in meetings.

The Telephone
Approaching time management from the opposite direction, you need to find ways to eliminate time wasters. The telephone is one of the most common of these. The first thing you can do to prevent the telephone from wasting your time is to stop it from interrupting you when you are in the middle of something. Everybody has had those times when . . .
There are three methods you can use to stop phone interruptions. The first is to simply work away from the phone. Now this may be a problem if . . .

> The second method is to find a phone call interceptor. This is a person who can answer your phone and take messages. It doesn't have to be a secretary if you don't have one. Even a co-worker can . . .
>
> Another method of controlling your phone is to only return calls at specified times. This might be at the end of the day, or each morning, or right after lunch. There are a number of advantages to this . . .
>
> *Meetings*
> Directions: When you are sure that you have completed all of the objectives in this section, go on to the self-quiz on the next page.

Desktop Publishing

Beyond these considerations, most of SDL print formatting relates to how the package looks. Remember, there is no substitute for good-looking materials and no excuse for unattractive ones. Many books, articles, checklists, and so forth about formatting print materials have been published. You can find some of these listed in the Suggested Readings section. Our discussion here will hit the high points.

Good desktop publishing software, a high-quality laser printer, and a person who knows how to get the most out of such a system are three mandatory tools for producing any SDL print materials. The capability to do borders, shading, boxes, and so on that this hardware allows, along with the superior quality, will help make your packages more readable and more acceptable. Also, when it is time to revise your program, these items will be worth their weight in gold.

The cost is significant but not outrageous, and the benefits will be more than worth it. If you're a one-person department, there are plenty of classes on desktop publishing. Taking a few of these will pay big dividends immediately. Often, if you buy the hardware from a reputable dealer, it will have free classes for you to take.

If you have the budget, you might consider sending your

work out to a professional desktop/graphics service. The products produced by these shops are usually superior in quality to anything you can do on your own, and the operators are so familiar with the capabilities of their machines and programs that they will suggest ways to format your material that you might never think of. This know-how does not come cheap but is often worth it, particularly if desktop expertise is limited in your organization.

Reproducing Your Print Package

After making your master, how you reproduce your package becomes important. Poor copy quality automatically suggests that the program is second rate, even if it isn't. Copy quality control is a must. If possible, try to find a printer that has a direct electronic copying system. This process takes the material right from your disk and feeds it into the printing machines. The quality of these systems is far higher than that of ordinary photocopiers. In fact, it is almost as good as offset printing. The price will usually be less, and the mistakes far fewer.

If you need to go the photocopy route, be sure to triple-check your master before you send it out or begin to copy it yourself. Decide if you can logically use front-to-back pages. This saves paper and money and makes your package thinner, but it may be cumbersome for your trainees, depending on where they will be using your programs. It can also be a very complicated and easily botched copying process, particularly if you are doing it yourself. After the copies are made, you'll need to check each page of each booklet. That's right—*each* page of *each* booklet. I have seen photocopy machines do the strangest things, and printers do things that were even more bizarre. You may automatically check the copy you are sending to the CEO, but your trainees will be strongly affected by things like missing pages and blurred print. So give them a break by making sure their packages are right, and they'll return the favor by accepting your materials more readily.

Binding

Next, consider your binding process. Plain old stapled pages are cheap, and they look it. Putting your programs on 11 x 14 paper with a fold and staple is a bit more complicated, but it looks a lot better. Add a colored cover page on heavier stock that wraps around the back, and you have an attractive package that is cheap enough to toss out when a revision comes around.

Hot-glue binding is about the next least expensive process and can be done in your own shop. However, if your packages are going to receive a lot of heavy use, this system doesn't hold up well.

A plastic spiral binding system always looks good and can also be done at the office with a relatively inexpensive machine. Unfortunately, it is a time-consuming process, particularly if you need to make a lot of copies, and it doesn't lend itself to revising. Other plastic bindings are available as well but are a little more expensive.

Most expensive, but classiest, are preformed binders. These come in many different types, with rings, locks, posts, slip-on spines, and any number of other techniques for keeping your packages together. If you are in a learning center situation, these binders are usually a good idea, since you don't normally make too many copies of your packages. However, in a distributed system where you may need hundreds or even thousands of copies, they may become cost prohibitive.

I did run into a situation, though, where this wasn't the case. It was a distributed system for a trucking company with over ninety training sites. Revisions were almost continuous due to the fact that the material concerned a computer system that was constantly being modified to increase its capabilities. Every month, changes to the SDL package were necessary—sometimes a page or two, sometimes an entire section.

The designers found that the cheapest approach was to buy three-ring binders and just send updates of pages as they were produced. It was expensive in the beginning, but this approach more than made up for the initial cost as time went on, since it wasn't necessary to rebind new editions. The updating was also much faster, because printing time was decreased and binding time eliminated completely.

In the final analysis, binding must be a compromise between making your package look as good as you can, the price you can afford to pay, and your revision needs.

Graphics

Graphics are another way you can make your print package look good, as long as they are appropriate. The old saying about a picture being worth a thousand words is true, but make sure those thousand words are worth saying. I've seen some very good programs that were badly served by incomprehensible or useless graphics.

Technical SDL packages are the biggest offender in this area. Often they are full of flowcharts, graphs, and diagrams only peripherally connected to the material. I've seen graphics that were so complicated and hard to understand that the trainees just gave up on them and, for that matter, on the whole package. When I asked the designers why they had included them, they replied, "We needed pictures to break up the monotony!"

On the other hand, I've seen some less-than-adequate packages made at least usable by good graphics. For example, programs that discuss how to read, use, fill out, or otherwise wrestle with complex forms (a very widespread use of SDL) work best with examples of those forms throughout the package. Graphics of full forms, cut-down forms, and spotlighted line items help make a highly confusing and often deadly boring package more user friendly.

The key is to use graphics, but only graphics that fit and reinforce or add to the material presented. This doesn't mean that every graphic has to relate exactly to the material. Cartoons and other diversionary graphics can help you make points in less obvious ways, or just relax the trainees. Use them, but plan them for that purpose and don't get carried away with them.

Techniques for Including Graphics in Your Programs. Unless you enjoy cutting and pasting, the best way to deal with graphics is to buy a good digital scanner. Once again, this sort of equipment is not cheap, but if you do any graphics at all, it will pay for itself the first time you do a revision. I did a quick analysis once and found that on one program alone, the scanner had saved my clerical staff over thirty hours of form designing and cutting and pasting.

You can also do some things with a scanner that would be

almost impossible otherwise. For example, how would you like your CEO's picture on the first page of your package, right there with the memo that he or she wrote explaining why this program is important to the company? With a scanner, such creativity is no problem, either the first time or during revisions. Even if you get a new CEO, as long as you have his or her picture, you can put them in your program!

Other suggestions for attractive print materials include the use of shading and blocking. This can be particularly effective in setting off directions, activities, or quizzes. Also, consider varying font sizes to set off titles and thought breaks, or font characteristics such as boldface and italics to stress certain points.

Adding Color to Your SDL Package

Another consideration is color. There is a lot of controversy about color: Is it needed? Does it distract? How much should be used? Are trained artists the only ones capable of using it correctly? My basic philosophy is use color when possible.

Color print is easy on the eyes after so much black and white everywhere else. Colored paper, even if it's only one color, can make your packages look better. In some large systems I have developed, color coding was used, so management packages were one color of paper, basic skills packages were another, and customer service a third. Color graphics and multicolor pages are attention grabbing. Use them if your system and your budget allow it.

The Need for White Space

The final aspect of print formatting that we'll discuss here is white space. Many SDL packages fail in a usability test not because they haven't been analyzed, objectivized, or even chunked properly, but simply because they are just to daunting to read. The pages are filled with words, words, and more words. A graphic may be thrown in occasionally, but then it's back to the words. You can guard against this tendency by using plenty of white space.

Don't be afraid to use up a little paper; it's recyclable. Paragraphs should be separated by an extra line. Add headings and

---

An SDL Simulation

With your content done and your package laid out with directions, introductions, and slots for evaluations, you now use your desktop publishing software and laser printer to create a master of your SDL package as it is constructed to this point. You add graphics of your own design and from other sources.

---

subheadings in bold type to break up the monotony. Start new thoughts on new pages. Use borders, graphics, and anything else you can think of to break up the text.

The one drawback to this is that it will make your packages look bigger simply by having more pages. There is a good argument that if the package itself begins to look too "fat," it will intimidate the users just as much as too many words on a page will. You'll need to strike the right balance, and that's a matter of personal preference and experience. However, remember the process of chunking. If you're getting a package that is too fat, possibly you need to chunk, and chunk again, until you have the right number of packages.

White space is important in CBT as well. I have seen countless programs that are just screen after screen of fifteen lines of verbiage—or thirty if they are single spaced. The same fundamentals that help create good print materials will work for verbiage on computer screens, too. With disks, you don't run into the "too-fat" problem, so use a few extra bits for white space when developing computer-based SDL.

Suggestions for Other SDL Media Formats

This section will provide you with some hints on the development of SDL media formats other than print. Once again, its purpose is not to make you an expert at any format but simply to provide you with some ideas that I've collected through years of developing SDL packages in various formats. More detailed infor-

Table 4.1. A Summary of Media Formats.

Format	Description	Strengths	Weaknesses	Notes
Print	Bound workbook or study guide, most often with diagrams, line drawings, or pictures.	Revises easily. Cost and time effective to produce and disseminate. Easy for trainee to use if literate.	Difficult to branch. Trainee interest lowers quickly.	Lots of white space needed. Don't rewrite your lectures. Watch reading level.
Audio	Cassette recordings, often accompanied by either workbooks or readings.	Production cost and time relatively low. Dissemination costs low. Excellent for nonreaders.	Difficult to branch. Interest level low. Must redo entire tape to revise.	Multiple voices help. Music good, too, if not overwhelming. Beware of "in-the-car" programs.
Print and slide	Workbook with slide augmentation.	Interaction of book and slides keeps up interest and opens up other interactive possibilities. Can show pictorial examples. Slides relatively cheap to produce in quantity. Revisions fairly simple.	Hardware becomes more expensive and more difficult to use.	Explicit directions needed for use of slides.

Medium	Description	Advantages	Disadvantages	Comments
Slide/audio with or without print	An integrated slide and audiotape program, usually pulsed for automatic operation and often combined with a trainee workbook.	More interaction possible. Branching possible but cumbersome. Visual integration increases trainee interest and learning. Useful for nonreaders.	Takes more time to produce. Equipment costs higher. Slightly more difficult for trainees to use. More difficult to revise.	Voice or print slide change commands can substitute for pulsing. Do-it-yourself slide and tape production and reproduction possible and inexpensive.
Video	Videocassette programs produced specifically for the customer by an outside agency, bought as a total package off the shelf, or reworked from various materials. Often have no workbooks but usually at least a minimal study guide.	High interest level if kept short. No better format when action is needed. Easy for trainee to use. Relatively cheap to disseminate. Playback hardware inexpensive.	Not branchable. Time consuming and expensive to develop well. Revision difficult.	Chunk for better learning and easier revision. Use only when action is required. Augment with workbook.
CBT	Computerized programs, usually developed with the help of an authoring system and accessed through a PC or workstation.	Branching excellent. Interaction good if done well. Trainee interest can be high. Revision not too difficult. Low-cost dissemination.	Hardware expensive. Computer phobia a problem for some trainees. Very time consuming to develop.	Watch for computerized page turners. Consider use of existing or secondhand equipment to reduce costs.
Video interactive (CD ROM)	Laser disc with video segments or still pictures integrated with a computer to create a marriage of CBT and video.	Highly interactive. Excellent branching. High trainee interest. Superior for performance skills.	Hardware very expensive. Cost and time for development high. Difficult to revise. Expensive to disseminate.	Have a professional do it for you.

mation for each format can be gleaned from sources listed in the Suggested Readings section. Table 4.1 summarizes many of these points for all formats, including print.

Slide-Tape Formats

The most basic of the alternative formats is the slide-tape combination. I've more or less skipped a slightly less involved format, the interactive audiotape. Most of the suggestions made here for the audio aspect of slide-tape are the same for the audiotape without slides. The other portion of an interactive audiotape system is a print component, for which we've already provided development suggestions.

Slide-tape SDL packages have received less notice lately as more exotic formats like interactive video and multimedia have come on the scene. However, they are still a learning-effective and—more important—a cost-effective method for SDL.

I won't bore you with the oft-repeated studies and numbers that indicate the importance of visuals in the learning process. Suffice it to say that visualization is important in the learning process, and a slide-tape program can go well beyond any print graphics in meeting this need. It also costs less than interactive video and multimedia and takes much less time to produce and revise.

Print Piece. A good slide-tape SDL package has three components: print piece, slides, and audiotape. We'll touch on each of these. The print piece may be called a *study guide* or a *learner's guide* or whatever you wish. It usually contains instructions on how to use the package and anything else the developer sees fit to put in. I've seen examples that consisted only of the objectives, with space for writing notes after each objective. Though a rudimentary design, it was very effective for the learning of cognitive material.

Other guides may include self-quizzes; activities to be performed; internal directions for when to stop, start, or review an area on the audiotape; examples of forms; and anything else that might help the trainee.

One package I was asked to review had each of the slides duplicated in the guide but with labels or pieces missing. The trainees had to fill in these gaps as they observed the visuals and listened to the tape.

Another type contained fill-in-the-blank questions that were completed simultaneously with the tape and slide viewing.

I even came across one package where the entire audiotape script was reproduced with blanks for filling in key words and concepts. I considered this to be a bit of overkill but was assured by the developer that it was the best way to achieve mastery and that it worked well.

Slides. The second component of a slide-tape SDL package—the slide component—is a simple concept. There are only a few rules to follow. The main one is that, in most cases, more is better than less. Your purpose is to make a visual presentation, so use visuals. Temper this with a few subrules, however. First, the trainee needs time to assimilate the visual, or it is of little use. Second, at all cost avoid *cognitive dissonance*—that is, having your tape say one thing while your slide is showing something else.

These subrules tend to be interrelated. Achieving one usually depends on achieving the other. This interdependency is illustrated by the need to give the trainee time to digest the slide. I have seen programs where the slide is described on the tape, others where there is silence on the tape, and still others where the narrator notes that the trainee should take so many seconds to review the slide before moving on. I find this third method to be the most effective, particularly if the narrator mentions one or two key points to look for on the slide and then stops talking.

A third subrule is to avoid literal duplication by a visual of what is on the tape. Having overheads or slides that restate exactly what they are saying is a favorite trick of stand-up presenters. Presenters use these "word slides" in lieu of notes, or simply because they don't know what else to do for a visual. In slide-tape SDL packages, word slides should be kept to a minimum and used basically for emphasis. *If it needs saying, it can be said on the tape.*

If you've matched your slide to the narration, given the trainee time to assimilate the visual message before the tape moves on, and used all the visuals that these two concepts allow, you will have a good slide component.

Advantages. The advantage of using slides is that they are simple to make (all you need is a camera), cheap to duplicate (with about a $100 worth of equipment beyond your camera, you can make as many copies as you need), and easy to revise (shoot a new slide, take the old one out, and put the new one in).

They also show actual pictures of what you are talking about, and, as word slides, can add strong emphasis to what your trainee is hearing on the tape. In fact, these are two of the three types of slide you might use. Along with graphic representation slides such as diagrams, charts, and so on, a judicious mixing of word slides for emphasis and picture slides for showing reality will give you the visual component you need for an SDL package.

Disadvantages. There are some disadvantages to slides, too, since they can be awkward to handle, ship, and set up in a distributed system. The playback machines can get cranky at times, and if you decide to get fancy and have your slides computer generated professionally, they can become very expensive. But you can obtain close-to-professional results at home, and slides are definitely the quickest, cheapest visual for SDL.

Dealing with packaging problems. To handle the packaging problems, there are several products on the market expressly designed to hold and transport slides. They range from small plastic boxes and see-through vinyl sheets to hard-cover plastic binders that have a preformed place for the audiotape and slides and a pocket for your written materials.

These products make storage and shipping easier, but they don't solve the problem of how the slides get into the carousel once they reach their destination. This is of particular importance for distributed systems using slide-tape SDL packages. I've numbered slides, put little dots on them, given specific directions, and even tried an audiotaped set of step-by-step directions for getting slides into the carousel correctly. Still, I've found slides out of order, backward, or upside down when I visited the training site.

Sending already-loaded carousels is cumbersome and can be disastrous, since they are breakable. I thought the cube slide projectors might solve this problem, but they had some sticky technical problems. Distribution is one disadvantage of the slide-tape process that I don't have a solution for.

Audiotapes. The third component of a slide-tape SDL is the tape. The tape portion of an SDL package must absolutely match the objectives. The tape is really not much different from what you would write if your SDL were using a paper-and-pencil format. In fact, the key to a good tape is to write a script. (For more information on script writing, refer to the Suggested Readings.)

After completing your script, you can match up visuals to go with it. I've found this to be the best approach for producing slide-tape packages for SDL. Write first, review, revise, and validate your information, then add visuals. Make sure your visuals fit the material, add them to your script in the form of a story board, then narrate.

Narrating. Just as important as a good script is a good narration of the script. A lot of slide-tape SDL packages fail simply because the narration is poor, or boring, or can't be understood. The best remedy for this is to get a professional narrator. You can find good narrators at local radio and television stations or listed in audiovisual magazines. They range from cheap to expensive, with the quality being about equal to the price, but almost any of them will be better than a nonprofessional. If you must do the narration itself, I have three hints: practice, *practice*, PRACTICE.

Music and sound effects. Beyond narration, you can enhance your audio portion with music and sound effects. Doing things like this takes time and a bit of money, but if you have a little of each, your program will be much more interesting to the trainees. This is an important consideration when you remember there is no instructor to make boring material interesting through teaching style.

Another approach is to use multiple voices if possible. I've seen this done between chunks or within them. Either way seems to work, though it is much more difficult to change voices during a chunk of content. Alternative male and female voices can also break up the tedium.

Equipment for the slide-tape format. Recording and play back equipment are important considerations, too. There are plenty of different types on the market, and your best bet is to work through a good audiovisual equipment dealer. Some types of equipment will perform multiple functions like acting as a projector as well as an individual viewer, or being a recorder as well as a playback machine. Some of these extra features are useful and can make things less costly, but in the end I've found that simplicity is usually better. I've learned that fewer buttons make playback equipment less daunting to the trainees, and fewer choices and settings make recording equipment more foolproof for me. Does anyone out there, short of a real audiophile, know how to use a graphic equalizer?

You can buy relatively simple equipment to add a silent signal to a tape so that the slide changes when you want it to. You can even have the tape stop automatically if, for example, you want the trainee to spend some time with a slide, as we discussed earlier. This equipment is cheap, easy to operate, and gives professional results.

On the other hand, if you want slide changes or tape stops to occur through a direction to the trainee in your print material, there is nothing wrong with this technique, either. The point is that for little money, and with a bit of creativity, you can add an entire new dimension to your SDL packages.

Video

Recently there has been a marked increase in the use of video by a significant number of corporations. One study found that over 80 percent of the companies surveyed use or plan to use video for training. In any training situation, video is a complex medium to produce and use effectively. In SDL, this complexity is multiplied by such factors as the need for a properly written script; program length considerations; the need for stop, start, and review capability; the relation of the video to the written materials; and particularly revision needs. Add to this the price of production and the price of playback equipment, and I find it difficult to recommend video as an SDL medium, with one exception.

The Need to Show Action. That exception is when you need to show action. For example, suppose you wanted to train employees on the twelve steps to opening a pump cover. Slide-tape would work well here, unless you had to show how to twist the pump cover off in just a certain way to avoid breaking the gasket attached to it. If this were the case, your choice would have to be video. The need for a particular action would almost demand it. On the other hand, if you only have to unfasten twelve bolts and lift the cover, why spend the time, energy, and money on video?

I've seen hundreds of SDL packages that are like the second

example. They could have been done more easily, certainly less expensively, and possibly more effectively with a different medium. But they used video and bored the trainees who watched twelve bolts being loosened. When asked why they used it, most developers responded that they "needed" to have a video.

There are many reasons for this "need," ranging from "we have the equipment, so we have to use it" to "I always wanted to do one." Barring some deep internal or possibly external motivation, good SDL development suggests using video only when absolutely necessary for the visual presentation of an action. In all other cases, you can usually find another medium that is cheaper, easier to develop, and will serve as well.

Developing Video. When needed, video development closely follows the pattern of the slide-tape process. Scripts, storyboards, and a major emphasis on keeping to the objectives are of prime importance. For the all-important staging, shooting, and editing, professional help is a must. Home videos may be a big seller on television, but they won't be in an SDL package. Again, there is no instructor who can make up for what your video lacks, particularly in interest value. So spend the money and use the pros.

One possible exception to this advice is if video is only one of the formats that your program is employing. Short snippets of video that detail a simple action can effectively be done in-house with camcorders and simple editing. Going beyond this, particularly when using actors, is inviting disaster or, worse yet, laughter.

Of course, multiple media formats can complicate things for the trainee, so you need solid directions, which brings up another point. Video, like slide-tape, never stands on its own in SDL (or any other training design, for that matter). A workbook or learning guide component is mandatory for any SDL video process. The process of developing it is about the same as for slide-tape, but be sure you do it.

Other strengths and weaknesses of video include the following:

- *Difficulty in revision.* This can be somewhat mediated by producing your video in small discrete slugs, each of which can be changed without the need for redoing the whole program.

- *Ease of distribution.* Even with a print component, video can easily be distributed through the use of preformed plastic carriers that can go into a three-ring binder.
- *Flexibility.* Your trainees can take a video program home to play on their own machines.

Computer-Based Training

CBT is probably the most useful media format for SDL. It not only lends itself to SDL very well but is relatively easy to develop. It is also cost effective, at least from a hardware point of view, due to the proliferation of desktop computers and networks in today's corporate environment.

Many people get confused between computer-based training and computer training. Simply stated, *computer training* is training people how to use computers, while *computer-based training* is training people through the use of computers. Interestingly, the best "computer training" is usually "computer based." In other words, using the computer to train people on how to use the computer. (You can see why this can get confusing.)

The important point for the SDL developer is that CBT can be used to train on any number of different topics, not just on how to use computers. Anything that you put in a paper-and-pencil format can be put on a computer. Almost anything that you put on a slide-tape format can be put on a computer. Even video formats can use the computer, though in this case, the computer becomes just a high-tech learner's guide.

Advantages. One of the biggest advantages of CBT is that you can do it without professional help. There are several excellent authoring systems available to help you design SDL CBT-format programs. Most of these programs include branching techniques to further individualize your programs and make them more time and learning effective. They might also have built-in quiz correction and record-keeping programs to make you and your staff more efficient.

A second advantage is that CBT programs can run on machinery that in many companies is already in place. This saves on capital outlay in getting your SDL system started, and in an office environment, it puts training right on the trainee's desk. Training centers can also benefit, since most organizations usually have a few older-model computers that nobody uses anymore. These may not be the latest technology and may be a bit slow, but you can end up with half a dozen computer workstations in your center for almost no capital outlay.

A third advantage of CBT is size. If your entire program is on a 3½-inch disk, it's very easy and cheap to duplicate and send to other training sites. It's also easy to use for anyone who knows how to run a computer. The person just puts it in, pushes a button, and follows directions. Finally, the program is relatively easy to revise.

CBT Authoring Systems. Unfortunately, CBT can also be deadly boring, particularly when the developer makes it into an electronic page turner that is nothing more than page after page of text. You can avoid this problem by using a number of good development tactics. The simplest of these is to be sure you pick an authoring system that allows for branching, then put in as many branches as you can.

A step beyond branching is the process known as *HyperCard* or *Hypertext.* Authoring systems using these functions allow your trainees to request information as their learning needs require rather than to simply follow predetermined branches. (See the Suggested Readings for further detail.)

Your authoring system should also allow you to change screen colors. This is not only attention getting but can signal evaluation screens, important graphics, and other items to the trainee. As in print, use varying font sizes, italics, and reverse video for more emphasis.

Graphics. The most important development tactic, however, is the use of good graphics. Be sure your authoring system will allow you to transport both drawn and scanned graphics into your program. For diagrams, charts, and so on, there are computer drawing programs that are easy to use. Don't buy a fancy one initially. Start with a simple one that's easy to use, and learn what you need by doing. Most of the basic programs are cheap, and you can buy better ones later as you become comfortable with the process.

Another useful item for CBT, particularly when it comes to

graphics, is a digital scanner. We talked about scanners in relation to print packages, but they are also handy and perhaps mandatory for CBT as well. The reasons are essentially the same: personalization with company logos, ease of adding forms and other special documents, ability to take graphics from multiple sources, and so forth.

For an even wider range of graphics, you can buy electronic clip art that you load into your computer and then transfer to your program as needed. Examples include cartoons, line drawings, graphs that you can change, and a host of other professionally done illustrations. The point is, jazz up your CBT SDL package! Follow the rules of good graphics as we discussed earlier, but use your creativity, and the available technology, to make it interesting.

Disadvantages. On the negative side, computers are a problem for those who are not used to them. You should remember from the analysis phase that you need to consider your training audience and their capabilities before choosing this or any other format.

CBT also takes a lot of time to do it right. Designers give various ratios, ranging from 50 hours of development time per every hour of actual program that the trainees use, to 200 hours of development per hour of training. These proportions fluctuate, depending on how well the developer knows the authoring system and how much branching and graphics are put into the program. However, they are invariably greater than the five-to-one ratio for classroom development, the ten-to-one ratio for slide programs, and the twenty-to-one ratio for video programs.

One way to keep development time down is to hire a CBT expert to do some of the work. We've said that an advantage of CBT is that you can do it yourself. However, there are times—particularly when you are first starting out—that such an individual can be of real help. A good CBT specialist will be able to use the authoring system more efficiently, should have many ideas for enhancing your program that have been developed through years of CBT experience, and can teach you both the methods and the shortcuts that will make you more expert. Such talent cost money, but it can help you get your first programs out faster and make you a better CBT developer as well.

The important point with CBT is that if you don't have the

time, money, and/or expertise to do it right, with branching, graphics, and other good learning techniques, don't do it at all. In the eyes and minds of your trainees, using a computer will not make up for the fact that your program is nothing more than an electronic page turner. They will get bored with it and turn it off, which will turn off the learning. A good paper-and-pencil piece will take a lot less time to develop, will be more effective, and will be used more often.

High-Technology Formats

A word should be said about two other approaches: interactive video and multimedia.

Interactive Video. A level beyond CBT is the *interactive video* format. Interactive video uses a combination of a computer and a video player, usually a videodisc but at times a videocassette. The best of these programs allows the trainee to drive forklifts, pilot planes, and literally interact with computer-simulated people, all without leaving the workstation.

They require the trainee to make decisions that lead to other data branches, which creates the need for new decisions, which branch again, as often as the material or the developer's imagination dictates. The trainees see, hear, almost feel both mechanical and personal interactions, and find out the results of their decisions in most realistic ways. Ever have a simulated bomb go off in your face as you're trying to defuse it, or a simulated employee storm out of your simulated office threatening a lawsuit because you chose the wrong thing to say? For SDL, there is no superior media format.

Unfortunately, since it is a level beyond CBT in capability, interactive video is also a level beyond it in complexity. The programming, the video needs, even the writing necessary to take full advantage of the process are well beyond the abilities of most nonspecialists.

And you'll want to take full advantage of everything you can, because the hardware is very expensive and can be cumbersome to use. The cost of this professional expertise can be prohibitively high, and even with expert help, the development time can stretch into months for a single one-hour program. Added to all this is the immense difficulty in revising, particularly if you are using a laser disc system.

As with video, you'll want to be sure that this technology will increase the effectiveness of your SDL packages to the point that it is worth the time and effort involved before you invest in using it.

Multimedia. A technology that eliminates some but not all of interactive video's disadvantages is what today is being termed *multimedia.* Terms such as *CD ROM, DVI, CDI, digital video,* and so on apply to this category of media format. In multimedia, the entire program—including text, pictures, graphics, video, and sound—is contained on a single laser disc about the size of the ones used for musical reproduction.

The playback hardware is a somewhat modified but basically generic desktop computer. There is no need for a special video player, video monitor, and the larger videodisc of interactive video. This eliminates some of the awkwardness and expense of interactive video, making the final product much less complicated for you to send out and for the trainee to use.

Some multimedia programs can even be stored and run directly from floppy disks. However, the small storage capacity of these disks limits the ability of the program to include video and complex graphics.

Multimedia uses the unique ability of HyperCard and Hypertext to create decision and branching possibilities that are almost endless. With it, you can capture material from many sources—including books, television programs, and even old movies—to use in your training programs.

Multimedia definitely involves a "for professionals only" development process. My only suggestion is that if you have the need, and the money, this avenue is certainly worth exploring. The Suggested Readings section will give you some sources that can start you in the right direction.

Consultants and Prepackaged Materials: Shortcuts for Development

There is one other approach to SDL material development to consider: having others do the development for you. In the media section, we discussed formats that only full-time experts in those particular processes should develop and noted that these specialists could save you time. However, other types of SDL consultants can help you decrease your development time and enhance your SDL packages.

The Hired Gun

In Chapter Three, I mentioned I had hired a consulting firm that specializes in SDL to do an entire package for me, because I had neither the staff nor the time to do it myself. This is one of the two basic types of SDL consultants available.

The other type of SDL consultant, which is more common, is what I term the "hired gun." These are one- or two-person shops, usually local, that you employ to help do the grunt work of your SDL packages. They mainly perform material development but might also help with the job analysis or some of the review and rewrite processes. They use your design and format, at times your offices, and often your equipment. In the final analysis, they are really just temporary, specialized staff. You usually need to monitor them closely.

I've used this type of consultant often, particularly during a start-up situation when I needed a lot of SDL packages quickly, or before I could hire and properly train a staff. If you do your monitoring well, the hired gun will produce a quality product for you. A disadvantage is that monitoring takes time.

The Town Marshal

Town marshals are usually national, always expensive, and come equipped with the expertise, facilities, machines, and everything else needed to give you a finished product (that is, an SDL package) at the end of the contract period. With a good consultant of this type, all you need to do is outline the parameters, then sit back and wait for results. The first product you'll usually want to see is a preliminary draft of the SDL package. The following are some tips to keep in mind when employing town marshals.

- Be sure the project is well defined. If you realize that your analysis is not quite adequate, don't hire someone to come in and try to design and develop. You wouldn't do that to yourself and expect good results, so why would you do it to a consultant?
- Be certain the subject matter has been decided on and is relatively stable. Unlike you, the consultants don't know the company. They may not even be working in the same city. By the time they learn of changes to content or procedure, it is often too late.
- If possible, have a model of the design you want the consultant to use. There are as many ways to make an SDL package as there are developers doing them. If you want yours done a specific way (with objectives, for instance), be sure the consultant knows this.

It's an old but accurate adage: when dealing with SDL consultants, you should assume nothing. However, if you start them out right, the town marshal will produce excellent SDL packages for you and, more often than not, in much less time than you would have needed yourself.

Prepackaged Materials

While both types of SDL consultants, if used properly, can effectively shorten your SDL material development time, there is another shortcut that you can often take advantage of. Prepackaged or off-the-shelf materials can, in the right situation, be even more time effective and a lot cheaper. These materials, like consultants, come in two forms: purchased SDL programs and malleable programs.

Purchased SDL Programs. The first form of prepackaged material is the *purchased SDL program*, usually covering a singular topic. Some of these are general in nature, dealing with management subjects like goal setting, strategic planning, communications, and so on. Others are extremely specific and deal with a particular technical skill, such as tuning a car engine or troubleshooting a fluid pump. They come in varying media formats, and if they fit exactly what you need, they can save a lot of development time.

Even when they are close enough to your procedures to be useful, they are usually cost effective only in a learning center implementation. If you need to distribute the program to a couple of hundred or a couple of thousand training sites, they can become very expensive, despite licensing arrangements.

Malleable Programs. The second type of prepackaged material is what I call the *malleable program.* This is usually a program that was not made for SDL but that can be "hammered into shape" with a little work on your part. I had stated earlier that as a rule, video is only a time- and cost-efficient medium if your material demands action. Malleable videos are an exception to that rule. You purchase them from a distributor, then edit, add to, augment, or otherwise change them into good SDL programs that meet your analyzed needs. They are a tremendous way to save development time and energy.

If you are going to actually edit a purchased video program—and you usually need to, since off-the-shelf programs always contain material that you don't want—be sure to contact the distributor first. There is a possibility of copyright infringement. However, I've found that most distributors will give you permission, as long as you don't duplicate your edited copy without license.

A "tightened-up" video from an outside source, combined with a learner's guide that contains proper objectives, material relating to your company, and good evaluations, is an excellent SDL package. It can even be developed in less time than a simple print package.

While videos lend themselves best and most often to this fusion technique, other kinds of materials are available that can speed up your development process. Many companies put out workbooks, which you can use with little or no revision, depending on your needs. You can also transmute magazine articles, books, or book chapters into large portions of your content in a print format.

I have come across one distributed SDL system for management development in an accounting and consulting firm based in New York City that is simply a series of articles culled from management journals. Objectives and quizzes were added to the articles to make them into SDL packages. It represents an elegant solution for a company that wants to continue its development of managers who cannot meet as a group because there are 500 of them at locations throughout North America.

In summary, the process of SDL development requires you to take the tasks you identified in the analysis phase and use them to develop a complete SDL package that will help your trainees to learn those tasks. This means writing objectives from the tasks and writing content that relates to the objectives. You do this in a format that matches what your trainees can best use and what your company can logically support.

This is not easy. However, if you follow a good approach to SDL development, keep your eye on the objectives, and remember that your packages must do the job on their own, it's possible. What you will end up with is effective, efficient training, specifically designed to meet the needs of your trainees and your organization.

An SDL Simulation

While doing your research and writing your content, you came across two videos that said what you wanted to say on the topics of "prioritizing by helping your boss succeed" and "delegation." You already know from your format analysis that video players are available at your training sites, and so you buy the tapes, edit them so they fit exactly what you want the trainees to learn, and make them part of your program. You provide directions for their use and note them in the supplies list included in your package. These videos saved you development time and will give your trainees a break from reading. They increase the complexity of your package, but you feel your managers can easily handle the added format.

Exhibit 4.2. A Checklist for SDL.

Media Formatting

☐ Good print package development techniques have been used.
- Trainee instructions, supply lists, a table of contents, an objectives list, and a place for evaluations are included in your package.
- Your print master looks as good as possible.
- You've chosen a quality reproduction process.
- You've chosen your binding based on appearance, price, and the need for revision.
- You've added graphics where possible.
- You've used color where possible.
- You've included plenty of white space.

☐ Good slide-tape development techniques have been used.
- A good print piece accompanies your slide-tape program.
- The trainees have time to absorb your slides.
- There is no cognitive dissonance.
- Tape and visuals do not duplicate each other.
- You have solutions for any slide packaging problems.
- You have an effective tape narration.
- You've added music and sound effects where appropriate.
- You have the right playback equipment.

☐ Good video development techniques have been used.

☐ Good CBT development techniques have been used.
- You've avoided the "electronic page turner" syndrome.
- You've used branching where possible.
- You've used screen color changes for emphasis.
- You've used graphics where possible.

☐ The use of consultants—if feasible—has been considered.
- You've analyzed the type of consultant you might need.
- You're prepared to guide your consultant as necessary.

☐ Purchased programs and materials have been used where possible.

5

Evaluating Trainees

How to Assess Cognitive Mastery and Performance Improvement

Evaluation in SDL can be broken down into two types. The first is evaluation of the trainees, which is often termed *user evaluation* (Figure 5.1). The second is *package* or *system evaluation*. This is evaluation of the SDL process, which might involve a single package or an entire system, depending on the size of your SDL structure.

This chapter will deal with the first aspect, trainee evaluation. System or package evaluation will be considered in Chapters Nine and Eleven as it relates to each of the implementation schemes, and in Chapter Twelve for SDL as a whole. The evaluation of trainees and of the package logically overlap, but for simplicity's sake, I'll try to separate them as much as possible.

Trainee evaluation has two main components: cognitive evaluation and performance evaluation. We'll consider each in turn.

Cognitive Evaluation

Cognitive evaluation focuses on test development.

Developing Test Questions

If you are a traditional instructional designer, you may have already asked, "What happened to the test questions?" The ISD approach usually puts test question development into the design

Figure 5.1. A Model for SDL.

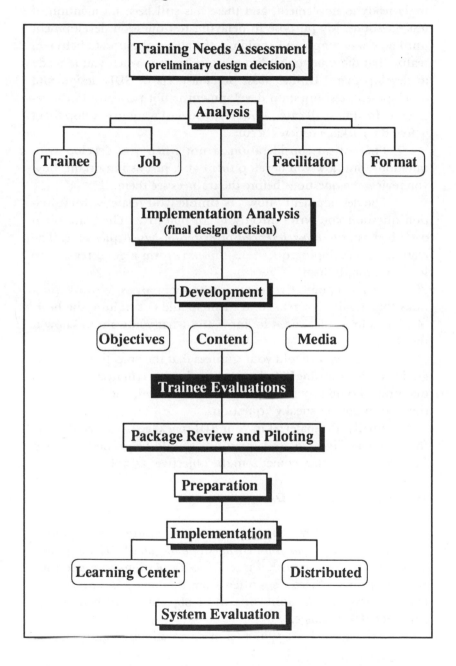

phase. Yet here we are in our SDL operation, packages done, seemingly ready to implement, and there has still been no mention of test questions. My purpose in delaying test question development until now was simply so I could use the above question to help you realize that the time to develop test questions is when you're ready to develop them. Unlike most other aspects of SDL design and development, test question development is not part of a linear sequence. In almost all cases, however, you will want to develop them before the package reviews occur.

The critical consideration is not when you develop your questions, but how you develop them and, just as important, how you review the questions before the trainees see them.

The development "how" is simple: you relate each evaluation question you write directly to an objective. These are often described as *criterion-referenced* or *criterion-based* questions. The reasons for developing questions this way form a good review, so let's go through them.

First, your objectives come from your analysis. Writing questions that are directly related to them should cut right to the heart of what your trainees need to know and what you want to know if they know.

Second, you've told your trainees that the objectives are their guide to the learning. If they believed you, criterion-referenced questions should provide them with no surprises, and you with no complaints about "sneaky" questions.

Finally, the material in your SDL package is written directly from the objectives, so your questions should be properly covered in the material if they come from the objectives as well.

Fourth Cornerstone of SDL

Criterion referencing—this matching of questions to objectives—is the fourth and final cornerstone of good SDL design and development. Adding criterion-referenced questions to a good job analysis, proper objectives written from that analysis, and content that you developed by following those objectives will help ensure a quality SDL package.

Writing good criterion-referenced questions is again a matter of practice. There are some references in the Suggested Readings section that you can turn to, but the only real way to learn the technique is to do it, review it, and do it again. You'll need the objectives in front of you, and the content as well. This is why I don't recommend writing questions directly after developing the objectives, as is the case in some versions of the ISD approach.

Use the verbs you've chosen for your objectives as your guide. If your verb asks the trainees to list something, the question should be list oriented, too. If your objective requires them to analyze, so should the question. Some of your verbs may be based on physical performance. In that case, you will want to develop performance-based measures, not questions. These are discussed in detail in the next section. Exhibit 5.1 provides you with some examples of good and bad criterion-referenced test questions.

A major controversy surrounding criterion-based questions concerns how closely they should resemble the objectives. For example, if an objective says, "Name the five parts of a widget," is it proper for a test question to ask, "Name the five parts of a widget"? My response to such a concern is "What else would you want the question to ask?" If your analysis indicates that this is what the trainees need to know, and your objective told the trainees that is what they are expected to learn, why would you want your test question to be different?

Some people say that this makes it too easy. Of course it makes it easy! The whole idea of good training is to make it as easy as possible for the trainees to learn! And if they have learned, why do you want to make it difficult for them to show you they have?

By the way, this controversy seems to occur only with respect to the lower-level cognitive skills with verbs like *list, state, define, name* and so on. When you get to the higher levels such as *apply* and *analyze,* your questions will almost automatically stop looking exactly like the objectives. Behaviors such as *examine* or *integrate* require more complex test questions to discern the trainees' abilities. However, this does not excuse you from making sure that these questions are as criterion referenced as those that simply restate the objective.

The method of developing test questions should be the same no matter what media format you use. CBT or interactive video may

Exhibit 5.1. Criterion-Referenced Test Questions.

Analysis	*Test Question*
State the blood vessel that carries oxygenated blood from the heart to the body.	The blood vessel that carries oxygenated blood from the heart to the body is: a. Trapezius b. Patella c. Ascending aorta

This is a good though simple example of a well-matched criterion-referenced question.

List three of the five functions of a reactor vessel.	Three of the reactor vessel's five functions are:

Another good criterion-referenced question.

Draw the four basic shapes for geometric figures.	The four basic shapes for geometric figures are:

A bad question. The verb asks the trainee to *draw*, the question to *list*.

Recognize the appropriate symbols for development of a flowchart.	The three most-often-used symbols on a flowchart are:

Probably a bad question. The verb asks the trainee to *recognize*, which means that examples will be provided, while the question asks the trainee to *list*, which usually means to list from memory.

Analyze the changes that occurred in American foreign policy after the death of President Kennedy.	In 500 words, formulate the probable response President Kennedy might have made to the 1968 Tet offensive.

This is a higher-level question, which, as we noted, will not necessarily resemble the objective. At times, that makes it harder to determine if it is criterion referenced. The verbs are different and fall at different levels on Bloom's taxonomy, but some would say that *analysis* can only be measured by what you can do with it—such as to formulate a theory. I feel that it is criterion referenced, though some test designers might disagree. Trying to stay as close as you can to your objectives when dealing with these higher-level verbs is the only safe alternative.

---

make it easier to create more interesting evaluation simulations, but if your objective does not match the question, the evaluation is not valid. For example, if you require the trainee to do a computer-generated role play, it must be linked with an objective that tells the trainee he or she is expected *to be able to* analyze factors in such a situation.

Developing a Question Pool

I've found that the best way to write test questions for SDL is not to write them for a test. In other words, don't decide that you need five questions for a quiz or twenty questions for a final test and then develop questions expressly for those instruments. Instead, get a rough idea of the total number of questions you will need for all the evaluations you are planning. Then divide the total by the number of objectives you have developed. Now try to write that number of questions for each objective, plus a few extra overall, just in case. In most programs, this works out to one or two or, in a heavily evaluated design, to three questions per objective.

Try hard to develop the number you have chosen for *each* objective. Some objectives lend themselves well to questions, while others don't. Your job is to strive to make your question pool—that is, all your questions taken as a whole—a fairly equal representation of all of your objectives. If you don't use this type of question development plan, you will end up weighing objectives unequally in your evaluations. The ones that are easy to write questions for will be overrepresented and those you had trouble with, underrepresented.

Within reason, this unequal weighing is not important, as long as you cover all of your objectives, but evaluation specialists will tell you that unequal representation will make your evaluations less valid. Since validity is a basic problem in any evaluation, I think it's wise to do what you can to keep it high.

I've found that writing each question on a 3 × 5 or 5 × 8 card is a practical way to keep track of your questions. This also makes it convenient when you need to create an evaluation instrument. You should code each question with the objective it refers to, since your cards will get mixed when you put together various evaluations. A good place to store your questions is in a card file used only for that purpose. This facilitates test security and makes it easy to develop a new test if you feel the old one has been compromised.

Reviewing Test Questions

Once you have finished developing your questions and before you ever use them, you need to have them reviewed. I say "have

An SDL Simulation

You develop your question pool:

Objective: Employ a daily "to do" list with priority symbols to plan and carry out each day's task.
Questions:
1. A "to do" list is used to . . .
2. What two times of the day are most often used for developing "to do" lists?
3. Two ways to prioritize your "to do" list are . . .

Objective: Discuss the importance of prioritizing activities that help his or her boss succeed as a good time management tool.
Questions:
1. Who is the person that determines your success and value?
2. What should you do each day if you are a good task prioritizer?

Objective: Effectively utilize the five-step method of delegation.
Question: Can you use the five steps to better delegation in your work environment?

Objective: Discuss the nine keys to improving reading skills.
Questions:
1. What is the best way to remember what you read?
2. How can the triple A attitude help you read better?

Objective: List three methods for decreasing the number of interrupting phone calls.
Question: List three methods for decreasing the number of interrupting phone calls.

Objective: Implement his or her own technique for reducing wasted time in returning calls.
Question: Describe the technique that you will use for returning phone calls.

Objective: Describe the importance of having a prepublished agenda for all meetings.
Question: What can you do before a meeting to make it run as efficiently as possible?

Objective: Discuss techniques for eliminating meetings.
Question: What characteristics are typical of a meeting that needs to be eliminated?

Objective: List ten ways to decrease the time wasted in meetings.
Question: List ten ways to decrease the time wasted in meetings.

them reviewed" rather than "review them," because you will have much better questions if you don't count solely on your own review to ensure their effectiveness. Since you wrote them, you'll probably have a difficult time reviewing them objectively. And that's what you need: an objective review of how good the questions are and whether they are relevant to the material they represent.

To accomplish this adequately, you really need three other people to review your questions, though one or two of them may perform double duty.

First Review. Your first reviewer should be a subject matter expert. Give the expert your questions and ask for a review of whether the answers are correct, from a purely subject matter point of view. You're not interested in whether the individual likes your questions or if your grammar is correct—only in whether the answers are accurate. Let the reviewer know this, so that he or she can concentrate on what you want.

Second Review. The second review should be done by a developer who understands question-writing technique. Give this person the questions and objectives. He or she will primarily be looking for an appropriate match between the objectives and questions. Beyond this, it is important to check for proper question construction, good grammar, relevant distractors in multiple-choice questions, clarity, and so on. Basically, this individual's job is to review the questions from an instructional design point of view.

Third Review. The final review should be done by someone

who has not been part of the development process and is not a subject matter expert. Provide this person with the questions, objectives, and materials. His or her responsibility is to make sure that the answer to each question can be found in the material. It should contain enough detail and keying to allow your trainees to answer the questions the way you expect. This review will make sure that is the case.

You may say this is what you did when you wrote the questions, and that's true. However, question writers—particularly if they are subject matter experts—tend to take things for granted that may not necessarily be there. A basic fact that is needed to answer the question may be obvious to you but not obvious at all to a trainee. As in piloting the entire package, this type of missing information is what a nonexpert review will point out in relation to your test questions.

This question review process is similar to the review process for the entire package, as discussed in the next chapter. You may be able to use your package reviewers to do your questions as well. However, no matter how you do it, an intensive test question review is a necessary part of question development in SDL.

Creating Trainee Evaluation Instruments from Your Test Questions

Once you have a bank of well-written, adequately reviewed test questions, you can choose the ones you need for each evaluation you have planned. Some designers do this randomly; others carefully consider the types of questions they want to use for each evaluation instrument. I've done both and have found each method acceptable, depending on the situation.

As discussed in Chapter Three, one of the most common uses of questions in SDL packages is to separate activities or chunks. Normally, such separations take the form of small self-quizzes or check quizzes, where the trainees answer the questions and then check their responses on their own. These self-quizzes act as both a summary and a review procedure. The answer key for some self-quizzes also includes references to where the trainee can find the correct answers in the previous material. Thus, if they miss a question, the trainees can go back and find the right answer. Other answer keys do not provide this information and direct the trainees to review the entire chunk if they do not achieve mastery level on the quiz.

The number of questions in a check quiz is up to you. I try to have at least one per covered objective. If you did a good job of chunking, you will have around three to five and perhaps as many as seven objectives per chunk, which should make the quiz easy to complete. I prefer the quizzes to be self-administered, though in some systems, a facilitator administers them. This is most common in a learning center implementation. In a distributed implementation, self-administration is normally the method of choice.

Beyond check quizzes, you may want to do user evaluations at almost any other time during an SDL process. Usually one is done at the end of a package or, in some complex programs, every week. I've seen packages with single questions put into the material on a random basis and with formal finals that were given at the end of fifteen weeks of SDL packages. Some systems use a pretest so that trainees can test out of basic packages. Others have an entire series of remedial tests that the trainees take each time mastery is not achieved. The key is to plan what you want in the way of user evaluations and then to make sure you write enough good test questions to fulfill your plan.

Trainee Evaluation and Mastery

Mastery self-quizzes and tests, which are standard in SDL, expect the trainee to answer a predetermined number of questions correctly before going on to the next chunk. Not meeting this level requires the trainee to review the previous material and again take the test or, in some systems, a different test. If you use this multiple-test approach, you will begin to see why you need many test ques tions in your pool.

I observed one training center–based SDL process in a hospital setting near Pittsburgh, where mastery of the material was so important that the facilitator administered both the check quizzes and a remedial quiz if mastery wasn't achieved the first time. She did this by simply drawing five random questions from the test

An SDL Simulation

You add your planned self-quizzes to your package by choosing from the question pool, deciding on the mastery level, and adding directions.

Section 1: Self-Quiz

Directions: Answer all of the following questions on a separate piece of paper without looking back through the section material. When you have completed all the questions, turn to the next page and correct your answers. If you missed any questions, go back to that area of the material and review it. Retake the quiz until you achieve the mastery level of 100%.

1. A "to do" list is used to . . .
2. Two ways to prioritize your "to do" list are . . .
3. Who determines your success and value?
4. What should you do each day if you are a good task prioritizer?
5. What is the best way to remember what you read?

Answers

1. Help prioritize your tasks.
2. Use different sheets for different priorities. Use color coding.
3. Your boss.
4. Make one task that will help your boss succeed a first priority.
5. Use the VRAC formula.

Section 2: Self-Quiz

Directions: Answer all of the following questions on a separate piece of paper without looking back through the section material. When you have completed all the questions, turn to the next page and correct your answers. If you missed any questions, go back to that area of the material and review it. Retake the quiz until you achieve the mastery level of 100%.

1. List three methods for decreasing the number of interrupting phone calls.
2. Describe the technique that you will use for returning phone calls.
3. What can you do before a meeting to make it run as efficiently as possible?
4. What characteristics are typical of a meeting that needs to be eliminated?
5. List ten ways to decrease the time wasted in meetings.

Answers

1. Work away from the phone.
   Use an interceptor.
   Just don't answer.

and so on

bank's 3 × 5 cards and reading them to the trainee. The expected answers were on the back. This was a highly labor-intensive way to quiz, but mastery of each chunk was mandatory (comforting in a hospital situation). The material they were dealing with was rather complex, as were the questions and answers. The hospital found this to be both an efficient and an effective method of checking trainee progress.

Achievable mastery level on check quizzes and tests can be quite high if the SDL packages are designed and developed correctly. I was involved in one system where mastery on check quizzes was set at 90 percent and on tests at 85 percent. Some practitioners may quail at such goals. However, the average achievement level in that system, which had around 200 participants a year, was over 90 percent! There are no hard-and-fast rules for setting mastery levels, but nothing can be accomplished if you don't aim high. I've seldom set mastery levels in my SDL systems below 85 percent.

Test Question Item Analysis

If you are doing formal testing, I suggest that you add a test item analysis to your review/revision procedures. This is a particularly important tool in a mastery testing process. Basically, it requires you to keep track of how many trainees missed each question over a period of time. The period depends on how many trainees you are working with and how much data you wish to have before making a decision. Questions missed by a significant number of your trainees should be reviewed again for appropriateness to the objective and to the content. At times, you may decide to change a question that was missed too often; at others, you might opt to beef up the content. Whatever the case, an item analysis provides yet another check on both questions and content. It helps you make sure your package is as effective and fair as possible.

This whole process may seem like a lot of effort for simple test questions, but remember that scores on tests are often the only way people judge the success of the trainee and thus of your SDL package. It's worth the time and energy to make sure your tools are as good as it is possible to make them.

Performance Evaluation

The second type of user evaluation common in SDL is performance evaluation. However, this may not be the best terminology. Many of the verbs that we consider to be cognitive—such as *draw*, *use*, *create*, even *count* and *list*—are also performance based. In fact, trainee objectives as a whole are often referred to as performance-based objectives. But for convenience, we'll stick with the term *performance evaluation*, defining it as evaluation by means of an instrument other than a paper-and-pencil test.

When Is a Performance Evaluation Needed?

The reason for this type of evaluation relates back to the task as it was first identified and then taught. If, for example, a task identified in the analysis phase was "The trainee must be able to disassemble and reassemble a valve," the use of written questions to evaluate the trainee's ability to do this would be difficult and probably not very valid.

However, observing the trainee "doing it" successfully would almost certainly fill the evaluation bill. Thus, performance evaluations in SDL are planned when the trainee needs to exhibit something that paper-and-pencil measures can't demonstrate. This could be as simple as showing that they know where a certain item in a store is located, or as complex as running a nuclear reactor.

Your indicator for a performance evaluation is as much the verb you have chosen for the objective as the task itself. If both of these indicate a physical performance, you need to design a performance evaluation. For example, a task such as "Correctly discharge an employee," with "State the five items you must receive from an employee when discharged" as an objective, is a good candidate for a paper-and-pencil evaluation. Another task, such as "Hold a proper performance appraisal meeting," with an objective of "Exhibit approved coaching techniques when discussing an employee's areas for improvement," obviously needs something more to evaluate properly. An objective that uses a term like *draw* falls in the middle. It is definitely a performance, but one that can be done in a paper-and-pencil format.

Where to Put Performance Evaluations in Your SDL Package

Performance evaluations, like cognitive evaluations, can be placed anywhere in an SDL package. They most often appear as chunk separators or at the end of a package. Like cognitive evaluations, they can be self-administered, though this technique is much more demanding to design properly. It's normally difficult and sometimes impossible for trainees to observe their own performance.

Usually when a self-evaluated performance occurs, it is considered more a practice than an evaluation. However, if there is a concrete result of the performance that the trainee can compare to a picture, diagram, or other ideal example, it can be self-evaluative. For example, a performance where the trainees are required to identify safety hazards in their workplace would be difficult to self-evaluate, since there is nothing to judge their findings against. On the other

hand, a performance where they had to stack boxes in a certain way—
if it came with a picture of how the final product was to look—could
be easily self-evaluated. Practices such as these, whether self-evaluated
or not, tend to make excellent chunk separators.

One of the most important times for a performance evaluation is after the trainee has gone back on the job and is using the
skills taught in the SDL package. This form of evaluation checks
for that all-important process of training transfer to the job. The
method for doing it is the same as with any performance evaluation;
only the timing (after the trainee has been back in the work environment) is different.

The concept of job transfer and the trainees' ability to use
what they learn back on the job will be revisited again in Chapter
Twelve, when we discuss system evaluation (though from the point
of view of evaluating the material, not the user's learning). As you
design your evaluation of both the user and the system, remember
that performance evaluations that check transfer of learning to the
job can be useful for both evaluative aspects. SDL's ability to provide the impetus for this transfer is one of its major strengths.

Performing Performance Evaluations

Formal performance evaluations are normally done by a fa-
cilitator/implementor of some type. Usually they are done in an on-
the-job setting, though I've seen simulations used for performance
evaluations in training centers, too.

The key to a good performance evaluation is to make sure
that the evaluator and the trainee are expecting the same performance. This can be difficult to achieve if your evaluator is a subject
matter expert who has his or her own notion of how the performance should be done. To guard against this, each performance
evaluation should be developed with a performance criteria sheet.
This sheet can be a checklist, a series of statements, even a relisting
of the objectives if they are broken down far enough to be useful.
It is developed to make sure the evaluator evaluates what the trainees were suppose to learn, in the way they were suppose to learn it.

Exhibit 5.2 contains some examples of well-designed performance criteria lists. Note not only the reliance on observable behav-

Exhibit 5.2. Performance Criteria Lists.

Pharmacy Duties for Associates
Observation Checklist

Directions for the Store Manager

Getting the Trainee Started:
Take the trainee to the pharmacy and give him/her an orientation to the paperwork and equipment he/she will be using. Have the trainee read the directions on the Pharmacy Duties for Associates Job Aid. Also tell the trainee that you will be using this Observation Checklist to coach and observe him/her through the process. Make sure you tell the trainee if he/she has any questions at any time, to stop and ask you.

Your Role as Observer:
Let the trainee perform the task. Do not walk him/her through it; let the Job Aid do that. Answer any questions immediately. Let the trainee make minor mistakes; stop him/her only if he/she gets into major trouble. It's important for the trainee to learn how to follow the Job Aid through the process. As you observe the trainee successfully performing each of the tasks below, make a check mark in the box. Once all tasks are checked off and you feel comfortable that the trainee can use the Job Aid to perform these duties in the pharmacy, sign and date the bottom of this form and file it in the employee's personnel folder.

The SDL Completion Record
Under the employee's name and next to the appropriate SDL, place a foil star, your initials, and the date in the box.

The Trainee Is Able To:

☐ Take in a Refill when the bottle or vial is available

☐ Take in a Refill when the bottle or vial is not available

☐ Take in a new prescription

☐ Take in a prescription for a new customer

☐ Take refills over the telephone

☐ Screen and route Doctor's office calls appropriate

☐ Thoroughly check all necessary information
prescriptions

_____   has successfully comp
Trainee's Name   program.

II

Recalls — Observation Checklist

Directions for the Store Manager

Getting the Trainee Started:
Choose an actual Recall for the trainee to complete; then give him/her any required equipment and paperwork. Have the trainee read the directions on the Job Aid and tell the trainee that he/she will be processing an actual Recall using the Job Aid. Also tell the trainee that you will be using this Observation Checklist to coach and observe him/her through the process. Make sure you tell the trainee if he/she has any questions at any time, to stop and ask you.

Your Role as Observer:
Let the trainee perform the task. Do not walk him/her through it; let the Job Aid do that. Answer any questions immediately. Let the trainee make minor mistakes; stop him/her only if he/she gets into major trouble. It's important for the trainee to learn how to follow the Job Aid through the process. As you observe the trainee successfully performing each of the tasks below, make a check mark in the box. Once all tasks are checked off and you feel comfortable that the trainee can use the Job Aid to process a Recall, sign and date the bottom of the form, place a foil star on the SDL Completion Record and file this piece of paper in the employee's personnel folder.

The SDL Completion Record
Under the employee's name and next to the appropriate SDL, place a foil star, your initials, and the date in the box.

The Trainee Is Able To:

☐ Set up the Telxon

☐ Create a Recall Transfer

☐ Review/Modify a Recall Transfer

☐ Print a Recall Transfer

☐ Delete a Recall Transfer

☐ Select an appropriate carton

☐ Properly pack the merchandise for shipment

☐ Enclose one copy of the scanning document in the appropriate place for shipment

☐ Correctly label all cartons in a Recall

☐ Complete the Warehouse Bill of Lading and obtain proper signatures

☐ Properly file all remaining paperwork

_____   has successfully completed the Recalls training program.
Trainee's Signature

                                 _____
                                 Store Manager's Signature   Date

II

Exhibit 5.2. Performance Criteria Lists, Cont'd.

PRESCREENING APPLICATIONS

I have observed the trainee accept and prescreen an application form from an applicant on the date noted below.

Date	Trainee	Coach

TEAM SUPERVISION

I have observed the trainee participate in THREE ROLE PLAYS giving feedback and listening on the dates noted below.

	Date	Trainee	Coach
1.			
2.			
3.			

TEAM SUPERVISION

I have observed the trainee demonstrate giving constructive feedback and listening on a daily basis for the previous three-day period.

Date	Trainee	Coach

	PAGE	1
PERFORMANCE TEST	of	2

STRUCT A PERFORMANCE TEST

nstrate mastery of this task by doing the following:

1. Tell the instructor you are ready to take the performance test and schedule a time and place for it.

2. For the agreed-on task, explain and construct a performance test.

3. Enter the completed performance test on the PERFORMANCE TEST from, and hand in by _ _ _ _ _ _ _ _ _ _ _.

ITEMS TO BE EVALUATED	MASTERY REQUIRED:		%
		YES	NO
1. Are the directions clear and concise?			
2. Is the testing situation described?			
3. Is the trainee told exactly what to do?			
4. Are any special restrictions mentioned?			
5. Is any time limit mentioned?			

ITEMS RELATING TO THE PROCESS:

6. Are only important items (to the process) included?

7. Do items begin with an action verb in the past tense?

8. Are the items based on the steps in the task analysis?

9. Is each item objective and observable?

10. Can each item be rated yes or no, with the desired response?

11. Is only one step per item included?

Signature	Program	Attempt	Re-Certify date:	Instructor's Signature
		1 2 3 4		

iors in these examples, but also the emphasis on directions. With performance criteria lists, as with most of SDL design, it is important to assume as little as possible.

The examples I've given are relatively simple, but I have seen much more complex tools that were really evaluation job aids. They not only provided the basic checklist but went into detail on what the evaluator should look for, do, not do, and how much help to provide. You might call this process *evaluator hints*.

If mastery is critical for your program, or if you are using evaluators who might not be subject matter experts, these more complex performance criteria sheets may be necessary. However, I've found under most circumstances, as long as the evaluators understand the subject matter, simple tools are the best. A little general instruction on how to evaluate should be all that's needed to prepare the evaluator.

Another Controversy

Another of those strange disagreements that seem to abound in SDL design relates to performance evaluations. "Should the trainee know what's on the performance criteria sheet?" How would you answer a colleague who asked you this question?

If your answer is anything other than absolutely yes, you have not mastered one of the most important concepts of SDL. You need to go back to the beginning of this book and start over! The purpose of SDL is to help the trainees learn, not to be tricky. Trainees should not only know what's on a performance criteria sheet but also should probably have a copy of it to aid in their learning. (This question was also an example of how you can put random evaluation questions into your SDL material.)

Reviewing Your Performance Evaluations

Finally, as with cognitive questions, you must review your performance evaluations before using them. Have subject matter experts review your criteria checklists. Check on the ability of your facilitators to administer a performance evaluation using them, either as part of your pilot or separately. One of your most important tasks in the pilot is to make sure the performance can be both exhibited and evaluated in the actual environment in which it will be done.

In a complex evaluation, where you have machines or other devices that need to be set up, you may have to literally observe the evaluation occurring in the workplace. A mistake often made in performance evaluations is to make them so complicated that the facilitator/evaluator just doesn't have the time to do them correctly. Checking the real-life problems involved in doing your performance evaluation will help stop you from making this mistake.

Conclusion

To summarize, two types of trainee evaluation exist: cognitive and performance evaluation. Both are useful anywhere in your SDL package, but they are usually found as chunk separators or as formal examinations at the end of large chunks. They are based on the tasks and the objectives you have identified earlier. They can be self- or other evaluated, depending on what you feel will best serve the needs of the trainee. But most important, they are developed in a way that allows the trainees to be fully aware of exactly what they will be evaluated on.

An SDL Simulation

While developing your trainee evaluations, you find two objectives that you feel have a performance component that needs to be evaluated. You evaluate them by adding a performance demonstration and directions to your package.

Section 1: Performance Demonstration

Directions: Objective 3 requires that you utilize the five steps of effective delegation when you return to the job. To evaluate you on this, your supervisor has been given those steps and will ask you to arrange for an observation time when you can exhibit your ability to use this process. After you have shown that you can perform this task, he or she will be observing you from time to time in your regular work assignments to evaluate whether you are still using the steps effectively. Your supervisor will use the following checklist as an evaluation tool.

Checklist for the Five Steps to Good Delegation
- Did the supervisor explain why the job is important?
- Was the task delegated in terms of expected results?
- Was the delegated authority defined and deadlines set?
- Was feedback asked for on steps 1–3?
- Were proper controls provided for to ensure progress?

Section 2: Performance Demonstration

Directions: Objective 6 asks that you implement your own technique for reducing wasted time in returning calls. Question 3 of the Self-Quiz asks you to state this technique. To evaluate your mastery of it, you are responsible for giving your answer to this question to your supervisor in written form. The supervisor will then observe your performance from time to time in returning phone calls and will evaluate you in 30 days on your effectiveness in following your stated time management plan for this time waster.

Exhibit 5.3. A Checklist for SDL.

Trainee Evaluation

☐ Cognitive trainee evaluations have been developed.
- Evaluation questions have been criterion referenced.
- A large enough question pool has been created.
- The questions have received three separate reviews.
- Self-quizzes and tests have proper directions.
- The right mastery level has been set and communicated.
- Item analysis is planned where needed.

☐ Performance evaluations have been developed where necessary.
- Performance evaluators have been determined.
- Performance criteria sheets have been developed.
- Performance evaluations have been properly reviewed.

6

Debugging Your Package
How to Make Sure It Works

The process of package review in SDL is probably more important, and more complex, than in any other training design (Figure 6.1). The reason is simple: your packages must stand on their own and therefore must be as faultless as possible. The purpose of reviews and pilots is to try to achieve this goal by finding weak areas, mistakes, or things that don't work in your packages before your trainees ever see them. Because of their importance, time for reviews must be factored into your overall development time. To skimp on reviews, or not pilot your SDL packages, invites disaster.

Reviews

Your packages should go through several types of reviews: content, design, editorial, and possibly organizational reviews. I will treat them separately, since a reviewer should be concentrating on one particular purpose in a review. However, the same reviewer may do more than one type of review, though preferably not simultaneously.

Content Review

The first of these reviews is a *content review*. This is usually performed by a subject matter expert. The purpose of this review is to make sure that you've covered the topic in adequate detail and that the information in the package is accurate and up to date and is not misleading.

Figure 6.1. A Model for SDL.

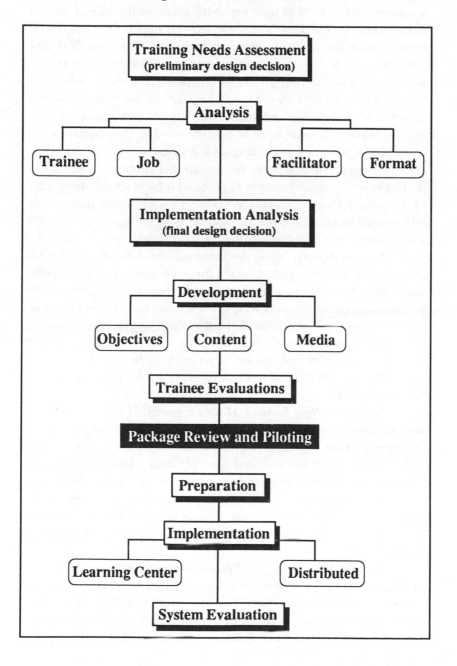

Limiting Content Reviewers. There are two problems with a content review such as this, and both relate to the role of subject matter experts. The first is that the experts may decide to go well beyond the scope of the objectives in reviewing. Particularly if they are new to the process, they might want to add entire concepts they feel you missed. They might also delete material they consider "too basic." These decisions were made back in the analysis phase and revisited while writing objectives, content, and test questions. The type of input you want now is simply whether the objectives are covered, not what new ones should be added.

There are several ways to control this problem. The easiest is simply to use subject matter experts who have already been part of the program's development as your reviewers. These individuals will already be familiar with the scope of your package and so won't waste time trying to argue for inclusions or deletions.

Your best choice is usually someone who helped with the job analysis but has not been directly involved since. He or she will understand the project and its limitations. Your worst choice would be the subject matter expert who acted as your content developer or content developer consultant. Such a person would be too close to the material and so would be unlikely to discern weak points in what he or she wrote or helped to write. Experts who helped you with other aspects such as test questions or media pieces would be your next choice.

Orienting New Subject Matter Experts. If such people are not available, your approach should be to start your novice subject matter experts by having them review the objectives. Do this without showing them the material and get their agreement that the objectives cover what needs to be covered on the subject. Now give them the material. Ask them to make sure the content covers the objectives in relation to the four criteria of accuracy, currency, no misleading material, and adequate detail. This should keep them on track.

Getting What You Need from Content Reviewers. The second problem with a review by a subject matter expert is that you will often get back comments like "This needs work" or "This isn't right." These comments aren't much help if you don't know what kind of "work" the package needs or how to fix what isn't "right."

Your reviewer needs to realize that you did the best job you could developing the material the first time. You didn't intentionally try to undercover a topic, make it confusing, or include factual errors. Therefore, if something isn't right, it won't help just to point that out. You need to know how to fix it.

This is probably the most difficult concept for content reviewers to deal with, because it means not only pointing out errors but correcting them. Such a process takes more time. When you recruit content reviewers, you need to make all of this clear from the beginning. They are not editors who are going to go through the material correcting punctuation and making notes such as "I don't like this." They are subject matter experts who must tell you what needs fixing and how to fix it. Their job is to help you make the material cover the objectives as effectively as possible.

A mistake made by many SDL developers is to send their package to an expert with a note that says, "Please review." *Review* means different things to different people. You will almost certainly get more than you wanted and less than what you needed from such a request. To be useful to you and your package, the expert reviewer needs to be picked carefully, trained well, and guided from time to time as the review progresses. At the very least, the reviewer must be adequately informed about your expectations.

Exhibit 6.1 contains a copy of a content reviewer job aid that I've used to train and help reviewers. If you analyze it, you will see that it has three specific parts: what is expected of the reviewer, what the reviewer should not do, and ideas to help the reviewer do it right. You may want to use something similar to this for your own content reviews. The important thing is that you use something to help the reviewers do the job the way you need it done.

Design Review

The second type of SDL package review is a *design review*. This review is done to make sure your program is instructionally sound. It must be performed by an experienced designer who understands how SDL should work.

Checking Objectives. Once again, the process starts with objectives. This time, however, the reviewer will not be looking at

Exhibit 6.1. Subject Matter Review Checklist.

Subject Matter Review

The Checklist on the reverse side is intended to help subject matter experts in the **content review** of written training materials. Your subject matter expertise is critical to the success of _____ training programs. We hope the checklist and the following suggested process will facilitate your review by helping to focus your attention on specific subject matter issues.

Suggested Review Process

Read the checklist
First, read through the checklist and become familiar with the areas you are to focus your attention on, such as *content accuracy* and *comprehensiveness*.

Read the Table of Contents
Once you are comfortable with the topics on the checklist, begin reviewing the materials by reading the Table of Contents. The Table of Contents will give you an overview of the scope of the content.

Read the Objectives
The objectives will identify the audience and the specific behavior changes that are expected of those individuals as a result of training.

Read the materials quickly
Next, quickly read the training materials from
reading will give you a good sense of how the tra
matter. As you read, make a check mark on the
review and attention.

Reread the materials for details
Finally, reread the training materials paying p
you checked the first time through. Use the top
Checklist as a guide to make any appropriate
training materials themselves.

The Training and Development Department th
expert advice.

Subject Matter Review Checklist

Value
Is the material **relevant** to daily operations?   ❑
Is the material **appropriate** for the intended audience?   ❑
Is the material **necessary** for the intended audience?   ❑

Accuracy
Is the content **accurate**?   ❑
Is any content **misleading**?   ❑

Comprehensiveness
Is there **too much** information on any one topic?   ❑
Is there **too little** information on any one topic?   ❑
Are there additional topics that need to be covered?   ❑
Does the content support _____ philosophy?   ❑

Coherence
Is the information presented in proper order and sequence?   ❑
Is the vocabulary appropriate for the audience?   ❑

Timely
Is the content up to date (concerning equipment, and so on)?   ❑
Does the content represent current policies and procedures?   ❑

Graphics
Are the graphics (illustrations, charts, tables) **accurate**?   ❑
Do the graphics **enhance** the content?   ❑
Do the graphics **detract** from the content?   ❑

Please review the attached training materials_____.
                                              (title of materials)

The intended audience for these materials is_____.

Please sign this form and return it, ALONG with the training materials to the
Training and Development Department by _____.
                                                            (date)

_____   _____
    (your name)   (current date)

them in relation to the subject matter. Rather, he or she should check to see how well they are written and how closely they match the job analysis from an instructional point of view. Use of correct verbs and clarity are the two important points the design reviewer is looking for here.

Matching Objectives to Material. Next, the reviewer needs to match the objectives to the material. While this is similar to a content review, its purpose is not to determine whether the objectives are covered adequately. The design reviewer is more interested in making sure that the objectives key the trainee into the content and flow logically with it. This is also the place and person for test question review if you didn't have it done as part of your question development process. Remember, your test question reviewer is looking for agreement between objective and the activity of the test question or process. If *demonstrate* is the verb, the evaluation should require demonstration.

Verifying Package Usability. Your design reviewer's next concern should be the readability of the material, both from a purely subjective approach and through the use of readability indexes, as discussed in Chapter Two. Clarity of directions, length and logic of chunks, and all the other instructional design considerations for SDL are the purview of the design reviewer as well.

Reexamining Media. The final task of your design reviewer is to reexamine the package's media. In printed materials, he or she needs to check clarity, white space, and all the other things that make a good print piece, as described in Chapter Four. If slides or video are used, accuracy and matching of visual to wording are additional considerations. If the program is computer based, the amount and logic of the branching can be added to the list.

Performing Your Own Design Review. This variety of tasks means that your design reviewer must be well versed in the techniques of SDL. If your training group has more than one designer, you are in good shape for this process. However, if you are a one-person show or if you're the only SDL specialist, you'll have to be your own design reviewer. I've had this happen to me and have found that the best solution is to develop a review checklist. The checklist should consist of all the items we've mentioned that need to be reviewed by the design reviewer. Add to this general list any

other items you feel are particularly pertinent to your package or
system.

Now sit down with your material and go through the list one
item at a time. It will be a temptation to skip around or try to do
two or more items simultaneously, but don't! Start with your first
item (for example, checking the verb match for your objectives) and
complete that for the entire package before moving on.

What you are trying to guard against is the destructive process of cross connecting assumptions. A noninvolved design reviewer will catch your assumptions and so stop your trainees from
getting caught in them. If you have to do it yourself, sticking to one
point at a time will detect the worst of your cross assumptions by
making you consider each design and development parameter
separately.

Editorial Review

The third review that must be done on an SDL package is
an *editorial review*. This is the one everybody likes to do and usually
tries to do if they are not properly prepared and directed. Basically,
it is a grammar review, with special attention to spelling errors and
typos. Nothing will undercut the acceptance and therefore the effectiveness of your package more drastically than these types of
errors. In the minds of those who matter most—the trainees and
management (especially top management)—such errors make the
entire package suspect.

Need for a Separate Editorial Review. You'll never eliminate
grammatical errors completely, but the best way to detect them is
through a review that is exclusively concerned with these problems.
Many otherwise competent designers make the mistake of assuming
that since they have had content and design reviews, the reviewers
must have caught any spelling mistakes or typos. This is a wrong
assumption. If the other reviewers were doing their jobs, they were
concentrating on things other than grammar. In fact, if another
type of reviewer points out many grammatical errors, I immediately
become suspicious of how well they did what I really wanted them
to do! Content reviewers should concentrate on subject matter, de-

sign reviewers on design criteria, and an editorial reviewer should concentrate only on grammar.

Who Should Do Editorial Reviews? The worst editorial reviewer is the person who wrote the package. Normally he or she will "read through" most mistakes. It's a good idea to have your editorial reviewer be someone who is not otherwise connected with the package.

I've often found good editorial reviewers among department secretaries. Most secretaries are used to proofreading, which is basically what this review is, and some are very good at it. As long as he or she didn't type the material to begin with, a secretary will usually start with a fresh approach and will thus be able to catch things others might miss. The best are also experts on rules of grammar, since this is part of their job. Secretaries often appreciate a break in their routine, and you can usually find a boss who will agree to let them do something like this.

Along with reviewing print material, the editorial reviewer should look at graphics, slides, videos, and any other media pieces. Again, misspellings, poor usage, and other language problems will be detrimental to your program. Be sure "media grammar" is as carefully checked as your printed words.

Organization Review

There is one final type of review that, in all probability, you'll want to do. I call it the *organization review*. Its purpose is mostly political: it is to make sure that everyone who feels the need to look at your material before it is used gets a chance to do so. These reviews are often done by mid-level managers, supernumerary administrators, and not-so-important VIPs. At best, they may help get people on the bandwagon for SDL.

I don't have a problem with organization reviews. In fact, I use them quite a bit. Since they seldom come back, let alone have anything in them that will cause you much extra work, they are usually harmless. My only caution is not to use them in place of the reviews we've already discussed. This type of review will not give you what you need to know about your package. Use organization reviews—lots of them if the political climate in your company demands it—but use them for the purpose for which they are intended, not to perfect your SDL packages.

All of these reviews take time and most often cannot be done simultaneously. I have found that you need about a month for review and accompanying revisions. This is an average; some packages take less time, some more, depending on size, media, and the time your reviewers have available. The important point is that they must be done, so plan for them.

Developmental Testing and Piloting

If you feel that after all the SME, design, and editorial reviews, you've done enough to ensure great SDL packages, you're mistaken. If you considered what we've done so far and then said, "Hey, how come everybody has reviewed these things but representatives of those that are most affected by them—namely, my trainees?" give yourself a gold star. To complete the review process, you need to make sure that the trainees can use your package properly and effectively. In SDL, you do this in two steps: the developmental test and the pilot.

Developmental Test

The *developmental test* allows you to find out if your package really works. Actually, you've been engaged in developmental testing ever since you began the review process. However, for simplicity's sake, we will call this first trainee review the developmental test to differentiate it from the pilot.

During the developmental test, you need to have the package completed exactly as it would be done in real circumstances, except in a controlled environment. Its purpose is to give you a chance to observe the package being done, to check for areas that might need improvement, and to get feedback concerning how difficult the package as a whole is and how challenging its component parts are for a trainee to complete.

Choosing Developmental Test Subjects. To do this well you need a test subject (or subjects) who resembles the trainee as closely as possible. That is, subjects should have the same basic background and knowledge as your intended audience. Your subjects should understand as little or as much of the topic as your trainees will when they use your package.

Obviously, the person who best fits these qualifications is a trainee. If you can beg, borrow, or steal actual trainees to do your package test, you will enhance its effectiveness. However, in many cases, particularly in a distributed implementation, it's difficult to get someone from the field to come to you for a day and be your research subject. Under these circumstances, you'll have to compromise, but try to find someone who is as close as possible to your intended trainees in learning characteristics and knowledge. The more removed from the typical trainee your subject is, the less valuable your developmental testing will be. One group of people you can't use as subjects are those who worked on the package or who might be considered subject matter experts on the material the package covers. The purpose of developmental testing is to see how well a package works and how easily a trainee can use it. Data from subject matter experts and designers who already know the material and the method are unreliable enough to make the whole process virtually worthless.

Preparing Your Subjects. Once you've picked the right people to be your subjects, they need to know what you expect. Ask them to follow the directions and go through the package from cover to cover as a trainee would. While doing this, they should take notes or jot down comments on problems they encounter. There may be special areas like a performance evaluation or a difficult concept that you want them to pay particular attention to. Let them know about these in advance. Generally, they are looking for parts of the package that are confusing or that they are unable to complete as directed.

The number of subjects needed for developmental testing is up to you as designer. I've found that two or three individuals, if they have the right background and learning characteristics, are usually enough to tell me what I need to know.

Observing and Debriefing. You will want to observe the subjects as they go through the package. This allows you to make your own notes on where they have problems. You might even want to interrupt the subject if you observe a particular difficulty. In this way, you can get immediate feedback concerning the problem and the subject's thought processes. I've found this personal observation to be a most enlightening approach. It often gives me data and insights that I would never have received otherwise. The developmental test is the only time this type of observation is both effective and nonintrusive enough to be a viable procedure.

When your subjects have finished, hold a debriefing session with each to discuss comments and ask specific questions you may have on certain areas or techniques. You need to plan the entire developmental testing process carefully. The key is to brief your subjects on those things you want them to consider while they are doing the package. During the debriefing period, ask them about areas that you wanted them to react to, without prior indication of their importance.

The Pilot

The second form of user review for your SDL package is the *pilot*. A pilot differs from a developmental test in that it is performed in the environment and under the exact conditions that the package will be used under. This may be in the learning center, on the shop floor, in the store, at a desk, and so on.

For the pilot, there is no choosing of a representative subject, no briefing, and above all, no interruptions. The SDL package is there, the facilitator is there, the trainee is there, and they do it. Under certain circumstances, you may be able to act as an observer, but be careful that your being there doesn't change the environment. *The main purpose of a pilot is to make sure your package works the way you intend it to, where it is to be done, and for those you targeted to use it.*

Pilot Considerations. A major consideration here should be how the package flows logistically. Can the trainees get started easily? Do they have the place and tools to do what needs to be done? Can they follow the package on their own? Are there areas where they bog down or seem to have trouble understanding the information? Are the performance evaluations "doable"? This is particularly important, since the pilot is the only time you will be able to truly check the functioning and effectiveness of the performance evaluations.

Look for the ease with which the trainee can get any equipment needed for the evaluation and can locate and ask questions of the evaluator. Observe how effectively the evaluator can use the criteria checklist and, more generally, whether the evaluation did what it was designed to do as efficiently as possible.

Determine whether your suggested timing for the package is reasonable. If this is an on-the-job environment, are your chunks discrete enough for a trainee to stop, do some work, and then pick the package up later? Finally, did the trainees learn what they needed to learn from the package?

Pilot Debriefing. The number of pilots you should perform is again optional. I like to plan one or two for personal observation. I have others done without my presence, which might possibly interfere with the process.

In either case, since you can't stop the pilot to ask questions, the debriefing is crucial. Handle it as you did the debriefing for the developmental test, with preplanned questions on areas about which you have the greatest concern. Be sure to include enough time for the trainees to provide all the feedback they consider important. I've seen the effectiveness of entire pilots significantly diminished because the designer had another meeting and so cut the debriefing short.

The facilitators' responsibilities are part of your program and so must be fully considered in the pilot, too. The facilitators need to be debriefed just as carefully, and with as much planning, as the trainees. Ask them if the instructions were easy to follow and whether they understood their role in the SDL process. Check on their ability to find necessary equipment and to do performance evaluations. Specifically ask them if the criteria checklists were complete and usable. The checklist in Exhibit 6.2 can help you to design and run a good pilot.

The two basic differences between a developmental test and a pilot involve who the subjects are and where the process is done. Ideally, your developmental test subjects should be trainees, though this is not always feasible. In a pilot, the subjects are always trainees. The actual facilitators must be involved as well.

Exhibit 6.2. Pilot Checklist.

Process

- Duplicate the exact training environment.
- Create the same conditions under which the training will occur.
- Use observation only if it is not intrusive.
- Plan enough time for debriefing.
  - ★ Does the package flow well?
  - ★ Can the performance evaluations be done?
  - ★ Is there easy access to the performance evaluator?
  - ★ Does the evaluation do what you planned it to do?
  - ★ Is the suggested timing reasonable?

Trainees

- Do not choose the subjects.
- Do not brief them.
- Do not interrupt them.
- Debrief them.
  - ★ Can they get started easily?
  - ★ Is there a place to work?
  - ★ Are the proper tools available?
  - ★ Can they work on their own?
  - ★ Are there areas they can't understand?
  - ★ Can they stop and pick up later?
  - ★ Did they learn what they needed to learn?

Facilitator/Evaluator

- They should be available as they would normally be.
- Debrief them.
  - ★ Can the evaluator use the criterion checklist effectively?
  - ★ Do the facilitators understand their role?
  - ★ Were their instructions easy to follow?

Pilots must be done in the exact environment that your packages will be functioning in. Developmental tests can be done anywhere. Combine these two evaluations with good content, design, and editorial reviews; make changes where indicated; print, duplicate, dub, or otherwise make enough copies of your packages to meet your needs; and you're ready for the next step in SDL: implementation.

An SDL Simulation

You have conducted content, design, editorial, and organization reviews. You perform a developmental test with three managers from your own location and two pilots with first-line managers from your other two locations. You make any necessary changes. You now have a completed package that is ready to implement.

Management Module 1: Time Management

Introduction

This is a self-directed learning package on time management. Its purpose is to help you learn to manage your time effectively. Since this is self-directed learning, there will be no instructor. You will be responsible for reading the material and showing that you have mastered it by completing the self-quizzes, performances, and final test. You will be able to take all the time you need to achieve this goal. If job duties interrupt you, you may put the material away and return to it when you have time. The important thing is that you learn the material, not how fast you can do it in.

The objectives that you will find at the beginning of each section will help guide your learning. All the quizzes and the test will be based directly on these objectives.

Please do not write in this book. Answers to the self-quizzes should be noted on a separate piece of paper.

Supplies List

Paper
"To do" list pads (three types)
Videotapes: *Time Management: The Reality* (12 minutes)
　　　　　　 Five Steps to Better Delegation (15 minutes)

Package Outline

Section 1: Time Savers
　　The "to do" list

Prioritizing by helping your boss succeed
Delegation
Improving reading skills

Section 2: Time Wasters
The telephone
Meetings

Module Objectives

The trainee will be able to:
1. Employ a daily "to do" list with priority symbols to plan and carry out each day's task.
2. Discuss the importance—as a good time management tool—of prioritizing activities that help his or her boss succeed.
3. Effectively utilize the five-step method of delegation.
4. Discuss the nine keys to improving reading skills.
5. List three methods for decreasing the number of interrupting phone calls.
6. Implement his or her own technique for reducing wasted time in returning calls.
7. Describe the importance of having a prepublished agenda for all meetings.
8. Discuss techniques for eliminating meetings.
9. List ten ways to decrease time wasted in meetings.

Section 1: Time Savers

Directions: Using the section objectives as your guide, read the material contained in this section. You will also need to watch the videotapes *Time Management: The Reality* and *Five Steps to Better Delegation.* When you have finished, complete the self-quiz found at the end of this section. Your learning time for this section should be approximately 60 minutes.

Section Objectives: The trainee will be able to:
Employ a daily "to do" list with priority symbols to plan and carry out each day's task.

> Discuss the importance—as a good time management
>   tool—of prioritizing activities that help his or her boss
>   succeed.
> Effectively utilize the five-step method of delegation.
> Discuss the nine keys to improving reading skills.

The "To Do" List

One of the most effective concepts in time management is prioritizing the tasks you need to do. This can be done on a daily, weekly, monthly, or even on a project basis. Usually people begin with a daily priority list, often called a "to do" list.

The first thing to do in using a "to do" list is to decide when you will make it up. This is usually done at the end of the day or the first thing in the morning. Many time-organized individuals will also take a few minutes at lunchtime to review and revise their list. If you make your list the night before . . .

There are as many methods for making a "to do" list as there are individuals who use them. We've included with this package three different types of preprinted sheets that might work for you. The first is simply a series of lines . . .

Other time managers find that a simple blank sheet of paper works best for their "to do" list. It can be full sized or simply a notepad, depending on your personal . . .

A newer application of the "to do" list is the computerized calendar/organizer. These software programs . . .

One of the important things you need to do with your "to do" list is to find a way to prioritize the tasks on it. This can be as simple as listing the first priority first, the second, second, and so on. It might also be as complicated as three lists, one for first-priority tasks . . .

Another technique is color coding. For example, first-priority tasks can be in red ink or on red paper, second-priority green, third-priority blue. The advantage of this system is . . .

Prioritizing by Helping Your Boss Succeed

One way to help you to prioritize your tasks has been postulated by Henry Sipes in his book *Time Management: The Reality.* He states that the best time managers are those who realize that they must be superior performers if they wish to get ahead in their company. To be a superior performer, you must be seen as a successful person, and the individual who determines your success and value is your boss.

Thus, the good time manager finds out what it is that will help the boss succeed and treats tasks that perform this function as his or her first priority. Sipes states that every day, one of your first-priority tasks must be to do something to make the boss look good.

Delegation

Improving Reading Skills

Directions: When you are sure that you have completed all of the objectives in this section, go on to the self-quiz on the next page.

Section 1: Self-Quiz

Directions: Answer all of the following questions on a separate piece of paper without looking back through the section material. When you have completed all the questions, turn to the next page and correct your answers. If you missed any questions, go back to that area of the material and review it. Retake the quiz until you achieve the mastery level of 100%.

1. A "to do" list is used to . . .
2. Two ways to prioritize your "to do" list are . . .
3. Who determines your success and value?
4. What should you do each day if you are a good task prioritizer?
5. What is the best way to remember what you read?

Answers
1. Help prioritize your tasks.
2. Use different sheets for different priorities. Use color coding.
3. Your boss.
4. Make one task that will help your boss succeed a first priority.
5. Use the VRAC formula.

Directions: When you have mastered the self-quiz, go on to the performance demonstration for this section, which is located on the next page. You may proceed on to Section 2 before completing the performance.

Section 1: Performance Demonstration

Directions: Objective 3 requires that you utilize the five steps of effective delegation when you return to the job. To evaluate you on this, your supervisor has been given those steps and will ask you to arrange for an observation time when you can exhibit your ability to use this process. After you have shown that you can perform this task, he or she will be observing you from time to time in your regular work assignments to evaluate whether you are still using the steps effectively. Your supervisor will use the following checklist as an evaluation tool.

Checklist for the Five Steps to Good Delegation
- Did the supervisor explain why the job is important?
- Was the task delegated in terms of expected results?
- Was the delegated authority defined and deadlines set?
- Was feedback asked for on steps 1–3?
- Were proper controls provided for to ensure progress?

Section 2: Time Wasters

Directions: Using the section objectives as your guide, read the material contained in this section. When you have finished, complete the self-quiz found at the end of this section. Your learning time for this section should be approximately 30 minutes.

Section Objectives: The trainee will be able to:
List three methods for decreasing the number of interrupting phone calls.
Implement his or her own technique for reducing wasted time in returning calls.
Describe the importance of having a prepublished agenda for all meetings.
Discuss techniques for eliminating meetings.
List ten ways to decrease the time wasted in meetings.

The Telephone
Approaching time management from the opposite direction, you need to find ways to eliminate time wasters. The telephone is one of the most common of these. The first thing you can do to prevent the telephone from wasting your time is to stop it from interrupting you when you are in the middle of something. Everybody has had those times when . . .

There are three methods you can use to stop phone interruptions. The first is to simply work away from the phone. Now this may be a problem if . . .

The second method is to find a phone call interceptor. This is a person who can answer your phone and take messages. It doesn't have to be a secretary if you don't have one. Even a co-worker can . . .

Another method of controlling your phone is to return calls only at specified times. This might be at the end of the day, or each morning, or right after lunch. There are a number of benefits to this . . .

Meetings
Directions: When you are sure that you have completed all of the objectives in this section, go on to the self-quiz on the next page.

Section 2: Self-Quiz

Directions: Answer all of the following questions on a separate piece of paper without looking back through the section material. When you have completed all the questions, turn to the next page and correct your answers. If you missed any questions, go back to that area of the material and review it. Retake the quiz until you achieve the mastery level of 100%.

1. List three methods for decreasing the number of interrupting phone calls.
2. Describe the technique that you will use for returning phone calls.
3. What can you do before a meeting to make it run as efficiently as possible?

4. What characteristics are typical of a meeting that needs to be eliminated?
5. List ten ways to decrease the time wasted in meetings.

Answers
1. Work away from the phone.
   Use an interceptor.
   Just don't answer.

and so on

   Directions: When you have mastered the self-quiz, continue on to the performance demonstration for this section.

Section 2: Performance Demonstration

   Directions: Objective 6 asks that you implement your own technique for reducing wasted time in reducing calls. Question 3 of the self-quiz asked you to state this technique. To evaluate your mastery of it, you are responsible for giving your answer to this question to your supervisor in written form. Your supervisor will then observe your performance from time to time in returning phone calls and will evaluate you in 30 days on your effectiveness in following your stated time management plan for this time waster.

Final Test

   Directions: After you have met with your supervisor to plan and begin the performance demonstrations for this module, you will be eligible to take the final test to prove your mastery of this topic. Your supervisor will administer and grade the test, then review it with you. Mastery on the final test is 85%. If you do not achieve mastery, you should review the material in this package and take the test again.

Exhibit 6.3. A Checklist for SDL.

Package Reviewing and Piloting

☐ Proper package reviews have been completed.
  • A content review of the package material has been done.
  • A design review of package objectives, flow usability, and media has been done.
  • An editorial review has been completed.
  • Any organization reviews that were necessary have been done.

☐ Developmental testing has been done.
  • The right subjects were used.
  • A good briefing and debriefing were held.

☐ Pilot(s) has been done.
  • The correct environment was used.
  • The right subjects were used.
  • Trainees and facilitators were debriefed.

Part Two

Ensuring
Successful Implementation

7

Preparing Your Organization
for Self-Directed Learning

So far, we have discussed the definition of SDL, its advantages and disadvantages, and how to design and develop it in the context of a learning package. Our next task is to consider the methods for getting your SDL package into the hands of your trainees. The instructional design term for this process is *implementation*.

The thinking and planning for implementation began during the analysis phase, when you did an implementation analysis. At that time, you decided whether you were going to use a learning center or a distributed implementation. It probably didn't seem like much of a decision at the time. However, almost every development decision you made was affected by your implementation decision in some way. This was true when you considered the cost of materials, types of binding, use of facilitators, media formats—even how you planned your evaluations.

Now you'll need to transform that decision into a plan that will effectively and efficiently control your SDL process. If you were consistent in referring to the implementation analysis as you made your other decisions, this plan will be fairly straightforward. It won't be simple, but at least you'll have a good idea of what you need to do.

If you weren't careful, you may have material that won't work, media that you can't use, and facilitation needs that can't be met in the setting where your training must occur. As you plan your implementation, you'll have to go back and correct these problems. Either way, you still have many factors to consider and mechanisms

Figure 7.1. A Model for SDL.

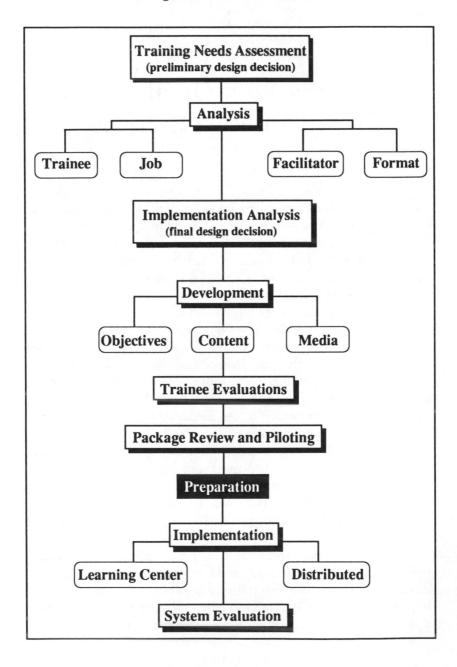

to put in place before you achieve the primary purpose of implementation—making the training happen.

In this chapter, we will set the stage for implementation by considering how to prepare the various levels of the company (Figure 7.1). Then, in the following chapters, we will take a close look at the two most common SDL implementation scenarios: the learning center and distributed implementation.

Preparing Corporate Management

There are three distinct groups in your company that you will need to address as you prepare for an SDL implementation: *corporate management, direct supervisors,* and the *trainees* themselves. You may also need to prepare your current field trainers, but since this is more critical to a distributed implementation, it will be discussed in Chapters Eight and Nine.

Preparation Versus Initial Support

At first glance, you might consider this area, in fact this whole chapter, to be a little out of sequence. The design and development work on your program is done, and now you're going to try to prepare company management for it!? Well, yes and no. We're not discussing selling the *concept* of SDL to management here. If you remember, we did this earlier when we considered the matching of training needs with strategic objectives and eliciting buy-in from senior management for the concept itself.

During the assessment and analysis processes, we determined how SDL and training fit into organizational objectives, and we discussed the general idea with senior management to get input and feedback. We talked about the advantages that SDL would have for the company, particularly in the forms of cost savings and training efficiency. Without this process, and their approval, we would not have gotten beyond analysis in our design model. Buy-in will be revisited again as a specialized part of a learning center implementation, but it is not the immediate issue.

At this stage, we are attempting to gather support, not for a concept, but for the actual training itself—that is, for the implementation. Much of what we discuss here can apply to selling the concept of SDL as well, but the one big difference is that now you can show your management something concrete. You will be asking for their support in making actual training work, not support for an abstract concept. Your ability to display completed packages, talk about distribution time lines, or specifically discuss the what's and how's of getting people to a functioning learning center will help you gain that support. Now you can discuss cost savings in terms of real dollars as well: how much it cost to develop the package and to get it to the trainees versus the price of a classroom approach with travel costs for instructors and trainees, room costs, and time lost away from the job.

The important point to remember is that your management is not made up of trainers. They may have approved the concept simply because they trusted your judgment and because it was a bit hazy to them. Now you're asking for something very real and very current. You want their time and money and their support in doing the training according to a systematic plan, so speak to them with concrete examples and in a language they'll understand. You particularly want to make sure you get their support, since this is the basis for the success of any SDL implementation, for it creates control.

Need for Control

Control is particularly important in a distributed SDL implementation, since the implementation is much more complex than in a learning center process. A distributed implementation is often widespread; thus, it needs much tighter control and oversight procedures than does a learning center, where you have full-time facilitators to make sure things are going right. Your programs are being used out in the workplace. Site implementors are responsible for several of their functions. Therefore, you should carefully develop procedures to guarantee they are being used correctly, or at all. These procedures must be enforced by managers at all levels in your organization. This is where the process of support comes in.

I visited a company that used SDL packages for its basic technical training of machine operators at eleven plants in the United States and Canada. When I asked what kind of control measures they had to ensure that the packages were used correctly, they told me that the direct supervisors of the trainees were the package implementors. "Control," they said, "was inherent in the design." I had my doubts about this, having made the same mistake once myself. However, they assured me their evaluations found that all was well.

I suggested that as a special evaluation, they talk to the trainees about the usefulness of the SDL packages. To make a long story short, they found that some of their trainees had never seen a package. Others had simply read them like a manual. The supervisors felt that reading the material, added to the tried-and-true method of "pairing them up with someone who knows," was enough training. It was also faster than having them do all that "stuff" in the SDL packages. The managers reinforced these feelings by never checking on how the training was going or whether the trainees were doing it "by the book."

This is an example of what happens when the management is not well prepared for a distributed SDL implementation. Everyone from the CEO to the first-line supervisor may agree with the concept, but concepts have a way of getting lost in the day-to-day business environment. Your job in preparing the management for a distributed SDL implementation is not only to have them recommit to the concept, but also to create the control that will make it work as a system.

This is not to say that support and control isn't important in a learning center implementation as well. Many centers have been underutilized to the point of extinction because management didn't support sending trainees to them, or because there were no controls in place to make sure the trainees came when necessary. Usage reports that upper-level management actually reads, and individualized training and development plans that are developed and followed with management support are the lifeblood of a training center.

However, these are fairly simple measures compared to what you need to control a distributed implementation. This being the case, control will be discussed in more detail in Chapters Eight and Nine. What's important now is to realize that control presupposes support from all levels of management.

An SDL Simulation

To gather top-management support for your SDL package, you send completed copies to each department head or higher. In a cover memo, you say a little about SDL and explain how the package will be used. Because this is a single-package approach and is not planned as a system at this time, you decide that this is all that is necessary.

To: _____

From: Training and Development

Enclosed with this memo is a copy of our new self-directed learning package on time management. This package will be used by all first-line managers to increase their time management skills.

Our recent assessment, which was conducted with managers and administrators from all three plants, revealed that one area where our managers needed improvement was time management, particularly as it related to prioritizing tasks and delegation. This package has been developed in response to that need and in response to requests for a program on this topic from both first-line managers and their superiors.

By designing the program to utilize self-directed learning rather than the traditional classroom, we have made the training more cost and time effective. Managers will not need to leave their facilities or areas to go to a central location for class; they can learn right at their desks when it is most convenient for them.

The training should also be more effective, since we have included the managers' supervisors in the performance component and in the evaluation of the learning. This will reinforce the learning and increase the likelihood that the concepts will be put into practice.

Please feel free to contact me if you or your staff have any thoughts concerning this new approach to training in our organization.

Techniques for Obtaining Management Support

As in selling the concept, the first step in garnering management support is to talk to managers at meetings. Now you have something to show, something they can get their hands on, not just a concept. If you've done your development work well, you should have attractive, user-friendly packages that will impress them. Once they have the packages in their hands, or perhaps have a tour of the learning center fresh in their minds, you'll need to explain what their role is and how the control measures will function. Then ask for their commitment to the enforcement of the discipline that it will take to make the system work.

This process starts with top management and should work its way down as far as you can logically go. Don't miss a chance to go to any meeting and talk. Stress the advantages of SDL and the importance of each level's help in controlling the process. If your organization is so large that you can't get to the lower management levels personally, find others who can. The best approach is to use a manager's direct superior to explain the program to him or her. Develop fact sheets concerning the system to help your surrogates do the job effectively.

And don't stop with one meeting. Use this technique to keep management involved by giving short reports on how the system is progressing. Ask for time at big gatherings like annual sales meetings or special full-management sessions to keep the concepts fresh in the managers' minds. Small reinforcements such as these will help maintain strong support at all levels. This in turn will help keep compliance with the system high. Your first-line supervisors won't question whether there is any way to do training other than "by the book"—the SDL book, that is.

Figure 7.2 is a planning tool you can use to help you strategize these meetings.

Preparing Direct Supervisors

The second group that you must prepare for an SDL implementation are the direct supervisors of your trainees. These individuals can have a great effect on your system in how they help to

Figure 7.2. Implementation Action Plan.

WHO	HOW (WHERE)	WHEN	WHAT (TOOLS)
EXAMPLE **Step 1** Solicit support from upper management • CEO • Vice Presidents • Assistant Vice Presidents	Board meeting	04/15/93	• Develop a slide presentation • Develop a sample SDL

prepare the trainees. They also influence compliance with your program as a whole. Basically, supervisors can supply some of the external motivation and guidance for the learners that they perceive as otherwise missing in the SDL process.

External control is a very touchy concept in SDL. I won't go into the battle of choice versus need or the issue of where motivation should come from here. Even (1982) covers this controversy in detail. Suffice it to say that in industry, certain material must be disseminated within specified time limits. A well-prepared supervisor who understands and believes in the concept of training by SDL can help prepare trainees to be self-directed learners and can keep them going when things get tough.

On the other hand, if you have not prepared the direct supervisors well, your problems may go well beyond their inability to help the trainees. The supervisors may actually decrease compliance with your system. Earlier, we discussed compliance and control from management's point of view. The supervisory level is where all those ideas are translated into reality. The supervisor creates the climate that helps the trainee take full advantage of the SDL process. Agreeing to comply with the procedures of your system and then actually doing it are what make the process work. Lack of commitment from the supervisors means a poor climate and possibly a failed process.

Characteristics of a Good SDL Climate

Steps necessary to create the appropriate climate for SDL include the following:

- Providing time to allow the trainee to do the learning or go to the learning center
- Allowing the flexibility to choose which packages seem most appropriate to the trainee's current and future status
- Empowering the trainee to use the material and skills gained in the learning
- Guiding the trainee to keep him on a path that is personally rewarding, while at the same time fulfilling the company's needs

Notice that these characteristics are stated in terms of something the supervisor needs to do. This is intentional. Without the supervisor's direct action, the proper climate will not be created.

Providing the time is a particularly critical factor. One of the real problems supervisors have in accepting SDL is that they see it as taking too much time. This is especially true in a distributed implementation where the supervisor can see the employee training. "Out of sight, out of mind" is not too far from the truth in training.

Part of your training of supervisors must be to convince them that SDL will save them time. They have to be bombarded with the time savings of SDL as downtime training, reminded that their quick employees will get back on the job sooner, and shown that it takes twice the time to train with the buddy system as it does to let one employee learn with an SDL package. I'm not sure why this is such a hard concept for supervisors to master, but I've always found it so. I've also found that if you can convince them of SDL's time effectiveness, they will become true believers, and many of your other problems will simply disappear.

Some adult learning theory, particularly as it relates to SDL, suggests that these climate and motivational factors are the domain of the learner's internal motivation mechanisms. In the reality of the business environment, they are also the province of direct supervision. For example, you may have an excellent training center where there are a number of programs available for the trainees' use. However, if the supervisors won't release them to use the center, the motivation to go will soon disappear. From a different point of view, if the supervisors won't acknowledge trainee professional development on performance appraisals, or counsel them as to what training will best help them achieve individual goals, it won't matter how many programs you have in the center. All the choices in the world will be inadequate.

Techniques for Preparing Supervisors

Gaining supervisors' acceptance of SDL and using their acumen to help prepare the trainee for the process require an appropriate approach and solid planning. An effective method is to utilize an SDL package on SDL. This approach is particularly useful when you have large numbers of supervisors in many different locations, as you might find in a distributed system. An "SDL on SDL" package can explain the basic concepts of your system to the supervisors while they are actually experiencing it.

After completing the package, the supervisors will have the background necessary to formally discuss the process of SDL with the trainees. This will make them more accepting of the concept, as well as clarifying what SDL really means to the company and to each position. Such discussions should also detail what the trainees' responsibilities are in the system. Exhibit 7.1 provides an excerpt from this type of package.

An approach that is useful in smaller distributed implementations, or in a learning center strategy, is to have the supervisors' direct superiors explain the basics of SDL and the procedures of the system to them. This is usually handled in a classroom environment or at a meeting. It's a good tactic for lending extra credibility to the entire SDL process as well. Knowing that your boss knows the system and is expecting you to set the climate and make it work— and more important, that he or she will be checking your success— is a great incentive to doing it right.

There are two problems with this approach. The first is that the manager must be sold on the concept. You did this earlier when you prepared management. However, it is better not to assume anything. Check to be sure, before you allow the managers to talk about your program.

The second problem is that the manager may miss a few points when explaining the system to the supervisors. To decrease the probability of this (you can never eliminate it), develop a lesson guide or fact sheet for the manager to use. Make it simple and short. Most managers are busy and don't have time for full-fledged lesson plans. It should cover the main points in big bold letters, with a bit of detail under each to remind the manager what it's all about. An example of this type of instrument, developed for a distributed system, can be found in Exhibit 7.2.

You can prepare the managers for their task, and check on their commitment, by going over the lesson guide/fact sheet with them. Do this at a regularly scheduled management meeting. You

Exhibit 7.1. Sample Chapter: SDL on SDL.

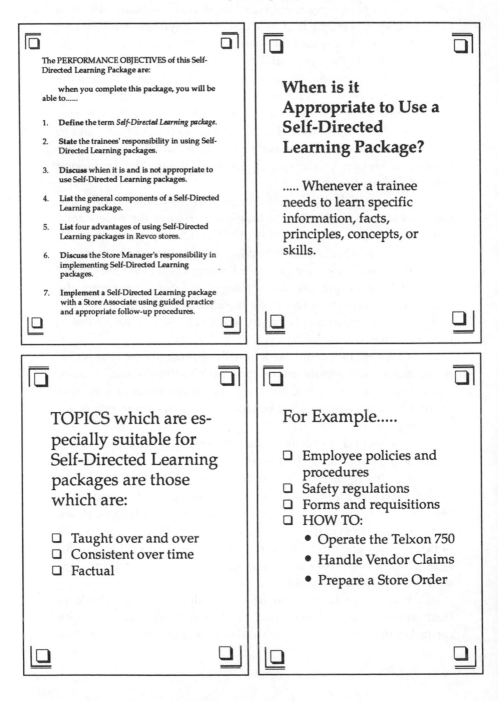

The PERFORMANCE OBJECTIVES of this Self-Directed Learning Package are:

when you complete this package, you will be able to......

1. Define the term *Self-Directed Learning package.*

2. State the trainees' responsibility in using Self-Directed Learning packages.

3. Discuss whien it is and is not appropriate to use Self-Directed Learning packages.

4. List the general components of a Self-Directed Learning package.

5. List four advantages of using Self-Directed Learning packages in Revco stores.

6. Discuss the Store Manager's responsibility in implementing Self-Directed Learning packages.

7. Implement a Self-Directed Learning package with a Store Associate using guided practice and appropriate follow-up procedures.

When is it Appropriate to Use a Self-Directed Learning Package?

..... Whenever a trainee needs to learn specific information, facts, principles, concepts, or skills.

TOPICS which are especially suitable for Self-Directed Learning packages are those which are:

☐ Taught over and over
☐ Consistent over time
☐ Factual

For Example.....

☐ Employee policies and procedures
☐ Safety regulations
☐ Forms and requisitions
☐ HOW TO:
  • Operate the Telxon 750
  • Handle Vendor Claims
  • Prepare a Store Order

Exhibit 7.2. Manager Fact Sheet.

DISTRICT MANAGER FACT SHEET
on _____ Store Operations Training
Self-Directed Learning Packages

What are Self-Directed Learning packages?

Self-Directed Learning packages are self-contained training programs.

Self-Directed Learning packages allow trainees to learn on their own without the help of a trainer. Training is available when it's needed. The number of store hours spent on training is reduced.

Self-Directed Learning packages allow trainees to learn at their own pace. Fast learners will complete the materials more quickly and will be back on the job sooner. Slower learners will take more time but will finish with a complete understanding of the tas

The purpose of Self-Directed Learning (SDL) is to put the responsibility for learning on the trainees. They will learn their jobs by using the Self-Directed Learning packages.

The Self-Directed Learning packages that will be distributed to the stores during the next year include the following topics:

Interstore Transfers

Order Receiving

Ordering

Pricing

Salvage

Merchandising

Outside Vendors

Photofinishing

Recalls

How do Self-Directed Learning packages work?

All Self-Directed Learning packages begin with a list of Instructional Objectives.

Objectives tell learners exactly what they should know or be able to do when they finish the SDL package.

A small section of information is presented and then the trainees are directed to practice what they have just learned by completing an exercise or activity. All new information is always reinforced by practice.

At the end of each chapter is a quiz that tests trainees' knowledge of the information presented in the chapter.

When trainees are able to complete the practice exercises and pass the quiz with no more than two incorrect answers, they may move on to the next chapter until they complete the SDL.

It's important to note that any time trainees are not clear about a procedure, or need more practice, they can stop to review.

Now, all that is needed is some guided practice. Either the Store Manager or his/her designate must observe the trainees as they practice the new skill, helping if necessary until they are capable of performing alone.

What are the benefits of using Self-Directed Learning packages?

- *They provide consistency in training*
- *Eliminate the need for one-on-one instruction*
- *Lessen errors in paperwork and pricing*
- *Reduce employee turnover through increased employee confidence and job satisfaction*

Exhibit 7.2. Manager Fact Sheet, Cont'd.

What are the District Managers' responsibilities in the training process

You will be asked to take an active role in the implementation of the Self-Directed Learning packages.

- First, your attitude toward the new training system will affect how your Store Managers feel about it. If you are enthusiastic and really believe that the SDL packages can make a difference, your Store Managers will be more likely to support the training process and will implement and maintain the SDL packages at store level.

- You need to ensure that the Store Managers understand the concept of Self-Directed Learning and correctly use the SDL packages in their stores.

To accomplish this, the Training and Development Department has designed a "Self-Directed Learning package on Self-Directed Learning for Store Managers."

This SDL package is intended to help Store Managers understand general concepts about Self-Directed Learning as well as specifics about the _____ Self-Directed Learning packages.

The package is also intended to give Store Managers first hand experience using Self-Directed Learning.

As a final activity in the package, the Store Managers are asked to complete an exercise, date, sign, and return it to the Training and Development Department by April 15, 1990. (A copy of the exercise is included at the back of this guide.)

- You will be notified if that activity has not been returned. **We are asking you to follow up with the delinquent Store Managers.**

- **On an ongoing basis you should monitor the SDL Completion Record each time you visit a store.** (A copy is included in this guide)

Every time a SDL package is completed, the Store Manager is to enter the employee's name and the completion date under the SDL title. **The Store Manger must initial each entry.**

What are the Store Managers' responsibilities in the training process?

- **The Store Manager has the ultimate responsibility to ensure that training occurs at store level.**

Store Managers are to establish the schedule for training. Specifically, they are to determine in which order the SDL packages are to be given to each employee.

There is no suggested order for completion of the SDL packages. The only requirement is that before new hires are assigned new tasks, they first complete the appropriate SDL and then ____ have at least one guided practice session with either the Store Manager or his/her designate before actual performing the job on their own.

- **Store Managers must also Initial the SDL Completion Record each and every time an SDL is completed in their stores.**

Additional responsibilities for facilitating Self-Directed Learning packages at store level.

Look at the attached checklist

This checklist must be followed each time an employee takes a Self-Directed Learning package. These responsibilities must be handled either by the Store Manage or by his/her designate.

don't want to call a special meeting that takes them away from their other duties. It shouldn't take you more than fifteen or twenty minutes (if it takes longer, your fact sheet is too complicated).

This idea of using regularly scheduled meetings for SDL discussions, introductions, and so on is relevant for any of the management interventions we've discussed. Try to make it just another item on a regularly scheduled management meeting agenda. Your materials and concepts should be strong enough that they won't get lost in whatever else is being discussed, and you obtain the advantage of not annoying your audience by forcing another meeting on them. It also makes the SDL implementation appear as if it is just another normal management responsibility, which is what it is and what you want them to believe it is.

An SDL Simulation

You've already planned for the trainees' supervisors to be your facilitators (site implementors) and evaluators. Since they will have some important duties, including getting the trainees started, evaluating the two performance demonstrations, and administering the final test, you meet with them to explain the concepts of SDL and their part in the package. You do this at their regularly scheduled monthly management meeting. At the meeting, you pass out the SDL package and a facilitator's checklist that they can use to help them administer the package.

Facilitator's Checklist
- Packages received
- Trainees introduced to SDL
- Video machine available and ready
- Trainee has initiated contact for delegation performance
- Delegation performance observation done
- Trainee has developed plan for returning phone calls
- Phone call performance observation done
- Final test taken
- Trainee mastery reported to training department

SDL and Performance Appraisal

One other method of garnering and keeping supervisory support for your SDL implementation is to make the training part of the company's performance appraisal system. Supervisors often have a hard time with the development portion of a performance appraisal form. If you can show them how using your SDL programs will make it easy to both plan and do development activities, you may get instant, highly supportive converts to your system. After all, you're making their job easier. They'll not only let their supervisees use your materials but will counsel them to do so when they fill out the performance appraisals. If you can formalize SDL as part of the performance appraisal document, it makes a great control measure for both implementation formats, and it is particularly useful for enhancing the credibility of your learning center.

Preparing the Trainees

In striving to understand what SDL is and how it works, we've paid only limited attention to the fact that there are learners involved in the process. That now changes, as preparing the trainees for SDL becomes a critical factor in the implementation process. We'll discuss reasons why trainees may have trouble with your SDL packages and how this knowledge can be used to make their transition to SDL easier.

Learners and Self-Directed Learning

As we've discussed, SDL covers a wide range of concepts, from the individualized classroom to CBT. However, whatever the definition or format, all SDL is designed and developed for use by a learner who needs to acquire knowledge or master a skill. And most learners have one thing in common: they are usually *not* prepared to engage in SDL. This isn't normally due to any psychological limitation. Rather, it seems to be an acquired response to a society—and especially a school system—in which the learner is spoon fed.

Babies, by way of contrast, are inherent practitioners of SDL.

Few parents set a curriculum and develop lesson plans for their newborns. Yet somehow, without such a regimented learning process, the child learns who's who, how to get food or just attention, how to walk, and, the greatest of all miracles, how to talk.

Self-directed, experiential learning is also the basic way that children learn almost everything. "Don't touch" seldom works until learners find out the reality of touching. And they will find out for themselves, when they feel they are ready, no matter how many times the concerned parent says no. You may call this form of self-direction instinct, but it is SDL.

Then suddenly, this self-directed learner is thrust into schools. Now learning becomes structured. There is a time for blocks, a time for puzzles, and a time for reading. If you choose to do your learning at the wrong time, you are ostracized by the group (I think the newest term is given "time out"). This punishment is decreed by a new authority figure called a teacher, who controls the learning time.

Soon there is a time for science, a time for math, a time for history, but no time to learn what you want to learn. The teacher decides not only when to learn, but also what to learn and even how to learn it. The price for failure to abide by these external controls is much higher than a quickly passing "time out." Grades, parental approval, and the chance to go to the right college replace wanting to know as the reason for learning. Self-direction disappears.

Simply stated, this learning acculturation process is why most learners have trouble with SDL. If you spend twelve, sixteen, or more years being told what, when, and how to learn, it becomes rather disconcerting to be told "You're on your own." Even if somewhere in the past it was once your natural way, you may no longer be comfortable with the idea.

The Learner's Point of View. To better understand the learner's difficulties in dealing with self-direction, we should look at the situation from the learner's point of view. A number of theoreticians have tried, drawing conclusions that range from "adults have a need to be self-directed" (Knowles, 1980) to "they are at times incapable of making their own learning decisions" (Snow, 1980).

However, I think the best way to understand the learner is to step back from being a designer, or a trainer, or whatever it is that you have become. Let the layers of experience and all the knowledge of learning theory peel away and once again become simply a learner.

You, the adult learner, probably feel a certain sense of freedom in being able to say, "I want to take charge of my learning," or "I want to learn at my pace and in my style." However, when you have been externally directed, externally driven, even externally motivated for years, how comfortable are you really with becoming responsible for your learning? How confident are you when no one has given you a specific plan to follow, no time span for "getting it done" has been set, and no instructor is there to lead and guide you? Since kindergarten and perhaps earlier, you have always relied on someone to tell you what you "needed" to learn, what was required to reach your goal, and how long you had to do it. Someone was in charge, to check on you, reward you when you did well, or punish you when you didn't learn what was "needed."

Suddenly, you find all those supports are being taken away from you. You're responsible for deciding what you want to learn and for getting started on doing it. You're responsible for setting your own timetables for completing the material as well as for evaluating your mastery of it. You're on your own, you're self-directed, and you're probably more than a little insecure.

Learner-Centered Advantages of SDL. The question is, how can the SDL designer help to mitigate the uneasiness you just felt as a learner? What can you do to build the learners' self-confidence, to increase their awareness of what SDL really is, and to give them the ability to understand how it will help them reach their goals?

An obvious answer is to sell the learner on the advantages of SDL. Unfortunately, most designers define advantages in terms of what the program can do for the company. Often this has little or no relation to the learner's needs. For example, an SDL package might be the most efficient way to train large numbers of employees in various locations on a new manufacturing technique. However, this is not of any major concern to the trainees. They want to know how it's going to make their job or at least the mastering of it easier. The fact that you'll be saving $60,000 in travel costs for the corporation will hardly be useful in quelling employees' apprehension at being thrust back into the world of self-direction.

Yet you can't chastise the designer too much for misreading the learner's needs. I have observed many classroom instructors who forget to concern themselves with their learners when they are sitting right in front of them. How much harder is it, then, for the SDL designer, who will probably never see the end users of his product, to consider the advantages of SDL as they relate to the learner. To be effective at this, we need to once again slip back into the persona of a learner.

Working at your own pace. So, as a learner, what advantages do you receive from SDL? The most obvious is the ability to work at your pace. This includes the latitude to repeat any of the material as often as needed for complete comprehension. It also means the freedom to control the information flow by simply picking the material up or putting it down. That will help you to understand the material better, allowing you to do a better job. If the boss needs you, you can stop and pick the package up later when you have the time to really learn it.

Availability when you need it. A second advantage is the availability of the material when you need to learn it, or what is currently termed *just-in-time training.* You don't need to wait for a class if you want to learn a new skill or prepare for a promotion. Better yet, you don't have to take a class long before you need the material presented in it just because that's the only time it's given. With SDL, when you or the boss decide that you need to learn a new skill, the training is ready for you, either in the learning center or at your workstation. You won't forget what you learned before you ever get a chance to put it to use.

Structure to help you learn more easily. A third advantage is that this is a structured learning experience, in which you are given the objectives from the beginning. Your anxiety or uncertainty about what it is that you really need to know is put to rest. The objectives are stated up front, and the content follows the objectives accurately and precisely. Related to this, you find that what you learn is what is evaluated. There are no surprises on the tests or performance evaluations. And speaking of evaluation and feedback, you can receive these at any time. You decide when you're ready, and you check your own progress. There is no more trying to figure out what things the trainer really wants you to remember, no more war stories, no more "Huh?" questions on the exam.

Long-term reinforcement and review. Another advantage is that the SDL materials can become your source for long-term reinforcement and review. If you haven't done a procedure for a while and you've forgotten some of its intricacies, you can refer to the exact place and the method that you used to learn it the first time. It's almost like having an expert on call, who you can confer with at any time. More important, you don't have to always be asking the boss.

Personal Development. Finally, particularly in a learning center approach, you have the ability to go well beyond just what you need and into what you want. Even a small learning center should have programs for self-development such as reading or writing skills. It will probably have programs that you can use to learn skills that make you eligible for promotion to the next level. It might also have packages on concepts such as stress reduction or wellness that can help you in everyday life. All of these are available to you when you need them and when *you* are ready to use them.

Learner-Centered Disadvantages of SDL. We've covered the advantages as seen through the eyes of the learner, but what about disadvantages? SDL, like any other design, does have disadvantages. Some of them are real and some only perceptions of the learners. Both need to be dealt with.

There is an argument whether these disadvantages should be hidden from or revealed to the learner. My feeling is that good SDL demands that the learner go in with as much knowledge of the situation as possible. However, I'll leave the final decision to each designer's own conscience.

Lack of an instructor. Most of the perceived disadvantages stem from the lack of an instructor. They relate to our earlier point that learners are not comfortable with SDL. These perceived disadvantages include:

- No one to answer questions
- No one to control the learning by explaining what is and isn't important

- No one to set a schedule for when to learn or a schedule for when to exhibit material comprehension
- No one to validate the learning through verbal or nonverbal feedback

A learning center approach reduces some of these perceived disadvantages through the presence of a facilitator, but the facilitator is not a controller. The learner who is used to having learning decisions made by an instructor will be ill at ease in a learning center, no matter how many facilitators are present. This apprehension is often characterized by an aversion to coming to the center. The learner is always too busy to make the trip, no matter how short it might be. The problem isn't time or the center's location; it's the perceived lack of structure in the learning. Often the excuse of no time can be translated into the lack of an instructor to control the time.

In a distributed approach, even the quasi-authority figure of the facilitator isn't there, making the perceptions doubly difficult to counter. The learner can no longer use the excuse that the center is inconvenient, since there is no center. The materials are right there at the job. However, "too busy" is still often heard as a rationalization. The underlying problem of discomfort with SDL cannot be easily dealt with. It requires systematic preparation of the learner for the process, as we will discuss later.

Poor reading and writing skills. There are some disadvantages that relate more directly to the learners' actual abilities and not perceptions. These include poor reading or writing skills, which makes it difficult for them to use SDL packages effectively. Dealing with these disadvantages may require you to look for alternative media formats for your SDL packages. For some learners, you may find that you have to abandon the approach completely.

You may have noted that many of the advantages of SDL also seem to be disadvantages, particularly when seen from the learners' perspective. This shouldn't be too surprising. Remember, we are dealing with individuals whose natural learning style has been disturbed, perhaps destroyed, by acculturation experiences. It's little wonder they're confused by SDL. They may want to take advantage of its benefits, but they see those same benefits as creating difficulties.

The disadvantages, and the advantages as well, are not exactly the same for all SDL concepts. Readers who are looking at SDL from a different perspective than that of a training package have probably recognized this. However, every system has its strengths and weaknesses as seen from the learners' perspective. If the designer is to prepare learners adequately, a solid analysis of these aspects must be done. Then a plan for smoothing the learners' transition into SDL based on this analysis needs to be developed.

Trainee Preparation

The key to preparing trainees for SDL is to develop a systematic plan for this purpose. This plan is based on an assessment of the advantages and disadvantages that your particular SDL system will have *for the trainees*. Remember, it's not what SDL will do for the company that will prepare the trainees, but how it will affect them personally.

Many times, this type of planning is simply overlooked. Even the best designers, who may spend vast quantities of time preparing the company and particularly the management for SDL, forget the need to develop a plan for preparing the trainees. After all, it is self-directed learning. When the trainees get the packages, or enter the learning center, they'll be self-directed and will learn.

From our previous discussion, I hope you realize that this is not necessarily or even probably the case. The designer must prepare the trainees by eliminating the confusion that will assail most of them when they are asked to once again become self-directed. A plan must be in place to emphasize the advantages and deal with the disadvantages. In other words, the trainee needs to be "sold" on SDL.

Selling the Trainee on SDL. The concept of "sell" is the real purpose of trainee preparation. You must first interest the trainees in the idea of SDL and then convince them of its usefulness by helping them envision using it. As the envisioning becomes comfortable, questions concerning the functions of this innovation begin to occur and must be answered. This is a classic representation of the selling process, and it should be the designer's goal in trainee preparation.

Depending on your implementation design, your plan is only limited by your creativity (and probably budget). Most effective plans have the common factor of being instructor mediated, preferably by the designated SDL facilitator/implementor. This may sound a bit illogical, having an instructor-led process to prepare for SDL. However, if you reconsider our earlier discussions concerning trainee readiness for SDL and SDL's perceived disadvantages, you'll understand why trainee preparation is best handled by a live instructor.

Preparing Trainees for a Learning Center Implementation. In a learning center approach, you might implement your plan on an individual or small-group basis. Or you could choose a classroom setting with a follow-up one-on-one process the first time a person enters the actual center. Your design will depend on the size of your organization and your time constraints. If a large number of trainees need to get started on special packages in the center, you'll be restricted as to how you can prepare them. These concepts are explored in more detail specifically for learning centers in Chapter Eleven.

Preparing Trainees for a Distributed Implementation. For distributed implementation, the most efficient execution is usually a classroom approach, instructed by your site implementor. You may opt for an individual approach, but since distributed systems are used most often in large organizations, the logistics of an individualized plan may be prohibitive. It may also be rather hard on the site implementor.

Four Steps for Trainee Preparation. No matter how you decide to execute your plan, the process usually consists of four steps.

Definition. In the first step, the instructor provides an overall *definition* of SDL, then discusses the definition as it relates to the trainees. It is important to point out the differences and similarities to what the trainees are used to. Then the instructor explores the things that will be easier due to the SDL system. The most important objective is to get the trainees interested.

Advantages and disadvantages. In step 2, the instructor discusses the *advantages and disadvantages* of SDL. The most important advantage—being able to work at your own pace without the aid of an instructor—should be stressed first. Both the positive and negative ramifications of this aspect are examined. The freedom to personally control your learning, combined with the responsibility of being your own guide, exemplifies this concept nicely. On the negative side, it should be noted that if results don't quite match expectations, there is no one to blame but yourself. Other advantages that flow from these concepts, such as the ability to repeat material until mastery is achieved and the personal control of material flow, should be discussed next.

This is followed by the less obvious advantages, such as the use of the packages for quick reference and reinforcement after the initial learning. Package adherence to objectives, which guarantees no unimportant material or surprise test questions, and learning availability when you need it should also be stressed.

If a learning center approach is in use, the instructor should emphasize the ability to go beyond "what you need" to "what you want" to learn. This area is completed by considering other possible disadvantages and how they can be overcome. This is where the trainees will begin envisioning themselves using the packages. The facilitator/implementor needs to be ready to answer questions as they come up to strengthen this process.

Package mechanics. With the vision begun, the third step details the *mechanics* of the learning package and implementation system. This will solidify the envisioning process. Start at the beginning with how to obtain and begin a package. Restress what it means to do the learning "on your own." Discuss the support that can and can't be expected from the site implementor or learning center facilitator, and how these roles are different from those of an instructor. Go over areas such as self-checks, performance evaluations, completion standards, record keeping, and any special aspects of package or system design that the trainee needs to understand.

Stress the importance of following the package as it is written to receive maximum value in minimum time. Like their supervisors, the trainees will look for shortcuts if they feel they are spending too much time. You need to convince them that doing it "right," by following the sequence as written and completing the quizzes and activities, will save time in the end by making their learning more effective. This is a key concept, particularly in a distributed system, where control over how a trainee completes a package is minimal.

Summary and reinforcement. The fourth step begins with a *summary and reinforcement* of the advantages of the new system. (Skip the disadvantages this time; they've heard them already, and this is the time for a little less fairness and a little more propaganda.) Be sure that all questions have been fully answered. Then conclude by restating how to get started.

A word of caution about using a learning center facilitator for your instructor is in order here. I've seen too many of these classes where the facilitator takes large amounts of time to explain the advantages of the SDL system for the organization. This is particularly true if the facilitator is the designer of the system. Though we've discussed this tendency earlier, it deserves repetition, since trainee preparation is a critical area where this often occurs.

While SDL can be a more efficient way to train in many circumstances and can save training dollars, make the training staff more effective, improve quality by improving consistency, and do all the other wonderful things you tell management, trainees seldom need or want to know this. They are interested in how SDL affects them and how they can use it to their benefit. Save the management speeches for management! Make sure your trainee preparation plan spends its time telling the trainees what they need to know.

In the final analysis, SDL requires the trainee to have characteristics such as self-confidence, self-awareness, self-reflection, and task orientation to succeed (Long, 1990). In the business environment, it often seems that most of the self-direction disappears from SDL because the trainee needs to master a specialized set of skills as quickly as possible. Even some of the adult learning characteristics that form the theoretical basis for SDL may seem to have been abandoned.

Be this as it may, such arguments do not mean that SDL designers can ignore the needs of the trainees for developing these characteristics. Nor do they allow them to abrogate their own responsibility for preparing the trainees by "selling" them on the concept.

Creating good, well-planned trainee preparation that presents the advantages of SDL in ways that help develop and enhance those possibly atrophied characteristics is part of your job. It will make your implementation of SDL easier and more effective.

An SDL Simulation

Your plan is for the trainees to be prepared by their supervisors, who are your site implementors. When you met with the supervisors, you gave them a list of concepts to cover as they introduce the trainee to SDL. You explained how to do the introduction. You do a random check of supervisors to make sure this trainee orientation has been accomplished.

SDL Concepts to Cover with the Trainee
- Define what we mean by self-directed learning
    Work at own pace
    No instructor
    Objectives are the key to learning and evaluation
    Use learning package
- Discuss why these concepts make it both hard and easy
- Talk about the advantages of SDL
    Saves them time
    More convenient, since they can learn at desk
    Work at own pace
    Can refer back to later for concepts forgotten
- Talk about the SDL package
    Where do they obtain it
    Where do they use it
    The video component
    Performance observations
    Quizzes and test
    Your role as facilitator
- Restate the advantages of SDL

Exhibit 7.3. A Checklist for SDL.

Preparing for an SDL Implementation

☐ Company management has been prepared for SDL.
- Meetings have been held with managers at all levels.
- The needed control measures have been agreed to.

☐ The trainees' supervisors have been prepared for SDL.
- The supervisors' managers have been properly prepared and developed.
- The trainees' role has been clearly defined.
- The advantages of SDL have been shown to them.

☐ The trainees have been prepared for SDL.
- The concept has been defined for the trainees.
- The advantages and disadvantages have been discussed.
- Package mechanics have been gone over.

8

Distributed Implementation

The Challenge of the
On-the-Job Training Site

Implementation, simply stated, is "making the training happen." A well-thought-out and well-executed implementation is as critical to the success of your SDL process as the four development corner-stones. But implementing SDL, particularly in a distributed environment, is complicated and often difficult to manage effectively. Many variables must be account for, and at times some will be beyond your control. This chapter will explore those variables as they are related to planning for a distributed SDL implementation (Figure 8.1).

There are quite a number of implementation variables, and some might not be germane to your particular system. Even the best-designed implementation will probably not be good enough to deal with all the problems you'll encounter, but you will need to at least *consider* all the variables as you do the advanced planning for your implementation. Never get caught in the trap of one trainer who summed up his implementation plan with the comment, "Hey, it's self-directed learning; I give to them, and if they are self directed, they learn it."

Recognizing a Distributed Implementation Scenario

The first step in planning a distributed implementation is to know that you have one. At first glance, the decision to employ a distributed implementation strategy would seem simple. If the

186

Figure 8.1. A Model for SDL.

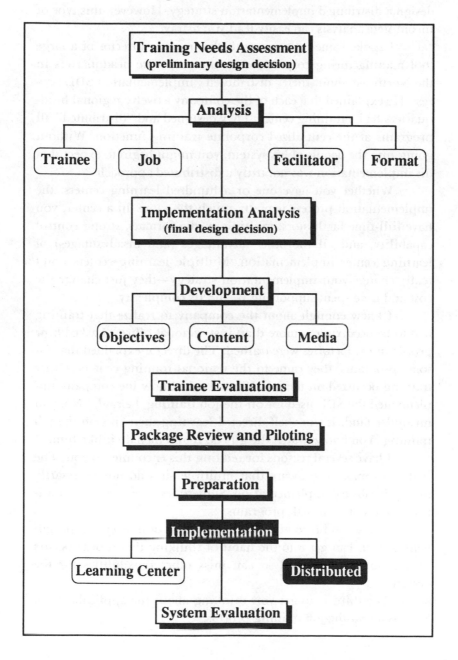

training needs to occur at more than one site, you will have to design a distributed implementation strategy. However, this type of incomplete analysis can easily lead you astray.

I spoke some time ago with the training director of a large tool manufacturing corporation at the corporate headquarters in the Northeast about their "distributed" implementation SDL process. He explained that each of the company's twelve regional headquarters had a training center. They designed and "distributed" all programs at the centralized corporate training function. Without going into the details of his system, you might begin to expect that his implementation was not truly a distributed approach.

Whether you have one or a hundred learning centers, the implementation process is pretty much the same. In a center, you have full-time facilitators, multiple media formats, strong control capability, and all the other advantages (and disadvantages) of learning center implementation. Multiple learning centers don't really change your implementation strategy—they just change the cost and time spent supporting it, and its complexity.

I knew enough about the company to realize that training had to be occurring at more than just regional offices. I asked how people in the factories were trained. The director explained that for some programs, they came to the regional training centers. Other training occurred on the job. When I asked how the company implemented the SDL used for on-the-job training, he said, "No, you misunderstand, it's not self-directed learning there, it's on-the-job training. You know, watch the guy do it and then do it like him."

I have several reasons for relating this encounter to you. The first is to make you aware that multiple sites do not necessarily mean distributed implementation. Sometimes they only mean multiple copies of your SDL programs.

The second is to give you an example of how even a proponent of SDL can get into the habit of thinking that it only occurs in a training center and so can miss other possibilities for the design.

The third is to get you thinking about the applicability of SDL as an on-the-job training process.

Distributed Implementation as a Training System

In reality, distributed SDL implementation is better characterized by where it takes place, or who is responsible for it, than by how many locations it takes place in. It is possible for a company with a single location, like a hospital, to need a distributed implementation strategy. As the previous scenario exemplified, the opposite is also true.

So what are the indicators of the need for a distributed implementation? The first one is elementary. Simply ask yourself if you have or will have an actual learning center. If the answer is no, you can't effectively use a learning center implementation strategy and will require a distributed implementation system.

But be careful! There are many different types of learning centers, ranging from entire buildings to closets. If you have a learning center, no matter how underfunded or understaffed, and you put your programs there, you are using a learning center implementation system. Even if people take the SDL packages home from your center, it's not a distributed implementation system. On the other hand, if you plan to ship your packages from a centralized location to sites that are not learning centers, you'll probably have to use a distributed implementation system.

That last word is where the concept of a distributed implementation really diverges from a learning center. While a learning center can be as simple as one package, or as complicated as an individualized development process with tens and possibly hundreds of packages, learning centers are seldom a training system by themselves. They can contain material that augments other training, provide packages that deal with the technical aspects of a position, even help prepare individuals for a new position. However, they rarely provide an integrated training system that furnishes a trainee with all of the training necessary to fulfill the duties of a current or higher-level position.

A distributed implementation, on the other hand, is most often a complete system. Its major emphasis is to create a trained job incumbent, chiefly through the use of the SDL design. The reason for this is to some extent revealed by your training needs analysis. A training need that demands a distributed implementation is seldom unique. It is usually just one aspect of a set of needs that require a training intervention.

For example, suppose you find that the sales reps at all ten of your branch offices do not know the procedure for filling out a refund form and that the only effective training design to deal with this need is an SDL package with a distributed implementation. It's more than likely that you've only isolated an indicator of other training problems. When all of these problems are revealed through a more in-depth analysis, you'll probably need a series of SDL packages, all done with a distributed implementation. In other words, you'll need to develop a system for training sales reps.

This might seem to be a bit of circular logic. A distributed implementation is a system because you use it where you need a system? Possibly so, but the final product usually justifies the concept. If you need to go through the complexities of developing an SDL distributed implementation, it will most often end up being a system for the total training of one or more positions. A learning center is normally more an adjunct within an integrated system of various designs, filling particular training niches where SDL is most effective.

If the previous discussion seemed overly complex, don't worry. Its purpose was mostly to help you realize that if you get into a distributed implementation and it starts getting bigger than you first planned, don't be alarmed. You've probably hit on a training system that your company needs to deal with a large-scale problem you may not have even realized existed when you started.

Work Practice as an Indicator of a Distributed Implementation

A second and more subtle indicator of the need for a distributed implementation than the lack of a learning center relates to what you have designed and developed into your SDL packages. If your SDL activities include practice in a work environment, you're probably going to need a distributed implementation system. Work environment practice—you might stretch the point a bit by calling it on-the-job training—usually needs to be done on the job. This

means that your packages are not used in a training center, but rather in a store, on the manufacturing floor, in the office, or wherever the job is done. Your implementation system must be designed to take these less formalized training settings into account, which is a facet of a distributed implementation.

This might seem like another "blinding flash of the obvious," and a flash that comes too late as well. In Chapter Two, we discussed the implementation analysis as occurring early in the SDL design process. Yet now we are saying that implementation depends on what you developed in the way of practice activities.

The point is that you can change your mind about the implementation if you find you must. In fact, you can change your mind about anything right up to the day the first trainee gets his or her hands on your package. You planned on a learning center implementation simply because you have a learning center and it seemed to fit your analysis parameters. But as you develop the package, you realize there are practices that must be done on the job. So you reconsider and distribute your package to be done on the job! You made that early decision based on the data you had available. With new data in hand, a change might be in order. Make it if it's needed. It won't be easy, but it's necessary if you want your SDL to work.

An exception to this "work environment means distributed implementation" rule occurs when the practice is done on a work simulator. Arguably, the simulator itself is a learning center and you revert to a learning center implementation automatically, but this might create some confusion for new designers.

Discounting the use of simulators, a distributed implementation system is almost always the right choice when you have included a work environment practice in your SDL. It's even more likely to be correct if the practice includes an observation/evaluation process, which we'll discuss later.

The Training Population as an Indicator

A third indicator of a distributed implementation is your training population. If the SDL must go to them on the job, because that's the only place that logistics allows, you need a distributed

implementation system. This might be due to the number of trainees you need to train, the distances you have to cover, the time span in which the training must occur, turnover considerations, or simply corporate finances.

There is no one main reason for needing a distributed implementation system. Rather, you need to do your usual careful analysis of all the factors and ask yourself, or your subject matter experts, the right questions. Most important, take nothing for granted. Wait until all the facts are in before deciding, then be flexible enough to change if necessary.

Distributed SDL Implementation
Compared to Classroom Learning

To better understand a distributed SDL implementation, it's helpful to consider how it compares to the other major distributed strategy—classroom instruction. In its implementation procedures, distributed SDL actually resembles classroom instruction more than it does a learning center implementation. That's not surprising when you realize that both strategies often fulfill the same purpose: bringing training to large numbers of individuals, in differing locations, in a short time frame.

Unfortunately, when most trainers have more than one site at which to deliver training, they reflexively think of a classroom approach as the only possible answer. They understand how simple it will be to develop a class at corporate headquarters, then send a cadre of instructors out to all thirty training sites to teach it. How simple, and how expensive!!

We've already considered the cost-effectiveness of SDL, particularly if you have a distributed implementation situation, so we won't restate that entire discussion here. It's worth repeating, however, that the most important advantage of a distributed SDL strategy over a classroom approach is cost-effectiveness. For this, if for no other reason, you should consider both alternatives before deciding on a distributed strategy.

Similarities

There are a number of similarities between distributed SDL and the classroom.

Efficiency of Scale. The first similarity is obvious—efficiency of scale. Both systems are designed to teach large numbers of trainees at the same time. This comment might seem a bit irrational at first glance. How can SDL, in which each person learns on his or her own, teach large numbers of trainees at the same time? The answer is that it all depends on what you design your SDL to do.

A classroom can be used to disseminate knowledge to 20 or even 200 trainees at once (let's not talk effective right now, just efficient). An SDL package can do the same thing—that is, if you reproduce 200 copies of your program, if each trainee at a location immediately follows the previous trainee in completing the package, or if your training occurs in 200 different locations at the same time.

In the final analysis, a well-designed SDL distributed implementation system can efficiently handle the same number of trainees a classroom design, and usually at a lower cost.

Need for Strong Program Documentation. A second similarity is the need for strong program documentation. In a classroom approach, you have lesson plans and trainee guides or handouts. In a distributed SDL implementation, you have the package itself. Each requires the same care in development. Both systems demand program documents that are accurately analyzed, correctly objectivized, concisely written, and properly used. Anything less and you will end up with little consistency in the way the material is presented and, more important, received.

Need for Control. Proper utilization brings up another similarity: the need for control. If your material is going to be presented consistently, both methods demand strong control processes, though their timing differs. In a classroom, the control is more critical during the actual presentation. Lesson plans are the foundation of this control, instructor training and continued instructor development augment it, and critiquing of instructors enhances and monitors it.

For a distributed SDL implementation system, control is more important in what you do before the trainee and the material come "face to face." Control measures for SDL are concerned with making sure that the materials are available, the site implementors and other ancillary personnel prepared, and the trainees prepared and enabled. Later, different controls are needed to make sure the training is actually accomplished.

While control problems would seem to be a disadvantage, a distributed SDL implementation is ultimately easier to control than a classroom implementation. You have different control issues, but you don't have the biggest problem of all: instructors who decide they know better than the lesson plan. If the trainees get to your information in a distributed SDL implementation system, they will get the information you want them to receive. Control problems particular to distributed SDL are discussed in more detail later, and they are critical, though not as difficult to deal with as overly independent instructors.

Differences

Of course, the similarities between the two distributed implementation systems are still far outweighed by the differences. In the long run, SDL will be cheaper than a classroom approach. Depending on your format, you will save a little and possibly a lot by sending training materials instead of classroom instructors to the trainee.

A distributed implementation system can be more time efficient than a classroom. If you have a wide geographical area to cover, you can usually get to all your trainees sooner with a distributed SDL implementation system than by sending instructors out to run classes.

Most important, a distributed implementation system will allow for continuous just-in-time training with review and refresher capabilities. A classroom will not.

Lack of an instructor, no need for a designated facility, and individualization are other differences.

The following list summarizes the major similarities as well as the differences between the two implementation systems.

Similarities

- Both are training designs
- Can train large numbers at multiple locations in short periods

- Produce efficiency of scale
- Need strong program documentation
- Need carefully designed control measures
- Good for cognitive material

Differences

- SDL more cost effective overall
- SDL lacks an instructor
- Classroom requires a designated facility
- Trainees need to be prepared for SDL
- Classroom best for affective materials
- SDL better for teaching psychomotor tasks
- Individualization simpler with SDL
- Material costs lower for classroom
- SDL has greater "just-in-time" training capability
- Classroom can utilize multiple media formats more efficiently
- SDL requires little instructor travel

Other similarities and differences exist, but the point of this comparison is that when you have a distributed implementation problem, you don't need to automatically think classroom. SDL in a distributed implementation design can be as efficient and possibly more effective.

Development Concerns for Distributed SDL

Using a distributed implementation will affect a number of your SDL development considerations.

Developing for the Lack of a Facilitator

The implementation's lack of a full-time facilitator can have important consequences. We've discussed some of the facilitator's activities in Chapter Two, so you should have an idea of the advantages the position provides when developing SDL for a learning center. Now, take the facilitator position away, and you will have a picture of the major distinction between the two implementation strategies.

Well-trained, fulltime facilitators are usually not part of a distributed implementation system. That's not to say that you will have no facilitator. In a distributed implementation, the supervisor, manager, field trainer, or some other appointed individual at the job site may take on some of the facilitator's duties. To differentiate between them and a full-time facilitator, we'll give these individuals the title of *site implementor*.

However, SDL facilitation is not the site implementors' primary job responsibility. They won't have the time to keep detailed records of program use, or to do detailed evaluations of either the trainees or the programs. They won't be able to devote a lot of time to setting up materials or machines. Basically, they will have the time to take what you give them and pass it on to the trainees as efficiently as possible.

Therefore, in your design you can't count on them to do as much or be as committed as your hand-picked, well-trained learning center facilitators. This will reduce the complexity of instructions that you can give them and the level of guided activities that you will be able to develop in your package.

The use of special supplies or preassembled materials also will become a more complicated implementation issue without a full-time facilitator. Your packages will need to be as self-starting as possible. Long, difficult directions and special machine or ancillary setups won't be a good design when there is no one to consistently do the preliminary organization.

You need to modify your user evaluation designs to reflect reduced facilitation as well. Evaluations of the trainee should be either self-directed or simple enough to allow a site implementor to administer them.

Finally, you should minimize the internal complexity of your packages. Everything the trainee uses must be easy to find at the start of the program. The content itself should not require continued reference back to centralized information from any source that is not within the trainee's easy reach as he or she does the package, since there will be no one to locate these references.

On the positive side, because a distributed SDL implementation usually occurs on the job, it is likely that your site implementors will be subject matter experts. They should be able to provide accurate answers to trainee questions. They also will be able to give and evaluate performance-based tests and practices if you don't make them too complex.

Control as a Development Concern of Distributed SDL

One of the difficulties that can arise when you use site implementors instead of full-time facilitators is the loss of control over how or even if your packages are being used. In a learning center, your facilitator can easily keep records on who uses them, how often, and for what. You can even get a pretty good idea whether they are being used effectively. In a distributed implementation system, you have reduced control over all of these processes. In fact, if you don't do actual observations at the training sites, you have little data on whether your packages are being used at all.

This creates a need for strong control tools that can be used by the site implementor. Sign-off sheets, manager observation forms, tear-out/send backs, and "training-done" reports become critical. All of these have their good points and bad, and all of them in one form or another are necessary. We've already discussed some of these mechanisms. In the next chapter, we will consider them in relation to a distributed implementation. It's important not to forget them as you plan your distributed implementation.

One control advantage you do have in a distributed system is that you no longer have the logistical problems of controlling a learning center. There are no large numbers and types of machines and programs to be monitored and cared for, either. Thus, part of the facilitator's job ceases to exist when you go to a distributed implementation system.

Media Formats in Distributed SDL Development

This lack of variety in hardware and therefore in alternative media formats is another development consideration. For a distributed implementation system, simpler is better in almost every circumstance. Multiple media packages are very difficult to execute. Even the ability to have two different formats in one program is sharply curtailed by the increase in complexity such a process engenders. Without a full-time facilitator, your SDL packages will be self-dependent. They need to be as simple as possible in both design and format to allow your site implementors to administer them and your learners to use them.

There are a few exceptions to the "keep it simple" approach for distributed implementation. One is computer-mediated SDL packages, commonly referred to as CBT. At first glance, CBT would seem to be a complex media process. It is a fairly sophisticated format and as such should not lend itself well to a distributed implementation. However, closer observation reveals that the machines are quite simple to use, self-starting, and highly reliable. They not only provide their own operating instructions, but also can monitor the learner as well. In some ways, they actually substitute for a full-time facilitator. Thus, from an implementation point of view, CBT is not a complex media format at all. It is well suited for a distributed implementation system. That is, of course, if you can afford the capital entry fee.

A second exception to the "keep it simple" rule for a distributed implementation are those processes that fall under the category of multimedia such as digital video interactive or interactive videodisc. Media formats here can be quite complex, mixing pictures, video, sound, graphics, and so on. However, all of this is handled on one machine. This machine, from the learner's point of view, is not much different from CBT hardware.

While simple enough in implementation, you again need plenty of entry capital for hardware. You'll need even more monetary and human assets to invest in program development. Unless you have a burning design reason for using this type of format, you should be wary. The start-up costs alone suggest that the basic rule of keeping your distributed implementation system formats simple is still your best approach.

Package Reproduction Considerations for Distributed SDL

Another development consideration affected by a distributed implementation is the use of off-the-shelf programs. In a learning center situation, these programs are relatively inexpensive, since the number of copies you need is small. Buying 200 sets for a distributed system will increase the price dramatically. Your best course is to stay away from off-the-shelf programs as much as possible, unless you can get a cost-effective licensing arrangement. However, this limits your sources of materials and programs.

This need for multiple copies also affects your package design as a whole. In most learning center systems, you'll only need a few copies of each package. Even if there are multiple centers, it seldom goes beyond a couple of dozen. For a distributed implementation system, the number can easily reach ten or one hundred times that many. Beyond the inherent duplication expenses that this causes, such mass reproduction reduces your ability to use specialized activities or materials within your SDL package. For example, something as simple as a purchased instrument can cost thousands of dollars if you need enough for 500 sites. Fancier bells and whistles such as models or a lab simulation become almost cost prohibitive. Without a proper facilitator, the effectiveness of these items is doubtful as well.

Developing Job-Specific Activities

The ability to develop job-specific activities, as mentioned earlier, is a design strength of a distributed implementation system. This is particularly important in technical training. Take advantage of this characteristic to make your training as job related as possible, with plenty of performance practices and strong performance-based evaluations. These help to ensure training transfer back to the job.

Your development of these aspects will depend in part on the availability and capability of your site implementors. We've discussed the difficulties of using site implementors instead of full-time facilitators, but there are advantages as well. If you are able to recruit good subject matter experts for site implementor duties, you can develop better and more detailed observed practices and evaluations.

Another approach is to try to obtain support for direct supervisors as implementors. This will not only allow you to develop stronger performance practice tools but can provide a detailed feedback loop for evaluation of trainee performance and program validity. However, be sure that you have a complete understanding of the time, energy, and expertise that your implementors can bring to the program before you design your activities and evaluations.

Planning Evaluations for Distributed SDL

Finally, a critical consideration is your system evaluation design, particularly as it relates to your implementors. A training center approach seldom goes much beyond the opinionnaire type of evaluation. These are nice for the facilitator and good for corporate reports, but they rarely answer the main evaluation question of "Are the packages working?" Getting this information requires a lot of time-consuming digging when you are operating a learning center.

In a distributed implementation system, your program is done at the work site and usually facilitated by a supervisor or other interested individual. The informal evaluation you can obtain simply by asking these individuals if the packages are working can be very useful. If you want a more statistical evaluation, use the compliance mode discussed in Chapter Twelve and ask the question, "Are you using the self-directed learning packages as planned?" If you want detail, particularly a critique of your program's strengths and weaknesses, develop a questionnaire for your implementors to answer. Chapter Twelve details who to ask and what questions to use for different evaluation purposes.

You can perform most of these evaluation strategies in a learning center implementation as well. However, supervisors in a learning center environment are not as well versed in the program or as apt to think the evaluation quite as important as are implementor/supervisors. The returns you get will not have the same depth or validity as evaluations from those who know the programs as implementors and the trainees as supervisors. Thus, such evaluations are worth the extra effort in a distributed implementation.

Costs to Consider When Planning
a Distributed SDL Implementation

Due to the nature of this form of implementation, we need to consider various cost aspects.

Special Costs Associated with a
Distributed SDL Implementation

There are several special costs associated with a distributed SDL implementation that you must consider in your planning. The biggest cost is for mass reproduction. The main advantage of a distributed implementation system is in its ability to train large numbers of people in many locations simultaneously. However, this means that you will need large numbers of packages. That type of cost may limit the format you can use by making reproduction of some formats too expensive for your budget. For example, a single video package that cost you $12 to produce with workbook and videotape will cost $6,000 or more if you need to send it to 500 training locations.

The second biggest cost is the time and money needed to introduce a distributed implementation system. You need to prepare supervisors, implementors, trainees, and many others before your first package appears. This requires traveling, talking, running orientation classes, and a whole list of other activities that have small or large costs associated with them. While this total may be beyond that of a traveling classroom, you need to remember that it is a one-time cost. The classroom cost is entailed every time you do a new program.

Distribution costs are small compared to those already mentioned, but in large systems, they can be significant. Even postage can add up, not to mention overnight fees for those training locations that never receive or that lose your packages. For a large distributed implementation system such as a retail chain of 500 or more stores, a clerical person can be kept busy just sending out packages and package revisions. Of course, such a personnel cost is likely to be much less than for two or three instructors who are out on the road.

Revision costs are also significant, since they include the largest of the reproduction and distribution costs each time you revise. A good rule of thumb is that if your programs are not going to have a two-year life span due to constantly changing policies and procedures, you may want to reconsider your decision to use SDL. Of course, after considering the alternatives you may have no other choice, but be aware of the impact of continued revisions on your budget and on the mental well-being of your designers as well.

Other Distributed Monetary Considerations

Beyond these four special costs, there are other dollar-related disadvantages to a distributed implementation system. One of these is the difficulty in using more exotic media formats, such as computers, without entailing high production, equipment, and maintenance costs. If you need a computer or even a VCR for every training site, your capital equipment budget can begin to look like the national debt. Even in-house media can get expensive in large quantities.

This doesn't mean you can't use these formats in a distributed implementation system. I know of a retail food distribution company in the Northwest that sends video SDL packages to 1,600 training sites. However, this arrangement requires heavy usage to be cost effective. Unless you are sold on one of the advanced media formats as being the "answer to all your training problems," you might want to think twice before expending the capital to purchase enough machinery for your mass distribution.

Also, the timing of expenditures can be a disadvantage. In a learning center strategy, your major expenditures are "up front." They occur when you equip the center and when you purchase or develop programs. Once your center is going and the programs are there, other costs are limited and easy to predict. In a distributed implementation system, you will find that most expenditures, particularly reproduction distribution and revision costs, come after development.

There are training costs for your site implementors as well, and certain introduction costs whenever you distribute a different program format. Often these costs are hidden from the first-time designer of a distributed system. They can be real "budget busters" when they occur and have not been adequately planned for.

All this doesn't necessarily make a distributed implementation system less cost effective. You have salary and upkeep expenses tacked onto a learning center or a classroom strategy as well. In the final analysis, I've found that even a medium-sized distributed SDL system can save you between 30 and 35 percent of the dollars that you would need to spend on a classroom implementation that covered the same training. Add to this the trainee time savings and the incredible efficiencies of SDL as "just-in-time" training, and an SDL distributed implementation begins to look very good.

However, the designer must be aware of the hidden "secondary" costs, since they can mount up quickly in a distributed SDL implementation. Even basic print packages can get expensive when you start talking about thousands of copies. The key here is to recognize these costs and plan for them.

Preparing Trainers for Distributed Implementation

We discussed preparing for SDL in general back in Chapter Seven. However, there are special types of preparation that must be done for a distributed system. The rest of this chapter will consider those processes.

Why Prepare Current Trainers for SDL?

In any business application of SDL, your current trainers— if you have any—are one of the most important yet least considered assets in making your SDL work. Often they have built strong relationships with the trainees and so represent the concept of training to them. If they do not understand and agree with the process of SDL, you lose a valuable support in the field. If they see SDL as threatening, they can easily become a negative factor in your system. Subtly and at times not so subtly they can affect the way the trainee perceives SDL, long before the first package appears.

Your current trainers will see your SDL system as threatening if they think it may replace them or at least change their jobs in a negative way. After all, until SDL came along, *they* represented training in the company. They went out and made it work. If they were good, they probably enjoyed the process, the give-and-take of the classroom, the interaction with the trainees. Now you're telling them that SDL packages will handle these tasks. The SDL packages will be the way the trainees learn. There won't be any more classes. *It's the new way!* So where does this leave them?

The Trainer as SDL Training Manager

There are several answers to this question. Some of them are probably more satisfactory than others from the trainers' point of view. The tack that I have found most rewarding, and most soothing to trainers' battered egos, is to help them to understand that they have a key role to play in a distributed SDL implementation. They are about to become managers of the training process.

In classroom-based training, they were responsible for managing only their classroom. In the new system, they are responsible for a number of training locations. Their new task is to go to these locations to guide, facilitate, analyze, evaluate, and do all those other things a manager does. There will be plenty of personal interactions with trainees, implementors, supervisors, and anyone else who is affected by the training. The only thing that will be missing is that feeling of power when they stand up before a class and impart their wisdom. If this feeling is what was most significant to them, it's probable that they were not very effective trainers anyway.

A Method for Introducing Your Trainers to SDL

To ensure that trainers provide a positive impact for your SDL, you must get them involved from the start. Begin with a special meeting at which you explain the basic concepts of SDL and explore its advantages and disadvantages. You'll need to give them a strong definition of what you consider to be self-directed learning and plenty of examples that they can work through to help them individually grasp the concept.

A particularly good way to provide to provide an SDL example for these individuals is to take a concept or topic that they personally need trained on and present it to them in an SDL format. For instance, since they are all trainers, an SDL package on how to write objectives, or perhaps test questions, will supply them with new knowledge and reinforce the advantages of the process. An excerpt from such a package, used for this exact purpose, can be found in Exhibit 8.1.

Explore with them their new role as training managers in the system. Discuss how they can help pave the way for SDL before it

Exhibit 8.1. Sample Chapter: Behavioral Objectives Used for the
Development of Regional Trainers.

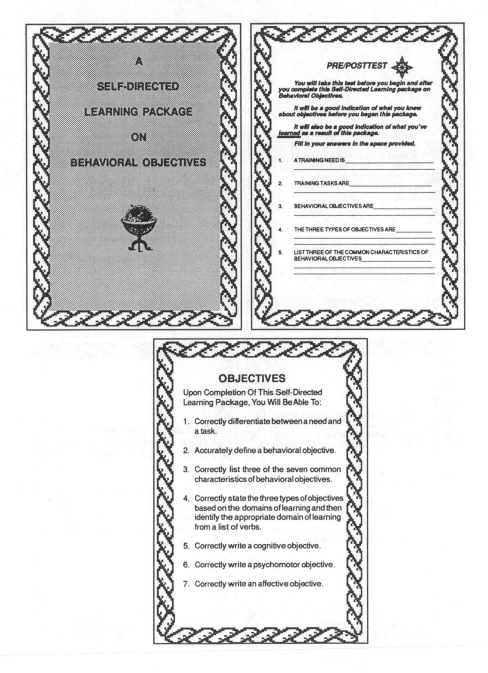

A

SELF-DIRECTED

LEARNING PACKAGE

ON

BEHAVIORAL OBJECTIVES

PRE/POSTTEST

You will take this test before you begin and after you complete this Self-Directed Learning package on Behavioral Objectives.

It will be a good indication of what you knew about objectives before you began this package.

It will also be a good indication of what you've learned as a result of this package.

Fill in your answers in the space provided.

1. A TRAINING NEED IS _____

2. TRAINING TASKS ARE _____

3. BEHAVIORAL OBJECTIVES ARE _____

4. THE THREE TYPES OF OBJECTIVES ARE _____

5. LIST THREE OF THE COMMON CHARACTERISTICS OF BEHAVIORAL OBJECTIVES _____

OBJECTIVES

Upon Completion Of This Self-Directed
Learning Package, You Will Be Able To:

1. Correctly differentiate between a need and a task.

2. Accurately define a behavioral objective.

3. Correctly list three of the seven common characteristics of behavioral objectives.

4. Correctly state the three types of objectives based on the domains of learning and then identify the appropriate domain of learning from a list of verbs.

5. Correctly write a cognitive objective.

6. Correctly write a psychomotor objective.

7. Correctly write an affective objective.

Exhibit 8.1. Sample Chapter: Behavioral Objectives Used for the
Development of Regional Trainers, Cont'd.

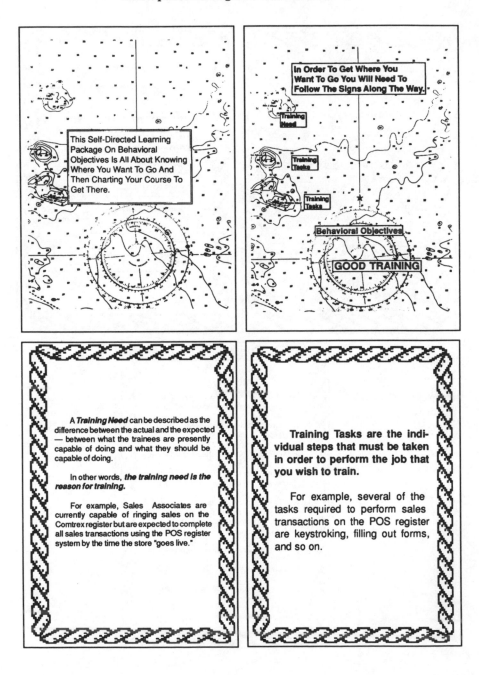

This Self-Directed Learning Package On Behavioral Objectives Is All About Knowing Where You Want To Go And Then Charting Your Course To Get There.

In Order To Get Where You Want To Go You Will Need To Follow The Signs Along The Way.

Training Need

Training Tasks

Training Tasks

Behavioral Objectives

GOOD TRAINING

A *Training Need* can be described as the difference between the actual and the expected — between what the trainees are presently capable of doing and what they should be capable of doing.

In other words, *the training need is the reason for training.*

For example, Sales Associates are currently capable of ringing sales on the Comtrex register but are expected to complete all sales transactions using the POS register system by the time the store "goes live."

Training Tasks are the individual steps that must be taken in order to perform the job that you wish to train.

For example, several of the tasks required to perform sales transactions on the POS register are keystroking, filling out forms, and so on.

Exhibit 8.1. Sample Chapter: Behavioral Objectives Used for the Development of Regional Trainers, Cont'd.

When you determine *Training Needs* and their associated *Training Tasks* you are performing what trainers like to call a FRONT-END ANALYSIS.

Take a look at the phrases on the next page and see if you can determine the *needs* from the *tasks.*

NEEDS & TASKS SELF-QUIZ

NEXT TO EACH PHRASE CHECK THE APPROPRIATE BOX TO IDENTIFY WHETHER IT IS A NEED (N) OR A TASK (T).

1 complete the IC-447
2. complete an interstore transfer
3. train all Store Associates to use ZON
4. use the cash key
5. write up a credit for returned merchandise
6. perform a cash refund
7. use the sign-on key
8. sign on and sign off the register
9. apply senso labels
10. correctly receive orders from outside vendors
11. enable every store to use the new gross margin forms by the beginning of the fiscal year
12. price sale items in less than two days

Check your answers on the following page.

NEEDS & TASKS Answer Key

1 complete the IC-447
2. complete an interstore transfer
3. train all Store Associates to use ZON
4. use the cash key
5. write up a credit for returned merchandise
6. perform a cash refund
7. use the sign-on key
8. sign on and sign off the register
9. apply senso labels
10. correctly receive orders from outside vendors
11. enable every store to use the new gross margin forms by the beginning of the fiscal year
12. price sale items in less than two days

gets to the field. Describe how they will help to introduce it formally. Deal directly with their fears and with how SDL will affect their current responsibilities. Spend plenty of time on role plays that reinforce how they will handle their visits to training sites. Discuss the problems they'll need to look for, both initially and as the system evolves.

If you can arrange it, have your CEO or some high-level administrator come in at the end of the meeting to reinforce management's commitment to SDL. If you did your job well in preparing the company management for SDL, you should have no problem getting support for this. It will help reemphasize the importance of the system and the trainers' key role in making SDL work.

I've found that it's better to bring management in at the end rather than at the beginning of these meetings. The questions that the trainers have at the start are best handled by you. Once the fears have been addressed, the mechanics have been taken care of, and the trainers have a reasonable idea of what's happening to them and to training, they will be more receptive to management's comments. The last thing you want to have are top-level managers bogged down in answering particulars that they probably are not sure of themselves. This invariably happens if your management representative is the first or an early speaker.

As a follow-up exercise to the meeting, ask the trainers to go back to the field and introduce SDL at their training sessions. Give them an outline of points to cover and make it their responsibility to begin the selling of SDL to the trainees in the field.

This first meeting with the trainers should not be your last. They'll have plenty more to do as your distributed SDL system progresses. You don't want to overwhelm them, so you should schedule at least one or two more follow-up meetings to discuss other roles they might perform and to train them in these roles.

Continuing Roles for Your Trainers in SDL

Three important roles that your trainers can fill in your distributed SDL implementation are as subject matter experts, package

review/revision specialists, and system evaluators. A fourth—
though less common—alternative is as SDL designers.

Subject Matter Experts. In many cases, your trainers will
have enough subject knowledge to be developmental subject matter
experts. Invite these individuals to work with you in writing SDL
packages.

Package Review/Revision Specialists. Over time, the trainers will grow into the role of reviewers, learning to assess and possibly help pilot completed SDL packages before they are released to
the field. As they learn more about the SDL process, they can also
evolve into revision specialists. In the early stages of this role, they
will be responsible for funneling back to you thoughts, comments,
and problems on each SDL package as it goes into the revision
stage. The subject matter expert review form from Chapter Six (Exhibit 6.1) can be used for this process as well. Later, as they get more
comfortable with SDL, the trainers will be able to perform the actual revisions themselves.

System Evaluators. System evaluation is another duty they
can perform. Get your trainers involved in the gathering of informal oral evaluations concerning system effectiveness and system
compliance. Written evaluations are important, but they often tell
you what the evaluators think you want to hear, not what you need
to know. There is no substitute for the personal observations and
discussions of a trainer who goes to the training site to find out
what is really happening. Work with your trainers to make them
superior oral evaluators, and you will get back the most valid evaluation data you've ever had.

An evaluation tool I developed for use by trainers as they visit
stores in a retail distributed SDL system can be found as Exhibit 8.2.

SDL Designers. You might also introduce your trainers to
SDL design theory. Only a few may actually become designers, but
this sharing of the intricacies of SDL design will help them understand the process better. They will begin to feel more like experts
when speaking about SDL with the trainees.

When this evolution is complete, you will have a group of
trainers who can not only revise but also originate new packages.
Show your trainers that there are personal growth possibilities for

Exhibit 8.2. Sample Trainee Evaluation Tool.

Regional Trainer Monthly SDL Monitoring

Directions: The purpose of store visits is to emphasize the SDL process, answer any questions the Store Manager might have, and assess the store SDL process. An entry should be made on this checklist each time you visit a store. Use the SDL Completion Record to determine the number of employees in the store and if each has completed the proper SDLs for his or her position based on the current SDL completion policy. If there are special comments you feel important to make concerning why a store is not up to date with its SDL completions, note them after the store number in the comments section of the checklist. This form should be returned to your RPD at the end of each month and a new form begun for the next month.

Date	District #	Store #	Number of Employees	Number Up To Date With SDLs	Number With Incomplete SDLs	Comments

_____   _____   _____
Trainer's Signature   Month   Date Sent to Region

them in the new system and you will have gone a long way toward making them SDL converts.

A good job of preparing your trainers will help pave the way for SDL by transferring some of their credibility as learning leaders to the packages that are to come. Ignore your trainers because you think they serve no purpose in an SDL design, and you risk starting your system with a handicap that you may never overcome.

Choosing and Preparing Site Implementors

As you prepare for a distributed SDL implementation, another group you need to consider is the system's site implementors. We term these individuals *site* implementors to indicate that their responsibilities are not to the system as a whole, but to the training that occurs at their particular site.

Tasks the Site Implementor May Perform in SDL

The site implementors have several tasks to perform in a distributed SDL implementation. One of the most important of these—introducing the trainee to the system—is discussed in the next section. Other duties might include:

- Keeping track of the packages and whatever minimum supplies are needed
- Making sure that the trainees can obtain the packets and that they return them
- Checking to see that the materials have been completed and evaluations done
- Administering evaluations, particularly performance evaluations
- Providing feedback to the designers on problems or augmentations to the packages
- Providing feedback to training administration on package usage and overall program acceptance

These tasks must be kept as simple as possible due to the nature of the site implementor position, but any or all might be important depending on your system.

Finding Site Implementors

Choices for site implementors vary. Probably the best choice is a designated senior person at each training location. For example, in a large banking organization it might be a senior teller, or in a manufacturing environment the lead machine operator.

Another possible choice is a supervisor. Though supervisors might seem to be the best choice due to the relationship between their responsibilities and the training of employees, there might be inherent time problems depending on the workload of the individual supervisor. Other possibilities are current field trainers or upper-level managers. However, these individuals are often not continuously at the training site, a critical consideration when choosing a site implementor.

Preparing the Site Implementor

Preparation of the site implementors is once again a process of good planning and solid training. As the main conduit between the trainee and the packages, the site implementors need more than a passing understanding of the precepts of SDL. The best way to produce this in-depth knowledge is through a combination of classroom training and SDL examples.

An SDL package on SDL, developed for the site implementor position, is a useful tool. We've discussed the use of this strategy before, so follow the same approach, but make it appropriate for a site implementor. After completion of the package, hold a classroom or, if necessary, a one-on-one session to further discuss the process and the implementor's role.

This is also a good opportunity for role playing the actual presentations that the site implementors will be making if their role includes introducing SDL to the trainees. It will help to prepare them and build their confidence.

Don't forget to document the presentation for your site implementors through solid lesson plans and training materials that will help them orient the trainees. Checklists, summary handouts, and written exercises are useful and necessary if you expect them to do a proper job of preparing the learners for SDL. Spend the necessary time going over these tools and how to use them.

Finish up the class with information on monitoring any performance practices and on what the site implementor's responsibility is in program evaluation.

An interesting variation of this process is to have your trainers run these classes. This helps to reinforce their understanding of SDL and recommits them to the process. It also allows the site implementors to discuss SDL with people who are much closer to the "reality" of the trainees than is a corporate SDL "expert." There is a danger here, since it is imperative that the trainer's instruction of the site implementors be both complete and very positive. Pick your site implementor trainers carefully if you use this approach and supply them with good lesson plans to follow.

As a final test of the site implementors' ability to handle their SDL responsibilities, have them practice the process of facilitation from start to finish when they get back on the job. A useful monitoring tool for this process is a tear-out sheet like the one in Chapter Nine (Exhibit 9.2) that you include in the back of your SDL package on SDL. The site implementors can follow, complete, and then send it back to you after facilitating their first trainee. This provides another reinforcement for them and a check for you that they can do the job.

To give them a hand with their new responsibilities, you might develop a site implementor job aid like the checklist shown in Exhibit 8.3. This particular list was designed to help site implementors administer SDL packages, but you can create them for orientation, evaluation, or whatever roles you have your site implementors playing in your SDL system.

Malcolm Knowles (1980) says that although most people are or want to be self-directed, and are capable of being so, it is not a good idea to just throw them into the strange waters of self-direction and hope that they swim. He suggests that learners should be prepared with an orientation session. This is the final step in preparing for a distributed SDL implementation.

Exhibit 8.3. Checklist for Implementation
Developed for Facilitators (Store Managers).

Checklist for Implementation of SDL Packages

Each time a store associate or new hire takes a Self-Directed Learning Package, use this Checklist as a guide to get them started.

1. Allow time for trainee to complete SDL.
2. Provide quiet space.
3. Explain that trainee is responsible for his/her own learning.
4. Give trainee an answer sheet from the front of the SDL box.
5. Explain that all answers are to be recorded on the answer sheet.
6. Check on trainee every 20 minutes.
7. Be available to answer questions.
8. Record the trainee's name, SDL title, and completion date on the yellow SDL Completion Record located in the front of the SDL box.
9. Have Store Manager sign the SDL Completion Record and replace it in the front of the SDL box.
10. Provide at least one opportunity for guided practice.

Preparing the Trainee for Distributed SDL

If you've followed a good distributed implementation plan up to this point, you have management groups that are committed to your SDL system. They have agreed to back up their commitment with control measures and the discipline to make the control measures work.

You have your field trainers well versed in SDL. If not "true believers," they are at least willing to go along with the program and give it a try. As they move through the field presenting their regular training programs or completing their assigned duties, they talk SDL. They are describing what is coming, enumerating the advantages of the new system, allaying fears, and discussing how it will affect the trainees. They are transferring the credibility they have gained over the years as instructors to the SDL packages.

You have supervisors who have been given a good introduction to what SDL is and how it works. At meetings they mention it, lending their authority to the process. At performance appraisals, they recommend that when the packages arrive, the trainees take advantage of them for self-development. When the packages do appear, they allow the process to happen by providing the time and encouragement necessary to get the trainees started right. They believe that it will be a time-effective training method.

And you have well-trained site implementors. Equipped with good lesson plans and tools, they complete the preparation process by holding orientation sessions with the trainees. These sessions formally describe the process to the trainees, solidify the vision of succeeding at SDL, and answer questions that arise.

We discussed these sessions in detail back in Chapter Seven. You might review that area before proceeding with the rest of this discussion. Remember that at the moment we are considering a distributed implementation, so contemplate the material as it relates to that aspect of SDL. As you review, reflect on some of the special problems pertaining to the trainees that occur in a distributed implementation. These include the following:

- The necessity of introducing all trainees almost simultaneously to the system rather than individually as they come to the learning center
- The use of site implementors for the introduction, with the likelihood that they will not all be consistent in their instruction
- The difficulties involved in starting individuals on their first SDL package when it is being done in a work environment
- Problems that might occur with site implementors evaluating trainees and recording package completions
- The need to gain the commitment of the supervisors to allow time for the trainees to do SDL
- Developing a belief in both the trainees and the supervisors that SDL, if done correctly, can actually save time

These problems should all be addressed by your system before the trainee ever sees it. Each should be gone over in detail during the part of the trainee orientation that deals with the mechanics of the system. We've discussed possible solutions, but each system is different, because it exists in a different corporate environment. You'll need to pick and choose from what has been presented here and create your own ways as well. The important thing is to do it in your planning and cover it all in your preparation. This will make it as easy as possible for your trainees to make the transition to an SDL approach.

Exhibit 8.4. A Checklist for SDL.

Planning a Distributed SDL Implementation

☐   You have properly planned for your distributed implementation.
   • One or more factors have indicated the need for a distributed implementation.
   • You have planned for the lack of a full-time facilitator.
   • You have planned for the increased control problems that will occur.
   • You have used the "keep it simple" approach for your media hardware plans.
   • You have considered the cost of package reproduction.
   • You have developed job-specific activities where possible in your package.
   • In your evaluation design, you have considered the advantages and disadvantages of a distributed implementation.
   • You have considered introduction, distribution, and revision costs for your packages.
   • You have decided how to use your current trainers in your distributed system and prepared them for it.
   • You have determined your site implementors and prepared them for your distributed SDL system.
   • You have prepared your trainees.

9

Managing the
Distributed Implementation
How to Facilitate
Delivery, Control, and Evaluation

In the previous chapter, we looked at distributed SDL implementation from the point of view of planning and preparation. This chapter will consider the techniques and problems that relate to the actual execution of the process (Figure 9.1). You will notice an overlap with the planning aspect in some areas, but this is to be expected. The carrying out of the implementation should be directly related to the planning you did, with as many of the execution problems as possible having been solved during the planning stage. The difference is that this is the stage when all your work must actually function in the reality of the training environment. Some of the concepts—particularly those associated with evaluation—will be discussed in more detail in Chapter Twelve. The goal in this chapter is to consider items as they directly pertain to a distributed implementation.

Delivering Materials to the Training Sites

Once you have completed package development and prepared everyone for a distributed implementation, your next task is to get the packages to the trainees. In most cases, this means getting them to the job sites. If you're dealing with a small number of sites or if they are in close proximity, this is relatively simple: you just

Figure 9.1. A Model for SDL.

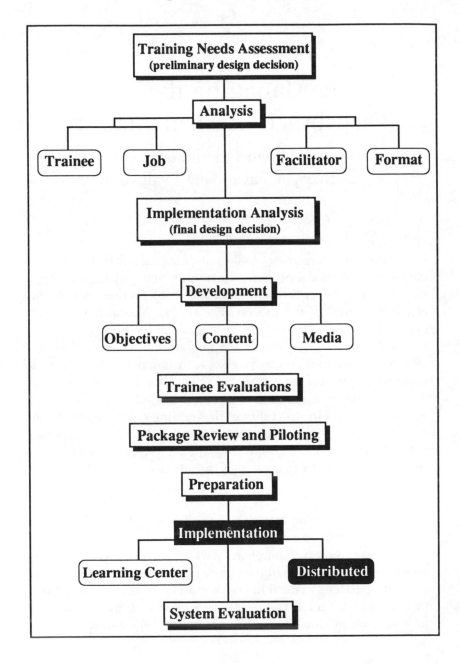

take them there. For a larger system, or one where the sites are highly dispersed, you will need to use other methods.

Hand Delivering Your Packages

You might wonder why you'd even spend the time hand delivering packages in small systems. The answer is that it would be time well spent. Each new package will probably have a few quirks or special instructions. This is a good time to brief your site implementors on these nuances. It also gives you a chance to do a little "unofficial" evaluation—to sort of poke around into how the SDL process is going. It's your decision as to how much time you can spare for package distribution and the other benefits that come with it, but if your system is small enough, it is well worth considering.

One SDL practitioner, who works for a medium-sized financial organization in Florida and now has a large system in place, related to me that the way she started was to personally take her first program to each trainee who requested it. She made sure that after delivery she "dropped in" on the employee's supervisor to explain why she was there. It wasn't long before the sharper supervisors were asking her for other programs that their staff could use without leaving the job.

As part of your "delivery" process, you might also want to take a minute or two to introduce trainees to the concept of SDL—if this is their first experience—and to explain how they should proceed through your package. Even if your package directions give the same information in detail, the personal touch is always a better way.

If you are implementing a small distributed system, try to look in on the trainees as they are working on the package, just to check for problems. But don't do it more than once! Remember, this is self-directed learning; the last thing you want to do is to hover over the trainees as they are working. It makes them nervous and leads to your providing too much assistance.

The trainer I mentioned earlier had a system where she looked in on the trainees right after talking to their supervisor. It was convenient, and sometimes the supervisor joined her. After they'd had some experience with SDL, she often asked the supervisors to check trainees on their own. As you will see later, this is an elegant—and some might say sneaky—way to develop facilitators in a distributed implementation, which is exactly what she used it for.

Other "Human" Methods of Package Delivery

If your system is too large, or if you don't feel you have the time, you need to get your packages out by a more indirect method. The best approach, no matter what the situation, is still the human touch.

Look for people who can do the delivery for you. Field trainers, if you have enough of them to meet your timing needs, are a good choice. If you've done your preparation correctly, they will be well versed in the general system, and you can easily explain the particulars of a package to them. They in turn can transmit those particulars to the site implementor.

You can still take advantage of some informal evaluation this way as well. However, you must be careful in your instructions to the trainers concerning what evaluation you are looking for and how they should do it. The last thing you want is to have your field trainers become known as auditors or "spies" at your training locations.

Cascading Your Delivery. Another "human" tactic is to use a cascade effect. This occurs when you give the packages and special instructions directly to a small group of individuals from the training sites who are meeting in a place that is possible for you to get to. An example from a retail situation might be a district manager meeting. In manufacturing, it could be the personnel representatives, or possibly the plant managers themselves.

The key is to give them the packages at a regular meeting that is being held for another purpose. In that way, you haven't reduced the efficiency of your system by spending corporate funds to bring this group together. Ten or fifteen minutes during the meeting should be enough to complete your task. These individuals in turn can give the materials and directions to the site implementors when they return to the training sites.

An SDL Simulation

You are using a distributed implementation, but it is small enough for you to take your packages personally to your users. You do this to exemplify the flexibility of your SDL process. As part of your "delivery" process, you also take a minute or two to talk to the trainees about the concept of SDL and the package, just to reinforce the supervisor's message. Later, you try to look in on the trainees as they are working on the packages, just to check for problems and compliance. If possible, you do this after a meeting with the trainee's supervisor, so that the two of you together can talk to the trainee about his or her training.

Pros and Cons of Mail Delivery

If none of these tactics are useful in your situation, you'll have to resort to even more indirect methods. The most obvious and cheapest of these is the mail. At first glance, this may seem a relatively simple approach. Put your package in an envelope, add a stamp, and send it.

However, there are some complications. One of them is that nonhuman problem. Since no one will be personally delivering your package, no one will be available to discuss special instructions. Your packages will have to be absolutely self-explanatory. Extra direction sheets or cover letters with special information are a big risk, since they can easily be lost or not passed on to the next site implementor.

And speaking of getting lost, be assured that a few of your packages will never get where they are going. The more you send out, the more calls you'll receive asking where they are. When printing a run of any package, figure on at least a 10 percent loss rate if you are using mail delivery and print accordingly. Speed is also not a strong point of the post office, so take that into account as well.

You can solve some of these problems by using UPS or other delivery services, but you'll increase expenses manyfold this way.

You will want to earmark some budget dollars for overnight or two-day delivery with a mail distribution. No matter what method you choose to get your programs out, you'll still receive phone calls asking for another copy. It will usually be needed yesterday because the first one was lost, stolen, or otherwise disappeared and no one realized it. Figure this cost into your plans when you're estimating how much you'll need to implement each package.

Distribution of More Complex Media Formats

Special distribution problems are associated with the more complex media formats.

Slides. As media become more complex, so do your distribution problems and costs. A paper-and-pencil SDL package requires nothing more than an envelope and a stamp. An audiotape will require at the least a padded envelope, if not a special container. Slides multiply the problem manyfold. They are cumbersome to ship in a carousel and can easily get out of sequence if sent by any more convenient approach like a slide box or plastic pocket sheets.

Video. If you are using video, a plastic "keeper" device of some sort is almost mandatory. There are several different types. Some fit into three-ring binders so you can send both print and video as one package; others are simply a videotape box. There are even binders made that have a pocket for a videotape impressed in the cover. Various distributors of these items exist. You'll need to find what's best for your situation. It's also a good idea to compare prices, since there is a lot of variation. However, no matter what the price, these devices will be more expensive than a simple envelope. Such distribution costs must be factored into your budget.

Direct Computer Downloading. There are some higher-tech methods available for distribution. I've seen them used with varying degrees of success. Possibly the "highest tech" is a networked computer-based system where you just download programs, and program changes, from a centralized mainframe computer.

The only problem I've been able to uncover with this method is that you need a computer-based system to begin with. For a

distributed implementation, such systems can be incredibly expensive unless they are already in place for some other purpose. In some manufacturing environments, they also might lack a certain portability when you want to use your package directly on the job. However, if you are using or plan to use a computer-based system with downloading capability, your distribution problems should be minimal.

I've read about one firm in Silicon Valley that uses a variation of this approach for software training. The computers at the desks of all their personnel are hooked into the mainframe, and the training programs reside there. Trainees call up programs as needed, and all completion records are kept by the mainframe.

Floppy Disks. Using floppy disks as a distribution medium for your computer mediated self-instructional packages has a number of advantages as well. Not the least of these is that they are small and easy to mail. However, disks can be demagnetized in the mail, and you still have the same problems that exist with mailing a paper package.

Computer-Assisted Paper Distribution. A rather exotic offshoot of direct downloading is what might be termed *computer-assisted distribution* (CAD). CAD is feasible in any system where you are using a paper-and-pencil media format and you have a computer network tied in to your training sites. Remember when we discussed earlier how useful it is in a distributed implementation to keep your formats as simple as possible? Well, this is where it may pay off for you.

The idea is to send your packages via computer to training-site printers. The packages are then printed out for use by your trainees. To do this, you will need training sites with networked computers, printers, and some sort of E-mail function.

Ten years ago, such a concept wouldn't have been worth putting into this book. Today many companies have computer networks connecting their branches. The beauty of this process is that you can use existing equipment. The most you may have to buy is an E-mail program that gives you some graphics capability. For this, you get a reliable, relatively cheap distribution process that also makes your paper-and-pencil SDL packages incredibly easy to update.

Fax. To round out this high-tech discussion, I'll mention one system I came across that uses a fax machine as the main distribution medium. There are some advantages to such an approach, but I'd recommend using it only if your machines have a plain paper capability. Also, the system I observed was using SDL packages that were just a step above job aids. The average size was eight to ten pages. I think expense and a certain unwieldiness would increase dramatically if you started using a fax distribution for large packages. Nonetheless, it's a good way to leave the subject, noting that you should never overlook any possible distribution technique. If it meets your needs, use it.

Control Measures

As already stated, control measures in a distributed implementation are the key to making sure your SDL process gets a chance to work. Because neither you nor a full-time facilitator will be at the training sites, these measures must substitute for the presence of a controlling individual. They can be as simple as where and how you store your programs, or as complex as management monitoring reports that remind everyone of the importance of completing the training packages. In the final analysis, you probably can't have enough control measures in a distributed system. We discussed their importance in the last chapter; now we'll look at how they actually work.

Program Location as a Control Measure

The first control measure is the physical location of your programs. More than one system has floundered because the packages couldn't be accessed easily or were literally lost after they made it to the training sites. This is not a problem in a training center where you have a facilitator to catalogue, shelve, and retrieve packages. However, in the work environment your programs can end up anywhere, or nowhere, if they don't have their own place. Expensive videos can disappear; even computer programs can get lost, either before loading or in the computer itself.

Importance of Program Access. An important factor to consider in where to locate your packages is availability. I observed a system at a multibranch savings and loan that had a two-drawer filing cabinet in each training location just for the SDL packages. The only problem was that the cabinet was in the branch manager's office. The manager was usually either busy in the office with the door shut or out of the office with the door locked. This meant that the site implementor, who was the head teller, could not get at the packages when they were needed—a rather strong deterrent to SDL's advantage of being just-in-time training.

However, the filing cabinet from the previous example was an excellent idea, just badly planned. What your packages need is their own place. It should be a well-marked place where trainees can find them easily and where new programs can be stored when they arrive.

Storing Paper-and-Pencil Packages. Your place doesn't have to be as extensive or expensive as a filing cabinet. For one paper-and-pencil system I developed, we used a simple plastic filing box. We sent the box out to each training site with the first few SDL packages already in it. It also contained a series of index tabs, each preprinted with the title of a package yet to come. As new packages arrived, the site implementor simply filed them behind the correct index tab.

The boxes were a bright yellow and had labels plastered all over them that indicated what they contained. We even gave advice on where the boxes themselves might be stored for easy availability. Over time, each became known as "the yellow box" (not creative, but descriptive). Employees immediately knew where to go when asked to get such and such a package from "the yellow box."

Just as a reminder of what can still go wrong in execution, even with good planning and preparation, I'll confess that at least two or three of the training sites—which were retail stores—sold the boxes to customers when they received them! I made the best of the situation by noting to management that the boxes only cost about half of what the stores sold them for, so this was a real example of how training impacts the bottom line. However, I still wonder about the customers out there who are filing their bills in boxes that are labeled *self-directed learning.* At any rate, the important point is that your first control step should be to make sure your programs have a specified place at each of your training sites that is as accessible as possible.

Storage and Access for CBT Programs. This concept can be generalized to higher-tech systems as well. One of the most difficult things in a computer-based SDL system is simply to find and start the training program. This is particularly true if the hardware is being used for more than one purpose, which is often the case in a distributed implementation.

One possible answer is to use a self-starting menu that the trainees can call up by simply pressing a certain key. They can pick the training program they want from this menu, and it will load and start automatically. Sometimes submenus might be necessary, but in every case, make sure the final choice is self-starting.

If the preceding discussion was confusing, but you aren't using computer mediated self-instructional packages, you need not concern yourself with it. However, if you are using or thinking about using a computer-based implementation, you may need more detailed information than can be provided here. Again, I refer you to the Suggested Readings section. Another source of information on high-tech training methods—or on any of the other training concepts discussed here, for that matter—are professional societies such as the American Society for Training and Development (ASTD) and the National Society for Performance Instruction (NSPI). You can also get in touch with the smaller, more focused industry groups that might be relevant to your field. These organizations often have a list of experts that know about computer-based training or other topics and who are willing to take some time to talk with you, share their expertise, and answer your questions.

Personal Observations as a Control Measure

One of the best control measures is for the training manager or director to do personal observations at the training sites. A rule of thumb I go by is that in a distributed SDL implementation, this person should be out visiting training locations at least two days a month. This applies to the rest of the training staff as well. Not only will visits by these individuals help control the process, but the staff will pick up valuable insights on how the packages are working and how to make them better.

Record-Keeping Techniques as Control Measures

After physical location and personal visits, the rest of your control measures are usually record-keeping procedures. They are designed to ensure that your programs are used, or used correctly, though often they help to reinforce the importance of doing the training as well. Remember, in a distributed implementation there is no one on permanent duty at the site to oversee the training. Your controls need to do this job for you.

Completion Card. The simplest record-keeping method is a completion card such as the one in Exhibit 9.1. As you can see, this type of document lists the packages and the individuals who need training and has a place to check off that they were trained. If you want to add a little accountability to the process, have the check-off box become an initial box. It should be completed by the site implementor or, better yet, the trainee's direct supervisor. To add more control, have the next-level manager responsible for reviewing the record on a regular basis. He or she should be trained to ask questions if package completion seems to be lacking.

If you want to centralize the control, you might have photocopies sent to corporate or some other intermediate location periodically. I found one training manager who asked for copies of his completion records to be faxed to him on a surprise basis. (Yes, it was the same person who sent his packages out by fax, and no, he didn't work for a phone company. However, he was a true believer in fax technology.) This approach does have a definite advantage. It makes it difficult for site implementors to fudge records when they are called in or if they know a site visit is imminent. This tampering with records can be a problem when site implementors or supervisors are held accountable for package completion.

Tear Out/Send Backs. A control measure that I've found useful at times is what I've already referred to as the tear out/send back. It is basically a checklist report that is completed and signed by the site implementor or supervisor. Quite literally, it's ripped out of a package and sent back to the corporate office. An example of

Exhibit 9.1. SDL Completion Record.

SDL Completion Record

Employee Name	Interstore Transfers	Merchandising	Ordering	Order Receiving	Outside Vendors	Photofinishing	Pricing	Recalls	Salvage							
Jane Doe	JM 3-9-90		JM 3-13-90						(Sample)							

In the boxes next to the employee's name, enter the completion date of the SDL under the appropriate SDL title. The Store Manager must initial each box.

one that was contained in an SDL package used to introduce SDL to site implementors can be found in Exhibit 9.2. I try to make these documents more than just checklists by fashioning them so they are relevant to something the completers have to do within the package or the program. They can also be expanded by asking for some form of reflective evaluation as part of the process.

Depending on the number of training sites and the number of packages you have, you may not want to use these tools on a continuous basis. You can easily overwhelm yourself with data, not to mention the sheer volume of paper and the record-keeping tasks

Exhibit 9.2. Tear Out/Send Back Form.

Exercise #4

Complete this exercise by filling in the blank spaces. Return the completed exercise to the Training and Development Department by April 15, 1992.

1. I gave the (title) _____ SDL Package to (employee name) _____

2. The SDL Package was completed in (time) _____

3. I had the trainee complete the SDL in the (location)

    _____

4. I checked back with the trainee every _____ minutes or so.

5. I spend (time) _____ providing a guided practice session with the trainee.

6. I recorded the trainee's name, SDL title, completion date, and my initials on the _____

7. In general, I feel that the Store Operations Training System Self-Directed Learning Packages will be _____

    _____

    _____

Your Name _____

Store # _____

Date _____

Exhibit 9.3. Site Implementor's Report.

Store Managers: We need your help in determining how well the Store Operations Self-Directed Learning System is working now that the first packages have been in the field for almost a year. Please take 5 minutes to complete the questions listed below. Return this survey to the Training & Development Department.

Region # _____   **District #** _____   **Store #** (optional) _____

Store Manager's Name (optional) _____

---

1. Have you used any of the Store Operations SDL packages?   Yes ☐   No ☐

2. How many employees have completed one or more of the SDLs? _____

3. What is the average length of time it takes an employee to complete an SDL package? _____

4. Are there any SDL packages that are particularly difficult for associates to complete or understand?

   Be specific please: _____
   _____
   _____

5. Do you think the activities and practice sessions are realistic and helpful?   Yes ☐   No ☐

6. Are the instructions in the SDL packages clear and easy to follow?   Yes ☐   No ☐

   Why not? _____
   _____
   _____

7. When your employees are working through an SDL package, how often do they need help from you or other employees?

   Never ☐   **Sometimes** ☐   **Frequently** ☐

8. Do you have any other comments about the Store Operations Self-Directed Learning System?

   _____
   _____
   _____
   _____
   _____
   _____
   _____

---

this paper entails. However, if they appear in 20 percent of your packages, or only in a certain edition, they can be useful for determining what's going on at the training sites. They'll also remind everyone of the importance of using the packages and using them correctly.

Site Implementor's Report. Another and perhaps more direct control measure is a site implementor's report. Usually, these are done on a planned basis, and their purpose is to check program usage and other statistical measures. They are often evaluative in nature and, as such, might be better mentioned in the next section. However, they have important control functions as well, particularly if you condense the facts they contribute and pass this summary on to a management level that is committed enough to the system to use the information. I have no special format or items for this type of report. Exhibit 9.3 contains an example of one I have used in the past. If you use one, design it so it fits your system and needs, but keep it short. Remember, your site implementors are busy people, and training is not their first priority.

Management Observation Checklist. A tool for formalizing management control in your system is the management observation checklist, completed by upper-level management at the training site. This list might include questions to ask trainees that will indicate if they have been trained, items to look for in the records, and questions to ask site implementors and direct supervisors. Corporate managers also can fill these checklists out whenever they visit a training site. Formal copies or informal comments can be sent back to you for compilation and analysis. Exhibit 9.4 contains an example of one of these instruments.

Training-Done Reports. Finally, there are the basic "training-done" reports that are filled out weekly, monthly, or in whatever time frame fits your system. If nothing else, they keep reinforcing the concept that management is interested in employees' progress.

Key to Control

The key to control is to do something with the information that the control measures provide.

And this something should be done by the people who can do it most effectively—namely, upper-level management. Once again we're talking about management support. In planning for a distributed implementation, you worked hard to get that support. Here is where you'll use it.

The purpose of control measures is to provide discipline:

Exhibit 9.4. Management Observation Checklist.

Please use this checklist to gather data on how well our SDL training system is working. Return it with your comments to the Training Department. Thank you.

Training Site _____   Date _____

Site Implementor _____

Number of Employees on site _____

Number who have used one or more SDL packages _____

Comments on SDL packages or system from employees interviewed:

_____

_____

_____

_____

_____

Comments from site implementor and/or manager:

_____

_____

_____

_____

_____

Your comments:

_____

_____

_____

Evaluator _____

The discipline to implement the training not just now but two years from now when it's no longer novel. The discipline to do it when the sites are too busy or too understaffed. The discipline to make training a priority, even when the company is in the middle of "something big."

This discipline comes from having higher management involved in your control measures. Such involvement indicates to everyone that your SDL programs are important. It comes from their acting on data from the control measures when things aren't happening the way they should. Particularly in a distributed system, the discipline that management brings to the process when they act as auditors of the training is invaluable.

I know of an excellent distributed system implemented in a multinational manufacturing, sales, and service company that was well thought out, planned, and developed but that was floundering in a sea of apathy. Then the CEO visited a few training sites and asked to see their training completion record. I was told the improvement in program compliance that occurred at all training sites after this one visit to only a few sites was amazing (and a perfect example of the efficiency of grapevine communications).

Your well-designed control measures will help create this type of management support, which in turn supplies the discipline necessary for a distributed SDL implementation.

Evaluation Considerations in a Distributed Implementation

One of the strengths of a distributed implementation is the effectiveness of the evaluation measures you can employ. As in the overall evaluation of SDL, there are two aspects to this: evaluation of trainee progress and package or system evaluation.

Evaluation of Trainee Progress

The main advantage a distributed implementation brings to evaluating trainee progress is its ability to include more realistic and more extensive skill performance evaluations, which in turn lead to better training transfer to the job. This is due to its on-the-job setting and may be one of the reasons you choose a distributed implementation for your SDL system. You need to plan carefully to take full advantage of it.

Tasks performed as part of training in a distributed implementation should be evaluated in real-life situations, not in simulation or role play. An expert such as the direct supervisor should be responsible for the evaluation—a procedure that is usually more valid than having a training center facilitator do the evaluation, since the facilitator can only evaluate "by the book." If you are using a distributed system, evaluated performance demonstrations should be found as often as possible in your packages, since this will greatly increase their quality.

Using the Trainee Evaluator Properly. One caution here is to avoid the mistake of putting too much emphasis on the evaluator's expertise as you design your performance evaluations. Many packages fail to achieve accurate trainee performance evaluation because the designer decides that the evaluator of the performance demonstration will "know what to look for." Thus, the package does not provide any criteria or tools for the evaluation.

This practice abuses both the evaluator, who must spend time deciding what to evaluate, and the trainees. Your trainees have come to rely on objectives to tell them what they need to know. Suddenly you are evaluating them on important performances without stated objective criteria. This will confuse them and damage all the previous work you've done in preparing them for SDL.

Performance evaluations in your packages should always provide the evaluator with guidelines or, for complex performances, with a criteria checklist, as discussed in Chapter Five. Also, remember that if the package is going to include performances, evaluated or not, your objectives must reflect that situation with psychomotor-based verbs.

When designing performance evaluations, be careful not to abuse your site evaluators. I said earlier that you should have as many performance evaluations as possible, since this is a strength of a distributed implementation. That's true, but moderate this goal with the knowledge that your evaluators have their own jobs to do as well. Too many evaluations that take too much time or are too complex will mean that often they won't be done at all. This strength of a distributed implementation can easily become a weakness if you make it impossible for your evaluators to do the evaluations.

Package or System Evaluation

A package or system evaluation is the second type of evaluative process that occurs in SDL. A distributed implementation offers a number of advantages for doing this type of evaluation as well. On the simplest level, you have the ability to go to training sites and simply observe if and how the packages are being used. You also have easy access to a number of people who can give you verbal answers to questions concerning the various evaluation phases (discussed in Chapter Twelve). Don't ask these questions of just the site implementor. Ask the supervisor, the next-level manager, and the trainee, too.

A combination of written and oral inquiry works even better. Send a simple two- or three-question usage evaluation form to all sites, then visit as many as you have time for.

Group Opinionnaire. A novel approach I came across that was used for evaluation in a small distributed system at a three-site plastics manufacturing firm was a group opinionnaire. In this process, the site implementor, supervisor, and trainee were asked to fill out a questionnaire together. In other words, this involved a group of people but only one opinion—or two at the most if there was a minority report. This led to a lot more analytical thinking by the respondents as they reflect on each other's thoughts and insights.

A more structured variant of this approach might be an area at the end of the opinionnaire in which each of the respondents could comment individually. This negates some disadvantages of "groupthink," such as one individual furnishing all the ideas, but it would tend to make the process more time consuming and unwieldy.

Obtaining System Evaluation Data from Supervisors. Opinionnaires, interviews, and checklists are usable formats in a learning center approach as well. The system evaluation process that really sets a distributed implementation apart is in the measurement of effectiveness. And the reason is that the best measurers of training effectiveness—the direct supervisors—are usually involved in the training system itself. This makes them able to evaluate both training applicability and transfer to the job.

In some systems, they are site implementors; in others, they sign off on training as a control measure; in still others, they are responsible for the performance evaluations of the trainees. Whatever the case, if you did your preparation work adequately, they understand the system and have probably been through the programs personally. In fact, it should be inherent in your implementation design that the supervisors are among the first to complete each SDL package as it becomes available.

Thus, supervisors are in a unique position to evaluate one of the most important evaluation parameters, package effectiveness, particularly as it relates to job transfer. This doesn't happen normally in a learning center approach or a classroom design. Only in a distributed SDL implementation are the supervisors this involved with the program—that is, if you did your design and preparation well.

Evaluating Package or System Effectiveness. Both oral and written evaluations are useful for gathering effectiveness data from the supervisors. The tools don't have to be too complex, since both you and the supervisor will be speaking the same language. What you are looking for are three pieces of information:

- Are the trainees using the skills they gain in your SDL packages on the job?
- What needs to be changed in any particular package to make the information more usable in the work environment?
- What can be done overall to make the information more transferable?

You can make the evaluation more formalized by developing a written opinionnaire. Use this type of tool to ask for comments and criticisms on single packages or on various aspects of the system. As in any written opinionnaire format, the more tightly you structure your questions, the more you'll get from the answers but the fewer replies you'll get. So design your pieces accordingly.

If you do oral evaluations with supervisors, you'll get more information. However, there is an objectivity problem, both in what your interviewees are willing to say to you and in how you hear what they do say. I've seen evaluation schemes that try to solve this difficulty by using a third party to conduct the interviews. The problem here is that it is difficult for noninvolved interviewers to ask good follow-up questions. Since the ability to ask follow-up questions is one of the main strengths of an oral evaluation, you've lost a lot by using a "disinterested" third party.

In any case, there are plenty of effectiveness data from sources that are closest to your packages and their intended results in a distributed system. Your only problem is to figure out how best to retrieve it.

Problems in Distributed SDL

There are two major evaluation problems in a distributed SDL implementation. The first is how to administer the evaluation mechanisms. The second concerns the evaluation factor of compliance, which is discussed in detail in Chapter Twelve but will be looked at here in relation to a distributed implementation.

Evaluation Administration. As to evaluation administration, you need to remember that you don't have a facilitator to keep track of program usage, hand out evaluations, or correlate data. Administration of this has to be automatic and must be the responsibility of a member of the design staff. This may mean you, if you are the design staff. You should not expect your site implementors to handle evaluation administration.

Your field trainers can help with this function, and in one system I viewed, it had been designated a supervisory responsibility. Whatever the case, someone must be responsible for distributing, controlling, retrieving, and analyzing your evaluations. As we mentioned, this is a key to control of a distributed SDL implementation, and there will be times when how well you can administer the process will be a limiting factor in your entire evaluation design.

Evaluating Program Compliance. The other evaluation problem in a distributed SDL implementation is in assessing compliance. This relates back to your inability to get reliable usage figures for your packages. Without these data, you have no idea how often or even if your programs are being used and if they are being used correctly.

I once designed a distributed SDL system in which I found out during site visits that at some sites the trainees were taking the packages home to do. Because each of the packages had a heavy performance component that could only be accomplished at the work site, I was concerned. Further inquiry indicated that the performances in the packages were being ignored.

Had this been a learning center, I would have known immediately from the facilitator that things were not going according to plan. But in this distributed approach, it was almost a year before I recognized this lack of compliance and was able to reeducate the site implementors about the importance of doing the *whole* package, with the performances.

This scenario might give you a clue as to who to ask about compliance. Your site implementors will be able to provide you with information about who is doing SDL and how it is being done. A quick list of questions that relate to compliance can be sent to them on a random basis. The questions you ask should be dependent on how your system is supposed to operate. Remember, though, you are looking for information on if and how your programs are being used, not on how effective or well liked they are. Make sure your questions relate to compliance, and save the other inquiries for a different instrument.

A mechanism that I've used to continually monitor compliance is the management checklist that we discussed earlier under control measures. This type of instrument can be tailored to compliance issues and then completed by visiting corporate management up to and including the CEO.

In one case, I was working in a retail chain where it is standard procedure for all levels of management to visit stores. I developed a very quick five-point checklist that any manager could employ to check for package compliance. It basically asked the visitor to check the SDL completion record and to ask the manager what the latest SDL package was that *the manager* had completed and what he or she thought of it. The same questions were asked of one or two store employees. The whole process took about two minutes.

You might see a hidden purpose in this approach if you remember our discussion of commitment and control. This type of evaluation tends to lend a certain importance to doing the training packages, particularly when the CEO uses the checklist on his or her visits to the stores.

In the end analysis, compliance evaluation and management control measures are really two sides of the same coin. Not paying attention to one in your design will cause problems when you evaluate the other. Both are major concerns in a distributed SDL implementation and require consideration that goes well beyond that normally used in any other training system.

Ensuring Continued Compliance and Support for Distributed SDL

Several tactics are effective for bringing about continued compliance and support.

Using Evaluation to Reinforce Compliance and Support

Your evaluation methodology, and how you communicate the data you receive from it, can help ensure continued compliance and support for your distributed SDL system. Your methodology itself can create continued support by involving as many people as possible in the evaluation. Asking people for data and viewpoints concerning the program will keep them interested in it and so will enhance their support. Sharing the data you receive from the evaluations with even more people will keep the program and their commitment to it fresh in their minds. In a distributed implementation, it is critical that your evaluation plan contains these or other methods to enhance long-term commitment.

One important technique is to never skip an evaluation. This holds true no matter how busy you are with other things or how sure you are that everything is working well. If you need another good reason for following your evaluation schedule, remember that doing evaluations reinforces the involvement of those who answer your questions. Sharing the evaluation information on a scheduled basis keeps management involved on a continuing basis as well.

Other Methods of Guaranteeing Continued Compliance and Support

Other ways of reinforcing compliance and support mostly involve a matter of good communications with your training sites. Managers, supervisors, and particularly site implementors need to know what's happening in the system, what changes you're planning, and how the system is working at other sites. I've used an SDL newsletter to great advantage for this. It doesn't have to be much of a newsletter. One page, distributed on a periodic or even random basis, works well. It should deal with current system information that might be of interest to the groups mentioned above. Hints on how to do things better and examples of how other sites have learned to do something a little different are also newsworthy items. You might even try little contests such as who has finished the most SDLs in the past month or which site has the highest score on tests. For some reason that I guess only psychologists can explain, contests seem to keep interest high.

However, the best method for keeping people informed and involved is personal contact. This has been mentioned before, but I don't think its importance can be overemphasized. Get out and see how things are going! Don't do this just during evaluation time, but all the time. Take 'em out to lunch. Talk to site implementors and supervisors, and don't forget the trainees. Ask them how they like the SDL packages and what can be done to make them better. Check the completion records, quizzes, and anything else you have in your system that can be checked.

Get to as many training sites as you can, as often as you can. Let them know that you're concerned, and they'll continue to be concerned as well. There are a number of methods that you can use to encourage long-term compliance and support, but they can all be summarized with one general rule: Keep as many people as you can as involved as possible with your system.

Revising and Updating

In Chapter Twelve, we will discuss revising and updating SDL in detail. For a distributed implementation, the basics are much the same, but some aspects become easier, while others present greater difficulties. These are considered in the following pages.

The main revision strength of a distributed implementation is that feedback from your site implementors and field trainers will enhance your ability to know when revisions are needed. You should also receive feedback directly from operations supervisors on what programs need updating—that is, if they are involved as closely as they should be with your distributed implementation. These sources can provide you with the basic information for your changes and formal revision reviews.

Revision Problems That Occur in
a Distributed Implementation

On the negative side, a major problem area with revising distributed implementation is logistics. You'll run into the same difficulties you had distributing your packages the first time.

Edition Control. To these obstacles, you can add correct edition control at the training site. No matter how often you request that your sites destroy outdated material, you'll still find old copies around and in use.

There is no way to eliminate this (I think it's one of Murphy's Laws), but you can minimize it. First, be sure that each new edition has a revision number prominently displayed. I have seen packages that have the revision number on every page, and I don't believe this constitutes overkill. For video or other media formats, the revision number is critical on both the box and the tape. Computer programs should have it on the disk and the first screen. If you're downloading your programs, this isn't as much of a problem. You simply replace the program that is no longer current.

Your next safeguard is to have a revision list located with each group of packages. It doesn't have to be complex. A page that lists each package and what revision number is current will be sufficient. Each time you send out a new package, send a new copy of the list. Remind site implementers, supervisors, and anyone else responsible for distributing the packages to check the revision list each time. Periodically send the revision list to each site implementor with instructions to examine all programs for currency.

If you feel the need for tighter control, have the list made into a checklist format that the site implementor can return when all items are up to date. A further check can be done by your field trainers. Make it part of their responsibility to examine all revision dates whenever they visit a training site. As I said, this won't do away with the problem completely, but it will minimize it.

Physical Design. Another area that may be a problem during a distributed implementation revision is your package's physical design. Because of the need for quantity inherent in most distributed implementations, your package must be simple enough to make revisions both physically and economically possible. We've discussed the importance of simplicity for distributed implementation before, but it bears repetition.

If revisions will be needed often, simplicity is paramount. Slides, videos, and other hard-to-revise media will be a problem. Even computer programs can be difficult to revise if you did not design them with this necessity in mind.

Simple print designs can present revision problems as well. In my first large-scale distributed package, I made the mistake of including a number of cut-and-paste graphics. When revision time occurred, the amount of clerical effort that went into recutting and repasting was mind boggling! If constant changes are going to be needed, keep your print packages as "revision friendly" as possible.

Revising Versus Updating

This brings up another revision decisions for print media: "Do I revise a whole package, or just a page or two?" This question becomes moot if your package is bound in a way that doesn't allow for page changes. A spiral binding with a three-color cover page is impressive but expensive if you need to revise often. And it's impossible to change just a page or two in such a package.

You made your packaging decision earlier in the design process, but now it will come back to haunt you if you didn't consider revision. A three-ring binder is more expensive than a staple or glue product, but it does give you the ability to change single pages. Whether you need that ability or not depends on what type of updates or revisions you need to make.

Another problem: keeping track of package revisions is bad enough; keeping track of page revisions in a large number of packages is close to impossible. You'll need very competent site implementors to give you any hope at all. A method you can try in some situations is to have the out-of-date pages returned to you. This is cumbersome and creates a heavy demand on clerical time, but it does work. In a large distributed implementation, though, it may be logistically impossible. However, it does give you more than just trust and hope as an assurance that materials are current.

I've seen revision and update problems handled in many ways, but the right way is always the way that works best for you in your particular situation. Like everything in an SDL design, the "right way" can only be found through strong analysis and good planning.

Exhibit 9.5. A Checklist for SDL.

Conducting a Distributed SDL Implementation

☐ An effective, efficient system of package delivery is being utilized.
  - The "human touch" is being used if possible.
  - Contingency plans for lost packages are ready.
  - Packages not delivered personally have explicit instructions.

☐ Effective control measures are being utilized.
  - The packages are in a good physical location and available when needed.
  - Record-keeping techniques are in place to maintain control.
  - Formal and informal management observations are being carried out at the training sites.
  - You are doing personal observations, site implementor reports, training-done reports, and other control measures as needed.
  - Top management is being kept involved to keep their support high.

☐ Specialized evaluation measures of both the trainees and the packages are being implemented.
  - Trainee performance evaluations are being done correctly.
  - Package effectiveness (training transfer) evaluations are being done.
  - Program compliance is being checked.

☐ Procedures to ensure continued compliance and support have been implemented.
  - The programs are being updated on a timely basis.
  - As many people as possible are being involved in and informed about the SDL system.

☐ Revision and updating procedures are in place.
  - Revision data from the sites are being collected.
  - Edition control procedures are in place.

10

Implementation Through Learning Centers

Pros and Cons of Centralized Training Facilities

The other major implementation strategy for SDL is the learning center (Figure 10.1). Like SDL, learning centers are called by many names. Designations such as resource center, individualized instruction center, learning laboratory, instructional resource center, and training facility are all used to denote a learning center. Some of these often contain processes that go well beyond simple SDL.

Characteristics of a Self-Directed Learning Center

For purposes of this book, we will define a learning center as a *specific location or facility where SDL programs are stored and where trainees come to use them.* While an organization may have a "learning center" that contains multiple learning environments and where various forms of learning take place, our considerations here will be limited to how the learning center concept affects and is affected by the SDL process.

The Learning Center as a Designated Facility

A learning center for self-directed learning is by definition a designated facility. Its *primary purpose* is to be a location where self-directed learning occurs. It may be of any size or shape, may be located in a basement or a closet, and may be as simple as a room

Figure 10.1. A Model for SDL.

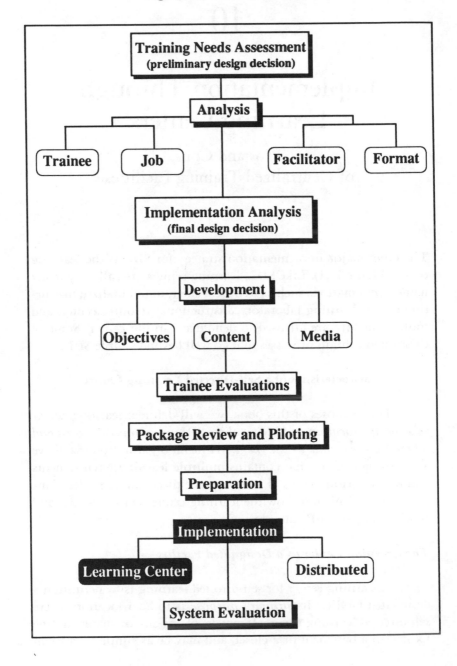

with a table or as complex as a simulator in a nuclear plant. Whatever its physical characteristics, it is a room, building, or other place designated specifically for the storage and use of SDL packages.

Learning Centers and Facilitators

The second major characteristic of a learning center is that it always has an easily accessible facilitator on duty when the center is in operation. This characteristic doesn't necessarily mean that the center must have its own staff. It does mean that when the center is open, a person whose *first responsibility* is to staff it must be readily available.

The terms *primary purpose* and *first responsibility* in the preceding discussion are important. Both the learning center and the facilitator may fill other roles. Neither of them has to be exclusively dedicated to SDL. However, if an SDL need arises, it takes precedence for both.

Examples of Self-Directed Learning Centers

Some examples might be in order here to help you understand these concepts. The smallest learning center I ever developed was literally a closet. It held one table with a videodisc interactive setup on it. There were only three programs available for the hardware. However, they were orientation programs. Everyone in the plant had to view them, either when they were hired or if their job location changed.

The "center" was staffed by two facilitators who were also classroom instructors. Their office was located around the corner. One was always on duty. When a trainee needed to use the equipment, it was the facilitator's responsibility to unlock the door, find the right disk, and turn on the machine. It was simple, but it worked, and it's a good example of a training center stripped down to its basics—a room with SDL programs and a facilitator to get the trainee started correctly.

A more complex illustration is a twelve-station SDL science lab I found in a university setting in Pennsylvania. The medium was slide-tape, and there were a variety of SDL programs that taught both biological and physical science. The room also included a laboratory in the back where the trainees performed experiments as directed by the SDL packages. There was an area with desks for testing (paper and pencil), a walled-off area for remedial testing (oral, with the facilitator asking questions), another walled area that served as a small classroom, and a facilitator's desk. The facility was open fourteen hours a day and staffed by four SDL package designers, who took turns at the facilitator's desk. Here you had a multiuse facility with full facilitation, where SDL was the primary function.

What a Designated Learning Center Isn't

These examples should suggest to you what self-directed learning centers can be and how facilitators might staff them. Looking at them in reverse can also give you an idea of what a learning center isn't. Self-directed learning centers are not machines tossed into a closet, requiring the trainee to search for a key, then a program, and then a place to set up. A center may be a closet, but the machines and programs are there, ready for the trainees, and someone who can help them get started is available when needed.

Nor are they contained in a room that has some other function that interferes with the SDL process. They are not part of a classroom. Learning centers may contain other areas within them such as a lab or a remedial conference area. They may even be part of an area such as a library. However, a center's usefulness for SDL must not be compromised by its location. This would negate one of the most important advantages of SDL—availability when the trainee needs it and is ready for it.

Learning Centers Versus Distributed SDL Implementation

Our self-directed learning center definition also distinguishes a learning center implementation from a distributed SDL implementation. With a learning center, the SDL packages are found in a designated facility, and the trainees come to them. In a distributed system, the packages are found where the trainees are, and there is no designated facility.

Beyond this obvious difference, most learning center implementations have two other characteristics that differentiate them from a distributed implementation. First, they usually represent a training augmentation rather than a training system. For this reason and because of the potentially large start-up costs involved, a learning center is more difficult to sell to management than a distributed system, which is in itself the training plan.

Second, learning centers are more capable of providing the trainee with the ability to choose the subject matter and method of learning that he or she needs and is most comfortable with. This is a component of SDL that we have to some extent slighted so far, but it can be a critical advantage of a learning center implementation.

As an example of what these differences can mean, let's compare two case studies of SDL implementation.

A Case Study of Distributed SDL as a Training System. The first example involves a Massachusetts-based manufacturing organization with roughly 900 dealers scattered throughout the country. This organization developed a distributed SDL system to train its new dealers on product advantages and disadvantages. Its goal was to provide better customer service by having more knowledgeable dealers and a measure of consistency in the promises being made about its products.

From this beginning, the organization quickly expanded its training concept. When it developed new products, an accompanying SDL package was also created. This went out to each distributor, *old and new*. As the system grew, product augmentations were added to the list of functions that required an SDL package. No product was introduced or changed unless the accompanying training package was complete and ready to use.

The training was done with SDL packages that went to the trainees at their job sites; no centralized facility was involved. Therefore, it was a distributed implementation. Except for the yearly new product exposition (where the firm gave out even more SDL packages), no other training was done for the distributors. Thus, it was a true training system.

A Case Study of Learning Center–Based SDL Providing Choice. The second case study involves a single-site metal fabricating company located in Ohio. The company developed a learning center to train its twenty-five or so managers and floor supervisors on quality techniques. This was not the only form of training in the plant, or even for these particular individuals; they also received supervisory skills classes and on-the-job training covering various machines. Thus, the center was not a training system but simply another component, one in which the trainees went to the packages instead of the other way around.

Over time, the center began to expand. Someone saw a good management videotape, which initiated the purchase of a whole management skills series on video. Then a computer station to teach a new software spreadsheet program to the clerical staff was added. Later an interactive video station, provided by a machine manufacturer to familiarize the operators with a new machine the company had just purchased, moved the center into the realm of high tech. The last time I talked to the center's facilitator (now one of two), she had just added a speed typing program, a computer literacy package, and three National Geographic specials to their collection. All 350 employees, from the janitors to the president, were using the center for specific training needs or for personal development. Though it is still an augmentation for their other training programs, the choice flexibility it allows them has made their center the most valuable of their training resources.

This particular case is one of the better illustrations I've found to exemplify the choice aspect of SDL. In truth, providing program and learning methodology choices such as these takes us well beyond our working definition of SDL. However, in a learning center implementation, the characteristic of providing trainee choice can be a strong HRD advantage of SDL. We will refer to it often as we continue our discussion of learning centers. No other training design can provide as much or do it as cost effectively.

Learning Center Implementation: Advantages and Disadvantages

Several advantages and disadvantages of a learning center implementation should be pointed out. Let's take the advantages first.

Advantages

The advantages can be grouped in at least four main categories.

Physical Advantages. Many of the characteristics we've already discussed are also advantages or strengths of the self-directed learning center. However, there are plenty of others; these include what could be termed physical advantages. One of the biggest is simply being able to avail yourself of a self-directed learning center as part of your design parameters. This is why I've stressed so heavily the idea that it must first be a location that is dedicated to SDL. Because it's there, with the relevant packages, your trainees can take advantage of it when they are ready to learn. Its "being there" also means that as an SDL developer, you can use its strengths in your package design. These strengths might include:

- Particular equipment that it has available so that you can format a package in the most effective way
- A centralized location that all your trainees can access and that you can control
- Increased trainee comfort in going there to use your programs as they meet with success in their first endeavors.

Advantages Offered by Facilitators. You also can't overrate the advantage of knowing you have a knowledgeable facilitator available when you are designing your packages and developing materials. He or she can help start the trainees off properly, watch for problems, provide equipment, evaluate, and do a multitude of other tasks necessary to the success of your packages. The facilitator will also help you control your SDL process more closely, in itself an advantage of the learning center.

Flexibility. I'm often asked what the difference is between SDL as I define it and self-instructional packages as used in a number of training applications. By now, I hope you see that SDL goes far beyond simple learning packages. It includes preparation, implementation, evaluation, choice, and a host of other concepts. This is the strength of SDL as an idea and a process. It is flexible enough to encompass self-instructional packages, learning centers, or multiple-country distributed training systems. It can be specific to a position or even to the "only correct way" to do a task. Yet it allows for choice in the professional development of managers or the personal development of each employee who takes advantage of a learning center.

SDL is the single print package in the hands of a nurse on a patient floor that teaches her the correct method for removing an IV. At the same time, it's the computerized learning center at a major university. Students use the facility to learn computer skills they'll need for the rest of their working lives. Professors assign its programs prior to class to make sure each student begins the session with the same background knowledge. Adults in the community who "only want to learn enough so I don't break the darn thing when they install it in our office" use it to overcome their fear of new technology and even to write their résumés. This flexibility is SDL's strength and is particularly the strength of a self-directed learning center.

Ability to Handle Varying Numbers of Trainees and Diverse Training Needs. There are many other advantages to a self-directed learning center implementation, but for the most part they can be illustrated by two possible training problems: you have too few trainees with too many different training needs or too many trainees with the same training need.

At first it might seem strange that the same training strategy can solve both these problems, but if you consider what a learning center can accomplish, it makes perfect sense. If your trainee population is limited but has a large number of needs, you have two choices. You can run many different classes in which you have only a few participants, or you can have SDL packages that address each need located in a learning center. Your trainees come in one or two at a time to learn from these packages in ways that are matched to their individual needs.

On the other hand, if you have large numbers of trainees with the same need, you can run a large number of classes in a short period of time to make sure you reach all of them in a timely manner. This will burn out your trainers and force your trainees to adhere to your schedule. Or you can have an SDL package that covers the needed information available in a learning center. The center is open all day, allowing the trainees to come in when they or their supervisors feel they have the time. Meanwhile, your trainers are busily involved in other projects instead of teaching the same old thing time after time.

I won't go into categorizing any more learning center advantages. As you may have realized, most are closely related to the general advantages of SDL that we've already discussed. Basically, if you're looking at a small number of training sites and/or a large number of training needs, you should consider a self-directed learning center as an option for your training implementation.

Disadvantages

Disadvantages of a learning center approach include the expense and time involved in setting the center up, the salary costs of the facilitator, and its lack of effectiveness for practicing on-the-job performances. These disadvantages and how to overcome them will be discussed in more detail in Chapter Eleven as we consider the actual operation of a center.

Summary

The following list summarizes all the strengths and weaknesses just reviewed. An SDL

- is a designated facility where SDL packages are used.
- has an easily accessible facilitator always on duty.
- can be as small as a closet.
- can be contained in the "right" type of other facility.
- is usually a training augmentation, not a system.
- can allow for trainee choice in subject matter and method.
- gives you more choices in your design parameters.
- is easier to control than a distributed implementation.
- is one of the most flexible of training processes.
- can be used if you have few trainees with many training needs.
- can be used if you have many trainees with the same need.
- usually has heavy start-up costs.
- has facilitator salary costs to consider.
- is not a good environment for practicing on-the-job performances.

These and other advantages and disadvantages need to be considered before you decide to go with a learning center implementation. The decision-making process is discussed in more detail in the next section.

Deciding to Develop an SDL Learning Center

Understanding the flexibility of SDL will help you to formulate reasons for using or not using a learning center implementation. The formal decision, as it relates to a particular training need, is made during the analysis phase of the SDL design process, as detailed in Chapter Two.

When to Make the Decision

As you may suspect, there is a lot more to the process than just deciding to use it. The implementation analysis decision is more a confirmation than a commitment to a learning center. Long before you ever get to that point in package design, you will probably have decided to develop a learning center and sold your company on the concept.

This is another one of those places in SDL design when the timing of decisions starts to become somewhat variable. The concept of a learning center could first arise anywhere in your assessment process; it often comes up when you are considering training needs from an overall point of view and relating them to corporate plans and goals. At any point in your development process, you might suddenly recognize the need.

Basis for the Decision

The important thing is not when but on what grounds you make the decision. The decision should be based on the answers to three questions.

Which Implementation Strategy Meets the Needs of My Training Environment and My Trainees Best? This is the first and most important question to ask. Sometimes the answer is simple.

For example, if you need to train five individuals in each of twenty locations, you probably won't want to set up learning centers. Or if the training demands that on-the-job practice and evaluation takes place, it might be wiser to plan a distributed implementation than to put your packages in a learning center that is separate from the job environment.

It's not quite as simple when you begin to increase the number of trainees, decrease the number of training locations, or add more packages. And if you find that your trainees need higher degrees of individualization, your implementation process becomes even more complex. Any or all of these factors might cause you to choose a learning center implementation. As an example, if you're a one- or two-site organization and you're going to use SDL for many forms of training, or perhaps for several development processes, you'll almost certainly want to use a learning center approach, if you have the funding.

Do I Have or Can I Get Funding for a Center? Which brings up the second question. In most instances, it seems cheaper at first glance to take the training to the trainees than to bring the trainees to the training. And often it is. Print SDL packages in the workplace will save time over print SDL packages in a learning center. Having the trainees come to a center costs time. And time truly is money when you're considering the cost of training. The center itself as square footage costs money. Equipping it and staffing it costs more money. You must spend a large proportion of the money at once to build and equip the center.

All of these factors can create both perceived and real problems when it's time to request funding. You'll need to know how to deal with all of them before you go to top management with the request to approve making your center a reality, and you must decide in advance how far you can compromise. For example, if you plan computer-based SDL packages and you need ten stations in your center but can only afford three, you may have to reconsider the approach. Perhaps the trainees can use the computers they have at their desks in a distributed implementation.

However, you always have the cost savings of SDL to fall back on as you try to sell your center to top management—not to mention the development processes that are available at reasonable costs for large numbers of employees through a center. We will discuss selling the center in more detail a bit later.

   Do the Learning Center's Advantages Correlate with My Program's Instructional Needs? The final factor, which is usually decisive if the previous two questions have not given you an answer, is the completion of the analysis question that determines your packages' instructional needs. If your packages demand strong facilitation, a learning center is the best approach. If you need strong control over who does the packages, how they do them, and how they are evaluated, learning centers shine. If you're moving into a more diagnostic development approach, a learning center is almost mandatory. If you're using a lot of prepurchased programs, a learning center is more cost effective. I could go on, but I think you get the picture.

   To sum up this discussion, before making a decision to use a self-directed learning center implementation, you need to:

- Consider what the training situation itself demands.
- Calculate your ability to fund a center.
- List the advantages of a center to your SDL process.

If things look right, you can begin to develop your center. Chapter Eleven contains information that can help guide you. But before you spend too much time and money, you'll need to consider the special problems you'll have in selling your SDL center concept to the decision makers in top management.

Selling the Self-Directed Learning Center Concept

   The first challenge you face after you decide on a learning center is that you immediately have to convince others it is a good idea. This wasn't as big a problem with a distributed SDL implementation.

Selling Your Learning Center Early

   The effect of choosing distributed SDL is not felt anywhere but in the training department, until the packages are about ready to be distributed and you have to begin your company preparation.

The fact that SDL is not a well-known training process actually works in your favor to some extent for a distributed implementation. Other than giving you the go-ahead decision, management will probably not want to get too deeply involved in something they don't really understand until you have concrete examples (like a package) to show them.

However, with a learning center, the effect on the company is immediate. First, you need a place—a "designated facility," as we have called it. This means room, furniture, interior changes, and other items that cost money. Next, you'll have to start considering a facilitator position. This means more money, and worse, usually a change in the head count of your department. Depending on your plan, you may need capital for equipment and possibly money to buy off-the-shelf programs as well. The "unusualness" of SDL will work against you here. Management will want to know early in the process what they are putting all this space and money into. It's difficult to explain the concept to the uninitiated if you don't have something solid to show them.

For these reasons and for a number of others depending on your specific situation, your most important job will be to convince the decision makers that your idea is a good one. You must sell your concept of a learning center to your company early and often. We discussed the selling of SDL in general in Chapter Two and considered how to gain top-management support in Chapter Seven, but you need to be much more proactive and aggressive in selling your learning center than when you sell a distributed implementation.

Defining and Isolating the Most Critical Needs

To do this, you first have to clarify for yourself why you need a learning center. Why this implementation strategy and not another? What advantages does it have for the organization? What training needs will it help fulfill? You did this somewhat informally when you were analyzing training needs and first considered a learning center. Now you need to do it in a more formal manner. Write down the answers to these questions. List the advantages. State them both in terms that will mean something to management. And prepare your responses to arguments that are likely to arise.

You may want to use a list of the needs you feel your center will meet as a handout. However, when you are preparing a sales talk to management, be careful not to get bogged down with too many possibilities. In fact, I have usually found that the best way to approach management is to isolate one very critical need that everyone agrees is a high priority. Describe how the learning center will meet this need.

This tactic will channel you into making that particular need your first priority in the learning center, so choose something that can be dealt with in a reasonable period of time. Otherwise, you may find yourself with a center that is gathering dust while you develop some vastly complex program to meet this need that everybody expects to see taken care of.

This caveat aside, focusing in on one critical need and then using the capabilities of your learning center to meet it will make it easier to sell the center concept. It will also convince your management that they made the right decision when they gave you the go-ahead. This can be very helpful the next time you come to them with a proposal for additional resources for your center.

An Example of Selling the Center Concept Through a Critical Need

A good illustration of this technique comes from a colleague who started her own learning center at a high-tech research company in Houston. She choose the corporatewide priority of basic supervisory training for the research center's eighty-five first-line supervisors to sell her center.

Taking advantage of the many off-the-shelf programs available, she suggested that center programs could augment the twice-a-year consultant the company brought in for classroom instruction. It could teach the basics of delegation, performance appraisal, coaching and counseling, and so on, bringing all supervisors up to a certain level. The consultant could then offer higher-level follow-up and skills practice in the classroom.

This scenario nicely illustrates the concept of picking something possible to do quickly and easily (find and buy supervisory skills programs). It also shows the center functioning as a training augmentation. This "piggybacking" on a currently accepted program is an excellent selling and initiation technique.

Our colleague went one step further in her selling process. She noted to her management that five off-the-shelf programs would cost approximately $2,500. This was the same cost as that of the consultant for one day. She pointed out that while the consultant could only handle fifteen or twenty supervisors in that day, the center could accommodate every supervisor, many times over.

Of course her cost advantages argument was incomplete. We've already discussed some of the other start-up costs involved. However, cost-effectiveness is a strength of learning centers. If you can use comparisons such as this effectively in your selling process, by all means do so.

Defining the Purpose of Your Center

Next, or perhaps simultaneously with focusing in on a need, you have to decide what the actual purpose of your center is going to be. This purpose must be stated clearly so that everyone has a chance to react to it. Maybe you see it used specifically for technical training, or perhaps management development. Will it only contain packages that are mandatory for skill positions, or will it be more of a choice process, as we discussed earlier? Is it to be a focused resource or personal development facility, containing materials that go far beyond the company's specific training needs? Will it be some combination of these and perhaps other purposes? You may decide for the present that you want to emphasize one aspect of the center— for example, technical training. The other possibilities can be left to evolve later as organizational priorities dictate.

Examples of general purposes for centers include the following:

- Technical training center
- Management development center
- Computer resource center
- General corporate learning center
- Career planning and development center
- Wellness center

- Productivity and quality resource center
- Sales and marketing resource center

After looking at this list, you may realize that you do want your center to be used for a combination of purposes. However, as in the case of training needs, my own experiences dictates that you should choose only one purpose for your selling presentation. I've found that when you start getting too involved in possibilities, it gets confusing. You create the possibility of too many misconceptions on the part of those you are trying to sell to. I usually pick the one purpose that I feel the management would find most important and try to sell the concept based on that.

Whatever you choose to do, write the purpose down on paper or, better yet, on an overhead. The overhead will force you to keep it short and simple, which is important. This succinct statement is what you want to present to the company's management.

Defining Your Center's Users

You'll also want to state who will use the center. This may be evident from your purpose, or it may not be. Either way, it is a good idea to specifically delineate who your training population is for the center. Will all positions in the plant receive the technical training that is the center's primary purpose? Will only first-line supervisors and up be eligible to take advantage of its development programs? Will you deal with requests from sales and marketing staff, or is your priority operations employees? Are the clerical staff going to be the audience for your computer software training, or will it be open to anyone who wants to learn about computers?

As with the aspects of need and purpose, most trainers are inclined to try to relate to as many audiences as possible. In this way, they hope to garner widespread support. However, this can again be confusing when you are trying to do your selling. It often leads to curious responses such as, "Well, do you really think just anyone should be allowed to learn about computers?" or "We don't need a learning center. All our people come to us fully trained or we don't hire them." To keep these tangential arguments from arising, it's best to focus on audiences that your assessments show need training. Let other audiences, like other purposes, evolve with the success of your center.

Defining Center Mechanics

Next, you will have to make some preliminary decisions on the mechanics of your center. It's almost a certainty that somewhere along the line during your sales pitch, you will be asked questions such as the following: "When will the center be open?" "Will people be allowed to go during work hours, or only before and after work?" "How will you serve second- and third-shift employees?" These will inevitably include that most important question of all, "How much is this going to cost?"

Estimating Costs

For that particular question, you will need to work up three different estimates:

- Start-up costs for machines, room changes, furniture, and so on
- Staffing costs
- An ongoing budget

Notice I said *estimates*. Unless your situation demands it, you normally don't have to be exact at this point. Some ballpark ideas should be sufficient, with a promise to present a formal budget later if the concept itself is approved. When estimating ongoing budget, don't forget funds for machine replacement and new programs. A little extra for expansion is also a nice idea if you can sell it.

If you're looking for real numbers, I'm unable to provide them in any way that would make sense. These costs depend on the size of your center, your location, and what you want to accomplish. It's important to consider all the factors we've discussed when making your cost estimates.

One thing you might consider to make the costs more palatable is a chargeback system in which each department that uses your center pays toward its operational cost according to that usage.

This is easy to implement for a center; you can simply charge by the hour. However, if you go this route, you'd better plan strong evaluative measures to show how effective your center and its programs are. Departments can quickly cut off trips to the learning center if budgets are tight and they do not see a good return on their investment. You really become customer driven when you go to a chargeback system. However, a learning center, with its inherent flexibility to meet the multiple needs of many trainees for both professional development and personal growth, is the perfect training design for a chargeback process.

Center Integration with the Training System

Finally, you'll want to be clear on how your center affects, and is integrated with, current training programs and systems. There are times when the learning center will literally take over some forms of training. At others, it is truly just an augmentation. You'll want to present the fit before asked to head off turf battles and hard feelings.

When you have decided on all of these items, you are ready to go to management and do your selling. Who you sell to, and in what order, will depend on your particular organization. However, never forget the importance of getting the CEO involved if at all possible.

Developing an Effective Presentation

Even with all of your well-thought-out purposes and plans, you'll still have the problem of presenting a concept that is not well known to your management audience. Of course, you'll want to discuss cost savings such as the number of trainees that can be trained from one purchased package versus sending them to a seminar, the effectiveness of SDL in general, and special advantages that your center will have over other training constructs.

However, you can add some substance to the abstraction of SDL in a center implementation by presenting examples of where a learning center approach has worked well, particularly in your industry. This will require some research but will be well worth it.

Such examples will make the concepts easier for management to relate to. Resources for finding such examples include ASTD, NSPI, other SDL practitioners, and bibliographies of books or articles on SDL.

It may take a little digging, but you should be able to uncover some learning center success stories. Most people will be glad to talk with you about them. You might even be able to get a slide or two of their facilities to help management visualize what you're describing.

I know of one case where the trainer was so interested in doing a high-power selling presentation that she went to three different centers and took video of what they looked like and how they worked. She edited this footage into a fifteen-minute video SDL package on learning centers and used it as part of her presentation. I wouldn't recommend this for everyone. However, she did inform me that when the CEO saw one particular center he liked, he asked if "theirs" was going to look like it. I don't think I have to tell you how her proposal turned out.

Using an Expert Guest Speaker. A variation on this theme is to have someone with experience in SDL and learning center implementation as a guest speaker during your selling presentation. I've been asked to do this a time or two and have been both flattered and glad to help another SDL process get started. If you use this approach, be careful to pick the right person. Explain exactly what you want your expert to talk about and how much time is available. Some people can talk for hours when they get wound up, yet never make the point you wanted your management to hear. Be sure your guest speaker clearly understands what you are trying to accomplish by being there. My experience suggests that if he or she can't accomplish your purpose in ten to fifteen minutes (twenty at the outside), you're trying to do too much.

Field Trip Approach. Another possibility is to take your key decision makers on a "field trip" to one or two learning centers. This is not as convenient as videotape or a guest speaker and may be a headache to arrange. However, there is no substitute for actually seeing a good learning center in action. Your managers should have the chance to question the creator of the center and the trainees as well. If possible, try to arrange a meeting between your managers and their counterparts in the host corporation. Their views on a center approach will carry a lot of weight with your decision makers, and they should interest you, too. Just be sure you pick places that are going to give the answers you want your managers to hear.

Don't forget that your ultimate goal is to get the support you need to begin to develop a learning center. How you do this depends to a great extent on your company and your particular situation within it. However, you will be successful if you follow these guidelines:

- Plan carefully and completely.
- Develop a simple proposal that focuses on one or two key points.
- Create an effective presentation that lays out the plan for your audience. It should provide enough solid examples to create reality from concept and vision.

The following list summarizes all the points that will help you with the process of selling your center.

- List the advantages a learning center has for the organization.
- Define and stress one need that management agrees is critical.
  Can the learning center meet the need?
  Can it be done in a reasonable amount of time?
  Is this what you want to do for a first program?
  Can you "piggyback" on an existing program?
- Calculate cost savings that may occur with the center approach.
- Clearly define and state the purpose of your center.
  What type of training will the center be used for?
  Will it be focused or include personal development?
  Write it down for all to see.
- Define who will use your center.
  Who will be the main audience(s)?
  Will other positions be able to take advantage of it?
  How will you deal with requests from other departments?
- Discuss the mechanics.
  Hours of operation?
  When will workers be allowed to go?

- Estimate costs.
    Start-up costs?
    Staffing costs?
    Ongoing budget?
- Discuss integration with current training designs.
- Try to find ways to provide concrete examples.
    Examples of learning center success stories?
    Expert guest speakers?
    Field trips?

In the next chapter, we will discuss how to proceed from your success in selling your learning center concept to making it a reality.

Exhibit 10.1. A Checklist for SDL.

The Self-Directed Learning Center

☐ The learning center is a designated facility.

☐ The learning center has a full-time facilitator.

☐ The learning center has a central location.

☐ The learning center will best meet the needs of the trainee population.

☐ Funding is available to start the center.

☐ A center will best meet the instructional needs of the SDL packages.
  - Strong control exists.
  - Diagnostic development is available.
  - Multiple media formats are being utilized.
  - Heavy emphasis is placed on prepackaged programs and materials.

☐ You have a good learning center selling plan.
  - A critical need has been isolated.
  - The center's main purpose has been defined.
  - The main users have been defined.
  - Center mechanics have been considered.
  - Cost has been estimated.
  - Integration with the current training system has been defined.
  - An effective presentation with concrete examples has been developed.

11

Building a Learning Center

What to Do to Make It Work

Once you've sold the idea of an SDL center to your corporate decision makers, you'll have plenty to do to make your idea a reality. This chapter will present methods and ideas for setting up, stocking, staffing, running, and evaluating an SDL center as an implementation strategy (Figure 11.1). Once again, some of the topics have been discussed previously, but we will see them now as they relate directly to the reality of running a learning center.

Setting Up a Learning Center

Setting up a learning center involves making decisions about location, size, furniture, and other considerations.

The Right Location

Your first step should be to find a location for your center. In most organizations, your choice will probably be limited to available space. There are several important factors to consider when comparing possibilities.

A Central Location. You want your location to be as central as possible in your organization. Remember, one of the advantages of SDL in a learning center is that it is convenient. It is a lot less convenient if the center is located in the basement of the facility or in a building at the edge of the campus. In fact, a centralized location is so important that you might wish to live with other deficiencies to get the best possible location.

Figure 11.1. A Model for SDL.

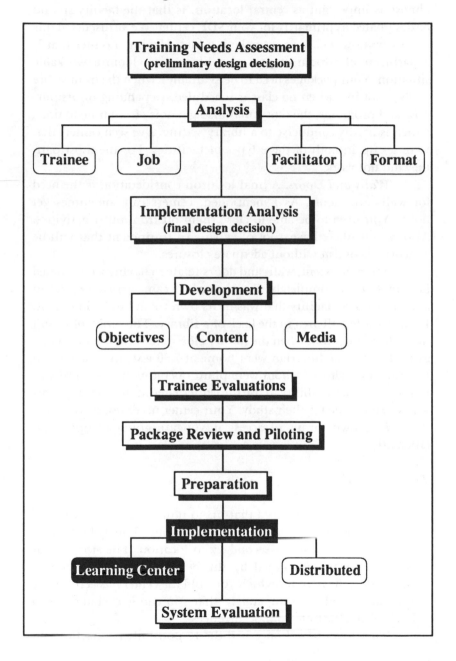

A Location Designated for SDL. A second consideration, almost as important as central location, is that the facility should be designated as primarily for your SDL center. We've discussed this in theory; now you have to make it a fact. Having a center that is a part-time classroom or part of a library is seldom a workable situation. Your packages need to be available "when the trainees are ready," not just when no class is scheduled. Depending on its purpose and programs, the center may also get noisy from time to time, which is hardly conducive to a library setting. I've seen centers that were set up in both of these types of facilities. For the most part, they did not work.

Walls and Doors. A final location consideration is the need for walls and doors. As I mentioned, centers can sometimes get noisy. You need to be able to close them off from other activities. Also, you'll likely have a lot of expensive equipment that will be a security problem without adequate closures.

To some extent, walls and doors relate to having a designated facility, but not completely. For example, I came across a center in a nuclear power facility that was in its own room but had no door. It was a walled-off area in the back of a library. The problem wasn't noise, but rather that when the library closed, the center had to close as well. Since the librarian went home at 7:00 P.M., this meant that the trainees (many of whom were plant operators that worked various shifts) lost the ability to use the center later in the evening. This was a prime time for their study. Your center needs doors for security *and* its own means of access if you are going to operate it efficiently.

The Right Size

You may have noticed that up to now, I haven't mentioned size as a factor in your location considerations. This is because in most circumstances size is secondary to location. The size of your center should be determined by the best location, and not vice versa—unless the need for which you sold the center has certain size requirements and is so imperative that you can get whatever you want. Let me illustrate both occurrences.

Two Examples. I once had the responsibility for setting up a temporary center to train 700 people in a short time. The training was critical, since it involved a new computer system that everyone would be using. We knew how many trainees we had to train and guessed what average hourly usage would be. We then looked for a room in a good location that could handle twenty-five workstations (the number we felt confident would allow us availability at all times). We found the right space, had the current occupants move to temporary quarters for two months, and brought in the equipment.

Unfortunately, this type of scenario is the exception. More common is a situation like the one in which I found myself with two possible sites for a permanent center. One was so small it not only left no room for growth, but would cause me to scale down my preliminary design. It was in an unused portion of a warehouse that was right in the middle of the ten-building manufacturing complex at which I was working. The other alternative was large, airy, and had a great view. It was on the top floor of the tallest, and least centralized, building of the complex. Many of the trainees were blocks away.

You can probably also guess which site I chose. Over time, I expanded my warehouse site (not without a lot of effort) and had a fine center. However, without the central location, I doubt if enough trainees would have come to the center to give me the usage needed to convince management that expansion was necessary.

Starting Small. This brings up another point concerning size and starting up a center. It's not bad to start small. Too many people want to create an impressive facility when they start planning a learning center. It has to have new furniture, carrels, computers, and special wallpaper. All of this increases start-up expenses, and that makes it harder to sell.

Unless you have isolated the aforementioned critical need, which is so overwhelming that money is not a consideration, you'll usually do better to by starting small. I've already mentioned the case of the center I started in what was literally a janitor's closet. We got rid of the brooms and mops, of course, but basically all it had in it was an interactive video setup and one program. Over a few months, we added a couple more computer programs (not interactive, just computer based). It wasn't too long before we added a videotape machine, then another computer. After that, we moved out of the closet and into a room with windows!

To be honest, I have to admit it didn't hurt that the interactive video program that started this particular center was mandatory viewing for the entire management of the organization. Nothing sells a learning center like being able to tell the VPs they can get *their own* training whenever they have time. And nothing gets you more room as fast as their having to go to a closet to get that training.

This case exemplifies two important points. The first we've already discussed. The interactive video with which we started the center dealt with a real need the organization had and so made selling the concept of a learning center easier. The second is that the concept became self-sustaining when the decision makers began to really understand how well it worked. Starting small does not mean you will stay that way long. If you have chosen the right approach, and if you know how to make it work, your center's growth rate can astound you.

I'm not suggesting that everyone should start their center in a closet. What you need for your preliminary learning center design depends on what your learning center is going to do and on how many people will be using it. Just as critical is what your company is willing to or can support.

Furniture for a Self-Directed Learning Center

I've seen perfectly serviceable centers that had nothing more than tables, chairs, and machines in them; in fact, I've done one or two myself. However, let's assume your situation is typical and discuss some of the interior items you'll need to consider.

On the average, you'll want a room, designated, centrally located, and with its own entry. It should be large enough to hold half a dozen or so carrels of varying sizes. This allows different numbers of trainees to share programs. It should also have storage space and an area for the facilitators. If the facilitators' area is going to double as an office, it's important to have glass walls to provide a little privacy. This also shuts off extraneous office talk, which can be distracting to the trainees. Several floor plans for small and large centers can be found in Figure 11.2.

Figure 11.2. Floor Plans for Learning Centers.

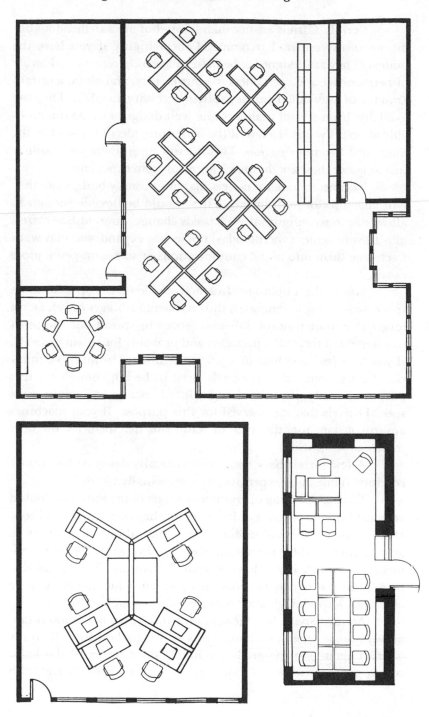

Carrels. Carrels are not mandatory but are a tremendous addition to any center. I recommend them highly if you have the budget. They are designed to be used in learning centers, add an air of permanence and specialness to your facility, and afford a certain amount of individual privacy, often necessary in SDL. They are available from several dealers, some well designed, some questionable at best. I've listed a few of the better providers I know of in the Suggested Readings section. This doesn't mean there aren't others just as good; these are the ones I know of from experience.

In general, look for carrels that are strongly built, since they will take a lot of punishment. They should be flexible enough to allow you to reconfigure as your needs change. Straight-line carrels may fit your center concept today, but as you expand, you may want to change them into island configurations or something even more exotic.

Size is also important. Interactive video takes up a lot more space than a simple computer, thus requiring a bigger carrel. Don't forget that your trainees will need room to spread out the print component of their SDL packages and probably for writing as well. If you have packages that are going to be utilized by multiple trainees at once, some of your carrels need to be big enough for this purpose. Finally, if you're doing a lot of testing, you might want special carrels that are reserved for this purpose. If your machines are in constant use, this type of setup can free them for the next trainee more quickly.

A few carrels have been ergonomically designed for trainee comfort. While more expensive, they are usually worth it.

Chairs. Speaking of ergonomics, one of the most overlooked yet most important pieces of furniture in the center are the trainees' chairs. Comfortable, *adjustable* chairs that allow the trainees to achieve correct tabletop height and eye level viewing of your equipment are a must. If you have a limited furniture budget, spend it here. Your center may not look as good, but your trainees will be able to sit long enough and be comfortable enough to learn.

Storage Space. Storage space for your programs is important as well. Some type of shelving units will usually suffice. If you're worried about your programs "walking away" (a particular habit of computer software and videotapes), you may need shelves with locking doors. Another way to solve this problem is to keep the programs in the facilitators' office, so that they are responsible for distributing them directly. We'll discuss this in more detail later.

Internal Environmental Considerations

Other center internal factors include lighting, HVAC controls, and interior decoration. Since centers are most often placed in preexisting structures, there is only so much you can do about these issues without incurring significant remodeling costs. However, if you are fortunate enough to be planning a center in a new structure, or are doing major remodeling, I refer you to Karen and Jim Leed's book *Building for Adult Learning* (1987), which you can find listed in the references. There are many ways you can make a new learning center—or any other learning environment—more "user friendly." This book provides such information for you in detail.

Light. For those who don't have the luxury of a new structure, there are still a few things you can do to the environment that will help the trainees. The most important of these is light. Your trainees will need light, but not too much of it, particularly if they are using slide or computer media. The best approach is individual lighting. Carrels often come equipped with their own light sources. If this is an option, buy it! If the carrel has no lighting option, think again about buying that particular carrel. If you're dealing with a table-and-chair center, desk lamps at every station will do the job well.

Room lighting should be as mild and inconspicuous as possible to save on screen glare and tired eyes. I once had a learning center in an old executive suite conference room. All the room lights were indirect, located near the top of the walls, and aimed at the ceiling. With individual lighting in the carrels, it was the best system I've ever had for lighting a center. You'll find this configuration hard to achieve, but consider shades or other ways to keep room light glare from the trainees' eyes. There are parabolic-shaped louver covers available for high-intensity fluorescent lights. They will help cut down on glare and make your room lights more directional. Check with your engineering maintenance people or industrial lighting dealers.

Another good piece of equipment to install is a rheostat. Rheostats are cheap, easy to put in (or have done), and provide significant lighting control for your center.

HVAC. HVAC (heating, ventilation, and air conditioning) in an existing structure is a lot harder to control. A window air conditioner can help if the room gets too hot. Barring this approach, the old reliable electric fan and the newly rediscovered ceiling fan can help a lot. Circulating the air will move the heat generated by tour machines away from the trainees.

If cold is the problem, try space heaters, but buy good ones with thermostats, internal fuses, and tip-off switches. Replace the room thermostat with a programmable one to heat or cool before the trainees (and you) come in. This is not expensive and is a useful technique, particularly if your room HVAC processes are not as good as they could be.

Speaking about thermostats, be sure your facilitator can control them. This may involve bribing the janitor or bringing in your own tools to take that little cover off, but it is a must. No matter what the building engineers say about the effectiveness of feedback systems, the only true indicator of the need for more heat or more cold is your trainees. When they complain, it needs to be taken care of, now!

Interior Decoration. Interior decoration greatly depends on your budget, but it's amazing what a few plants and posters can do for the learning environment. Paint and wallpaper are cheap. On more than one occasion I've had to do it myself, but it turned out pretty well. Keep to neutral colors, but try to make your center a little different from the rest of the building. It's surprising how a little change from what the trainees see everywhere else will affect their attitude and therefore their ability to learn.

Electricity. One other internal element is electricity. There is no substitute for enough electricity in a center. You need it for lights, possibly for extra heat or cooling, and of course for hardware. It is of critical importance if you are planning computer stations in your center.

A room not specifically designed as a center will never have enough wall outlets or have them in the right place. Extension cords can help solve the problem, but use them with care. They can be dangerous from an electrical point of view and can pose tripping or fire hazards as well. Some carrels come with electrical strips that will provide extra outlets safely, but these too need to be plugged into your usually limited wall outlets.

I have no magic answer to this problem. Electricity, because of the cost of electricians, is expensive to put where you need it, and you always need it where it isn't. My only advice is to remember that your setup budget should reflect any rewiring you must do. This includes not only what you need in your center today, but also power for your expansion plans as well. Doing it right the first time will save you a lot of headaches later.

Hardware Requirements for a Self-Directed Learning Center

The last area to consider in setting up a learning center is your hardware requirements. If all of your SDL packages are simple print formats, this is easy; pencils and some paper should do it. However, as your media become more complicated, so do your setup specifications.

Computers. The type of hardware or media you'll need, as you probably knew I would say, is dependent on what you plan to do with your center. More specifically, it depends on what media format the programs you'll have in it will be using. This may seem obvious, yet more than once I have seen trainers automatically plan to put computers in their center, because "that's what centers should have in them today." Once they were thus equipped, the trainers found they had no programs, at least none that any trainees needed, to run on the machines. They looked good, though, and the center was certainly "up to date."

To avoid this "technological herd mentality," go back to the need or needs that helped you sell your center. Decide what hardware will most closely match the way you plan to meet that training need and buy enough of this hardware to do the job. This will lead you into the analysis phase of designing SDL packages, and that's the right place to be when you need to make decisions on specific hardware for your center.

If this seems to you like one of those "chicken-or-egg" decisions, you're probably right. At times, usually when originating a center, the training you need to do will determine what hardware you have to purchase. In other situations, normally when you have a center already operating, the hardware there will make your decision about the media format for your packages.

Video. Generally, though, there are basic hardware pieces that belong in just about any learning center. The most pervasive of these is without a doubt the half-inch videocassette replay unit. Notice I did not say videocassette recorder or player. These terms are used interchangeably today to mean a video recorder. You don't need a recorder in your center if all you're doing is playing back tapes. For the same price as a consumer recorder, you can purchase an industrial-grade player that will last longer and need fewer major repairs.

This isn't to suggest that you shouldn't consider consumer machines. In most cases, there is little difference between them and the industrial models. However, the few truly industrial machines will give you longer service, especially in heavy-use situations. If heavy use is not a consideration and you can save money by buying a consumer model, do it. But be careful you don't end up paying for a lot of features you don't need in your center application. Look for a higher-grade machine rather than unneeded features. The better consumer machines will last longer and usually don't "eat your tapes" as often. There are consumer machines that are just players and that are less expensive than consumer recorders, but you'll have to look for them.

Of course if you plan to duplicate tapes, or you're doing some editing, you'll need a recorder or two. These machines can double as playback units as well. Just be sure that taking them out of service for recording doesn't affect your trainees' ability to use your programs when they need them. My suggestion is that if you can afford it, use recording machines as backups, not as everyday machines. If you can't afford it, do what you can, but remember that the trainee should always come first. Anything else defeats one of the most important advantages of your center and lessens its usefulness in the eyes of your trainees.

You might also have noticed that I said half-inch video machines. If I had been writing this book ten years ago, I would have cautioned you against half-inch in favor of three-quarter-inch tape. I suspect that if I do another edition in five years, I will be recommending 8-millimeter or something even smaller. At any rate, right now half-inch is the standard and three-quarter-inch is not really worth considering. Even for recording or duplicating purposes, half-inch in the form of super VHS is all you need. Mixing formats just makes things more confusing and more expensive.

Audiotape Recorders. The second piece of hardware that belongs in every center is an audiotape recorder. These machines are simple to operate and inexpensive. If part of the plan for your center is to purchase off-the-shelf material, there are literally thousands of audiotape programs available. These tapes are priced far lower than similar video or computer programs. They range from cassettes of presentations made at national conferences by world-class experts to complete, well-designed self-instructional programs on technical or management skills.

For your own SDL packages, audiotape can provide a cost-effective alternative to straight paper-and-pencil packages. Interactive audio workbooks that present material on audiotape and exercises or drawings through a paper component have been around for a long time. They are still effective for many training needs.

Other Media. Depending on your packages' needs and the purpose(s) of your center, you might include slide-tape machines in your inventory. This hardware provides you with a simple way to add a visual component to your packages. Many of these machines are dual purpose, able to project slides for a group as well as suitable for self-study viewing in a carrel.

The concept of group processes brings up the need for earphones. One pair for each machine is mandatory. Your trainees will almost always have to use them to cut down on noise in the center, so buy ones that are comfortable if you want them to finish your packages . . . and come back. If you will have small groups of trainees using a package at the same time, you'll need an "earphone block" for hooking multiple earphones into one machine. They are inexpensive, though be sure you buy the type that has individual volume controls. These setups will mean extra earphones, too. You don't want to have to borrow earphones from another workstation so that it is put out of service to meet the needs of a group of trainees.

Other hardware possibilities include the aforementioned computers of various types for running CBT, interactive video stations, CD ROM augmentations, and the newest media format— multimedia. A point to keep in mind is that each of these hardware applications increases your setup costs, particularly if you need a number of them to meet the planned trainee usage of your center. They may give you certain advantages, but they also increase the complexity of your learning center from program identification to trainee evaluation.

Importance of Diversity in Media Hardware Selection. What I usually try to do, particularly when setting up a multipurpose center, is to include one or two of every form of hardware I can find and/or afford. This gives you added flexibility in package design and allows you to see which types of media your trainees are most comfortable with.

In centers where you plan a lot of individualized development, this method increases your ability to use the various inexpensive types of programs that are available for personal development from different sources. For example, the U.S. government puts out hundreds of personal development programs on many different topics, in various formats. Most of them are free or very inexpensive. If you have the equipment to run them on, you can build your center's stock of programs and thus its usefulness quickly by taking advantage of this and other program sources.

This diversifying is also not as expensive as you might think. Many companies have some or all of the equipment you want sitting around gathering dust. Slide projectors, audiotape recorders, even old "slow" computers that no one wants anymore can fit nicely in your center. While these machines may be someone else's castoffs, they are usually free and can often do a more than adequate training job. Suddenly, with little capital outlay, your center can offer programs such as computer software training. This is good for your trainees and great publicity for your center.

Furniture and hardware don't have to be so expensive that they become a roadblock to your learning center concept. It's nice to have a brand-new facility with beautiful carrels and the newest computer technology, but you can start small and work your way up. The purpose of a learning center is to meet training and trainee needs. If you can accomplish this, it will impress those you want and need to impress (maybe with a little judicious publicity), and your center will grow.

Obtaining Materials for Your Center

At first glance, this might seem to be a confusing title for a section on self-directed learning centers. From all our previous SDL analysis and development discussions, it would seem obvious that the materials you put into your center are the SDL packages you create. However, depending on the purpose of your center, you may include materials you didn't develop. In fact, even if you have a center whose purpose is very specific, you may want to consider adding programs that expand its reach. The capability is there, and as long as your center isn't running at capacity, adding other types of programs can only benefit your trainees and your company. But what programs should you include, and from where?

What Materials Might You Want for Your Center?

The *what* is more or less up to you. You may choose to include only programs that relate to your center's primary operating purpose. For example, if you have a center that is responsible for the technical skills training of nurses, you may add other programs that are health related. On the other hand, you may choose materials that broaden your center's purpose.

An example of this is the management development center from Chapter One that had branched out into secretarial skills training by adding a speed typing program and a videotape on filing procedures. The key here is to determine what professional or personal needs your trainees might have, usually by the simple expedient of asking them. You can do this either formally on a survey or informally as they come to the center. Then find materials that meet those needs and add them to your center.

A word of caution is in order. Once a center "catches on," you'll have many people (trainees, supervisors, other trainers) who want various programs purchased. Some departments will even provide funding when they see what a center will do for them. You must be careful to control this growth. New programs need to be previewed, catalogued, placed, and evaluated. This requires facilitator time, which becomes more and more limited as trainee use of the center grows. Uncontrolled acquisition will expand your center but will lower its quality. Take the time to purchase quality materials and introduce them in the center correctly.

What Sources Are Available?

Which brings up the second question, *where* do you get these programs? You don't want to develop them yourself, particularly if it takes time away from developing programs related to the main focus of your center. Therefore, you need to look for outside sources of programs and materials. And there are plenty of them!

Vendor-Developed, Off-the-Shelf Self-Instructional Programs. The large variety of self-instructional programs available from vendors best match a center concept. These programs can be found in various media formats ranging from simple print materials to CBT and interactive video. Depending on the company, they may teach a technical skill as specific as how to do a pump valve replacement or as general as how to become a speed reader. Such programs are designed to be used in an individualized setting such as a center. If they are good and meet your needs, they can help increase your stock of programs dramatically.

Industry-Specific Professional Organizations. Another good source of programs and program materials, particularly if your center's purpose is directly related to your particular industry, can be your industry-specific professional organizations. For example, the American Nursing Association has many filmstrip-based self-instructional packages on various nursing topics. The Institute for Nuclear Power Operations publishes self-study books on topics related to the nuclear industry. I know of these two groups from my own experience, but it's likely your industry-based professional organizations have the same type of programs.

Other Vendor-Developed, Off-the-Shelf Materials. Beyond programs specifically designed to be self-instructional, there are thousands of books, audiotapes, and videotapes that you can use in your center with minor or major modifications. Often the change is as simple as adding a print piece with objectives and questions to a good videotape. Sometimes you may want to edit a videotape to remove areas that are not relevant, or simply to shorten the program.

I once produced an entire management development series for a center using prerecorded videotapes from several different vendors. I simply edited them to reflect my company's needs, then added a print piece to each. When I was through, I had a nine-session video-based SDL management development program that played as if I'd developed it specifically for my organization. It took me less time to do the whole program than it would have taken to develop just one of the packages from scratch.

Sources of Computer-Based Programs. If you are using computers in your center, you further increase the types of materials you can add and the sources for finding them. The tutorials that come with software packages alone increase your program diversity. While not always the best, instructionally speaking, having these tools available to teach people how to use software, and for computer literacy in general, automatically increases the scope of your center.

How to Find the "Right Stuff." There are many vendors that put out various types of self-instructional programs or quasi-self-instructional materials. Some firms deal strictly with video; others have multiple media formats. My advice is that if you're thinking about prepackaged or outside vendor materials for your center, go to some of the big training conferences like ASTD, NSPI, Best of America, and so on. In their exposition areas, you can meet with almost every vendor who produces any type of program material. You'll pick up more catalogues than you can carry home in a suitcase.

Often the vendors will give you special preview prices on their programs at these "expos," so you can evaluate their products in detail back in the office. Some conferences have even begun continual showings of off-the-shelf videos as part of the conference programming.

Taking this concept one step further, the ASTD national

conference for the last few years has been running a learning center. In it, you can view vendor programs on your own time schedule. The center has volunteer facilitators who can help you learn more about learning centers and how to create them. You can do this while actually observing and using a live learning center.

Copyright Laws

One final word of caution concerning vendor materials and off-the-shelf programs. Copyright laws are very confusing in the United States; I suspect they are as complicated in other countries. When you are using a distributed SDL implementation, it seems clear to me that you must buy one copy of a video, computer, or other program for each training site—that is, unless you can make licensing arrangements. This is the reason I've cautioned against using prepackaged materials to any great extent in distributed implementations. The same problem exists if you are developing multiple learning centers.

However, if you have just one SDL center, the issue is a bit more clouded. Once I would have said that, as a minimum, you were entitled to make a copy of any media product so that you did not use, and possibly damage, your master. Some lawyers tell me this isn't even true anymore.

What is definitely true is that you should never use your master copy in the center. Keep all your masters in their own separate place (under lock and key is not going too far, in my opinion). The trainees should use copies. My advice is that before you purchase *any* prepackaged program or vendor material, check and see what they will allow you to do with it. Be honest and explain what you feel you need. The best of these companies are highly oriented toward customer service. They will do all they can to help you so that you remain a customer. Some companies will even guarantee overnight replacement of damaged programs at minimal cost.

If a vendor takes the hard line of "all you're buying is the master," I'd seriously consider whether this particular program is so unique that you can't find something as good elsewhere. In any case, be sure you know your rights and responsibilities before copying, editing, or otherwise changing vendor materials.

Staffing Your Self-Directed Learning Center

One of the major differences between a learning center implementation and a distributed SDL implementation is the presence of a full-time facilitator. We have discussed in detail what a site implementor does and doesn't do and some of the advantages of a full-time facilitator. From this information, you should have a fair idea of what a learning center facilitator does. We'll cover some of those advantages again as we look at what a facilitator actually does in your learning center.

Responsibilities of a Facilitator

Like site implementors, learning center facilitators are there to help the trainees. They are not instructors and are usually not even subject matter experts. Don't expect them to fill in where your programs are weak or to be able to answer complex questions about technical subjects.

They will be able to get trainees started on programs, help them learn to use the machines, and troubleshoot problems. They can control the flow of programs, administer written and some oral evaluations, and in their spare time even develop packages. For subject matter problems, they may be able to refer the trainee to an organizational subject matter expert.

A facilitator's duties will depend on your particular center and on the abilities of the facilitator. Some of the most common ones are the following:

- Handing out programs
- Performing maintenance on machines
- Monitoring program use
- Performing evaluations of the usefulness of the programs
- Evaluating possibilities for new programs
- Creating and updating the program catalogue
- Helping trainees
- Administering evaluations
- Developing new programs

Finding and Developing Facilitators

From this rudimentary job description, you can see that the facilitator must have a number of different skills. It's unlikely you'll find a candidate who has them all. In most cases, you'll be lucky to find a person with more than half of the background skills needed. Your alternative is to look for individuals who have the skills that come closest to what you feel you need in your center and then train them.

My best facilitators have always been bright, personable individuals who are fresh out of college from an HRD or communications curriculum. I look for someone who is not afraid to try new things, is energetic, and seems to like working with people. Most of all, I try to find people who want to learn. These newly minted trainers are usually glad to do some of the more mundane work associated with facilitating a center in return for a chance to try some of the interpersonal and instructional design skills they learned in college.

My worst facilitator was a very experienced instructional designer who I thought could handle the chores of the center easily and thus spend most of his time developing new packages. The problem was he quickly grew to resent the "intrusions" that the center and the trainees visited on his package designing. He was "a designer after all, not a computer mechanic." Fortunately, before the situation got too bad, I convinced my boss that we needed another person. I hired a new trainer who was more than glad to work in the center for the chance to learn SDL design. It turned out my ex-facilitator was a fine mentor for her as well, making both of them (and me) happy—at least for awhile, but that's another story.

This brings up the question of job levels and salaries for center facilitators. If you start small, you'll need your facilitator to be a fairly strong "jack of all trades." A specialist job level requiring a college degree will be called for. Your company will make the decision concerning how much you can pay based on this level and the degree. Make sure the position is exempt, or you'll have serious overtime problems.

If you grow to the point where you can hire a second person, you may want to look at a clerical-level individual. By now, your specialist will probably want relief from some of the clerical tasks of the center. You may need someone who is expert at filing, typing, and all those things that you and your specialist did on a catch-as-catch-can basis. Having two or three facilitators, all with the same skills and expectations, is seldom the best approach. I've seen it work but usually only in a very large center that had outside clerical support as well.

What a "Full-Time" Facilitator Really Means

In all of this, we have not discussed the most important descriptor that goes with learning center facilitator—the term *full time*. It is imperative that your facilitator position be just that, a position. It won't work as an adjunct to the other duties of another position, or as something done by a part-time employee. The facilitator's primary responsibility must be to the learning center, and a facilitator must be continually available whenever the center is open.

This doesn't mean that he or she must constantly be standing in or walking through the center. As I noted earlier, the best center arrangement provides the facilitators with a private office built with enough glass for them to see and be seen in. The office needs to be adjacent to the center if possible, not down the hall or around the corner. This allows the facilitator to watch for trainees needing help. More important, it allows the trainees to find the facilitator when needed. Your goal is to make things as easy as possible for your trainees, particularly in the beginning when they are learning to be self-directed (see Chapter Seven). Part of making it easy is to make the facilitators highly accessible whenever the trainees need them. This means the right physical setup and a full-time facilitator on duty.

Staffing for Extended Hours of Operation

If your center is open longer hours, you'll need more facilitators. There is no getting away from this. You can't decide that since fewer people use the center at certain times, you do not need someone there. If the center is open, a facilitator must be available.

This is the key to having an efficiently run learning center, and one that is too often ignored.

One of the best center staffing processes I've seen was for a center that was open sixteen hours a day. It was staffed by four facilitators. These facilitators rotated the night and morning shifts so that no one had to do them all the time. At peak times (there were twenty-four stations, so peak times were really peak), two or even three facilitators were on duty. At other times, only one was available. However, at 6:00 in the morning when the center opened, there was a facilitator on duty to answer questions or administer exams. And at 11:00 P.M. when it closed, a trained facilitator did the closing—not a janitor, as I found in another situation.

What a Facilitator Does When Not Facilitating

The above situation was efficient because the off-duty facilitators spent the rest of their work time writing and revising the center's packages. This is usually an important aspect of a facilitator's job. Few centers require the facilitator to be constantly engaged in actual center responsibilities. In most of the ones I've run or observed, I doubt if 50 percent of the facilitators' time was spent on center tasks. The other 50 percent—or even 20 percent, if it's a busy center—can be spent working on new center programs, as long as the facilitator is physically available if a trainee needs something. This not only makes effective use of the facilitator's time, but also can double as professional development for the novice facilitator who is learning instructional design or SDL development.

The alternative to this is to have the facilitators sitting around waiting for something to happen or working on nonrelated projects such as stuffing envelopes. I actually saw one case in which, like a security guard on night shift, the facilitator sat back and read novels until a trainee needed attention. This is a tremendous waste of capability and diminishes not only the efficiency of your center but the position of the facilitator as well.

You need a full-time facilitator to make your center work properly. Hire the right person, train him or her carefully, provide avenues for professional growth, and your full-time facilitator can be that and a lot more. Just don't forget that a facilitator's first responsibility is always to the center and the trainees it serves.

Operating a Self-Directed Learning Center

The actual running of your center requires plenty of planning and advance decision making concerning a number of variables.

Hours of Operation

The first of these is the center's hours of operation. There are two concerns here: what your trainees need and your ability to provide facilitators. Many centers—particularly those with a personal development component—find it best to be open after or even before normal work hours. Those centers that run in a shift-work environment often need to be open before and after all shifts. Lunchtime is an excellent time for people to use your center. Closing it so your staff can all go to lunch together is not normally a good practice. You need to decide what hours best fit your trainee population needs, then plan your center schedule to meet them.

Sometimes this means that facilitators must work strange shifts, but there are often people available who might like or need different hours. I once worked as a facilitator in a center that was open from 7:00 A.M. to 9:00 P.M. Because I was going to school at the time and it fit my schedule, I arranged with the boss to come in at 7:00 and open the center. I went to classes during the midday and then worked from 5:00 to 9:00 to close the center. My colleagues loved this system, since they didn't have to come in early or work late, and it helped me get a degree.

Learning Cart as an Answer to Shift Operation. A special problem with hours of operation occurs in shift environments, particularly if mandatory training is going to occur in the center. These centers need to be open during all shifts. Yet few individuals will use them during second and especially third shifts, which are often understaffed. However, if it is open, the center must have a facilitator on duty. A cost-effective solution for this situation is the use of a *learning cart.*

This cart is simply a wheeled transport cart of no particular type that has shelves for holding some packages and one or two pieces of equipment. The carts are stocked with the mandatory programs and taken directly to the job site, where they are used as needed by the shift workers when they have the time. In the morning, the facilitator retrieves the carts and programs and puts them back in the center for day-shift use.

There are several problems with this method, not the least of which is that it is cumbersome. However, in certain situations it can be a lot easier and more efficient than staffing the center for three shifts.

One of the biggest concerns is that there will be no facilitator with the cart. Thus, the SDL packages and the directions for using the machines will have to be *very complete*. Learning carts are actually a distributed implementation, with all the attendant problems and advantages. You might even develop site implementors for the carts. These individuals would be responsible for procuring the carts for their area and for doing other site implementor tasks, as necessary. Use the concept if you need it, but be aware of its limitations and design differences.

Carefully determine the hours of operation you need, find the right staff to meet them, then post them *and keep them*. Nothing destroys confidence in a center quicker than a trainee finding it isn't open when it is scheduled to be, when he or she is ready to learn.

Sending Your Programs Home with Employees. Another consideration, both for shift workers and at other times, is allowing your programs to go home with trainees. Many people have video or audio machines at home for program replay. Certain reading-type programs, and even computer programs, can be used at home as easily as in a center. However, the problem of the lack of a facilitator still exists with this process. You've also inherited all the problems associated with a lending library, such as programs not being returned, coming back late, or getting lost.

My recommendation is to make it a policy that programs do not leave the center except officially on learning carts. Exceptions to the policy can be made on an individual basis, but only for a very good reason. If your center is open the proper number of hours, there should be little reason for trainees to take programs home, except in emergencies.

Scheduling to Control Trainee Flow in the Center

As part of your decision on hours of operation, you considered when the trainees needed to use the center. You also must consider how many trainees will be using it at any time—or what I call *trainee flow and control*. If you have a large center with plenty of every type of machine, this is not a problem. However, if you are like most of us, there are limits to your center's ability to handle trainees. These limits may be especially important when you add a new program that is going to be very popular or that is mandatory for a large group of trainees.

Scheduling Policy. My advice is that from the first day your center is open, you make it a policy that trainees can and should schedule times for machines and programs. They should be able to do this by stopping in the center or by phone. The time-consuming nature of scheduling by phone is another justification for a full-time facilitator.

Trainees should not be wasting time continually trying to reach someone in the center. I have often used an answering machine to back up the facilitators in case they are busy. In that way, one call is all a trainee needs to make, and the procedure was that if we didn't call back, you were to consider yourself scheduled.

The key to scheduling is not to demand it, but to make it a policy that the scheduled person receives first priority. Thus if non-scheduled trainees "drop in," they are free to use whatever they want, as long as they realize that they must vacate when a scheduled user arrives. This allows for flexibility and control at the same time.

Maintaining Schedules. There are any number of ways to maintain schedules. I've seen papers or erasable tablets at each workstation and sign-up sheets at the facilitator's desk or on a bulletin board in the center. I once tried sign-up sheets in the hall outside the center so those scheduling times would not disturb the center. This didn't work well, since we had a number of complaints concerning unauthorized erasures. If your scheduling needs to match trainees, programs, and equipment, you may need to have the facilitator control the schedule directly.

The newest technology is computer scheduling, kept by the facilitator and printed out each morning. Those who have used this technique report that the programs seem to work quite well. One problem with this method is that if the facilitator is using the computer for other purposes, stopping to call up the schedule can be a nuisance. Multitasking programs like Windows can solve this, but it is still an interruption.

Programs are available that not only schedule but that also keep track of trainee time in the center, grades on evaluations, individual development activities, program usage, and any number of other variables. Characteristics to look for include the following:

- Easy to use
- Quick to view
- Provide enough room for all the necessary information
- Have safeguards to prevent duplicate bookings
- Have multitasking capability

Sign-in Sheets. Another variable is whether or not you want to use a sign-in sheet for your center. Sign-in sheets are not part of, nor do they replace, your scheduling process. Their purpose is to keep track of center usage, either by total number of trainees, number of trainees per program, or number per machine. Managers also find the review of sign-in sheets useful to find out which of their staff are attending training. This is actually an evaluation process, and we'll discuss it in more detail in the next section. However, the decision to use a sign-in sheet, and the form you need, should be considered as part of your center operations planning.

Making Package Location Simple for Trainees

Once your trainees are in the center, the next step is for them to find the proper program. Again, this requires detailed planning. If they know what they want, it becomes a matter of simply finding the right package. However, if they are not sure or are just browsing, you need a system for them to find out what is in the center.

A booklet that lists the center's programs is useful, but I've found the best approach is some type of card catalogue.

Card Catalogue. Your entries in the card catalogue should contain the name of the program, possible uses, a brief synopsis, hardware needs, special equipment or supply needs, and average length of time for completion. If you have a self-service center, it also might provide direction on how to find the program. An example of a card that I've found useful can be seen in Exhibit 11.1.

Your card catalogue system can be useful for providing program and material information to the center facilitator as well, particularly if he or she is new to the job. I have even seen systems where the card catalogue's basic purpose was to provide information to the facilitators. It was their task to locate the programs and get the trainee started correctly.

Ease of Location as a Function of Package Storage. This brings up the variable of package storage that we mentioned while discussing learning center furniture. The important points to remember here are security and accessibility, which unfortunately are somewhat opposite in nature. You need to ensure that your programs do not walk away yet at the same time make them accessible to the trainees with minimum waiting.

I've seen centers where every package was behind closed doors, much like the rare books section of a library. The trainees had to ask the facilitator for the program, then sign a card testifying that they had received it. Each package had to be returned to the facilitator, who stamped the card "returned." You can see the problems that might develop in having to wait for a facilitator who was busy with something else.

On the other hand, I ran a center in an old library where the packages were on shelves that were accessible to all. The trainees found the program number using the card catalogue system, went to the proper shelf to retrieve the program, and sat down to use it. When finished, they returned the programs to the same shelf (sometimes, and therein lies a problem with this method).

You can decide to do something between these extremes—perhaps have only the programs that are "most likely to leave" on a request basis or have the facilitator reshelve the programs. Getting more high tech, you might use a security system such as many

Exhibit 11.1. Sample Card in a Card Catalogue.

CATALOGUE FILE CARD

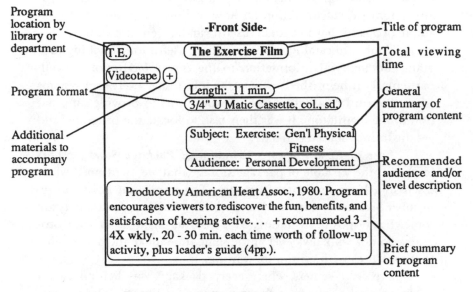

Program location by library or department

-Front Side-

Title of program

T.E.   The Exercise Film

Videotape +

Program format

Length: 11 min.

3/4" U Matic Cassette, col., sd.

Total viewing time

General summary of program content

Additional materials to accompany program

Subject: Exercise: Gen'l Physical Fitness

Audience: Personal Development

Recommended audience and/or level description

Produced by American Heart Assoc., 1980. Program encourages viewers to rediscover the fun, benefits, and satisfaction of keeping active. . . + recommended 3 - 4X wkly., 20 - 30 min. each time worth of follow-up activity, plus leader's guide (4pp.).

Brief summary of program content

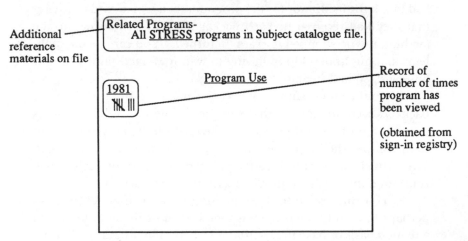

-Back Side-

Additional reference materials on file

Related Programs-
     All STRESS programs in Subject catalogue file.

Program Use

1981
卌 III

Record of number of times program has been viewed

(obtained from sign-in registry)

libraries have installed. I saw a center where they combined the instant access of open shelves with a magnetic security system. Reshelving was done by a facilitator to make sure the programs got back to where they belonged. This seemed to be working quite well.

Directions for Using the Center

There are several kinds of directions you need to consider developing to help your trainees use your center more efficiently.

General Directions. The first of these is the posting of general directions for the center's use. Instructions on filling out sign-in sheets, information on how to procure programs, and your scheduling policy should be stated on these posters. Your food and drink policy is another item for your poster. My recommendation is none, ever, and you know why if you've seen what a spilled Coke can do to a $5,000 computer. On your poster, or on the door, or better yet in both places, trainees should also find your hours of operation.

Program Directions. Directions specific to a single program or group of programs should be easy to find. Post them on the shelf or tape them to the program cover and make sure they're on your card catalogue cards, too. Special equipment or the need for a special type of machine to run the program are two items that should be included with program-specific directions.

Directions for Using Machines. Speaking of machines, directions for operation should be prominently displayed next to each machine. This will help reduce your facilitators' work load and make the trainees feel more self-directed as well. Be sure to disable, cover, or otherwise place off-limits buttons on machines that you do not want trainees to manipulate. There are always backyard mechanics in any group who like to "find out what these things do."

Center Orientation(s)

To augment your written directions, you may choose to have a formal orientation when a trainee uses the center for the first time. The orientation should cover all the "where's and how to's," as well as a little information on the purpose of the center and the SDL process. These orientations are most often handled by the facilitator on a one-to-one basis.

However, I have seen *Welcome to the Center* SDL packages that the new trainees use to go through all of the center's aspects on their own. I like this approach because it gets the trainees right into SDL, but you need to design it carefully. If you use it, you might consider having the facilitator administer a final quiz that certifies the trainee as ready to work in the center. This is the right time to check knowledge and answer questions, to make sure your trainees get off to a good start.

Center Start-Up Orientations. If you're just starting up your center, you might want to have group orientations at specific times. These are actually more useful for explaining and selling the center's capabilities than for training the trainees on how to use it, so we'll discuss them in the next section, which is concerned with publicity.

Publicizing Your Center

Every center needs publicity when it begins, and later as it expands and increases its capabilities as well. The more purposes and programs your center encompasses, the more publicity you need to make them all effective. Development centers in particular need to keep publicizing their capabilities to reach as many potential customers as possible as their needs change.

Publicity at the Start. Center initiation publicity can take many forms. The group orientation mentioned earlier is one of them. Consider how you might organize your groups to design orientations that are specific to their interests.

A *top-management* orientation, where they can see in action what they approved and backed with corporate funds, is always a good idea.

A *managers'* orientation spends time discussing the efficiency and effectiveness of SDL and the learning center concept. It should be aimed at convincing managers to go back and recommend the center to their supervisors.

A *supervisors'* orientation might focus on their part in allowing their employees to come to the center, as well as on what they themselves can get from it.

In *department-specific* orientations, questions about what future center programs can be developed to benefit each department are in order.

Corporate Newsletter. If you have a corporate newspaper or newsletter, you'll want to publicize your new center or new programs by that method as well. If the editor will agree, an issue devoted to the center, with pictures and quotes from users, is excellent publicity. Fliers on bulletin boards and in the lunchroom that announce your center's opening are also productive.

Lunchtime Publicity. One of the most effective publicity processes I have ever used also had to do with the lunchroom. Just after the center opened, we began a series of "brown bag lunch" seminars. For these seminars, interested individuals would bring their lunch to a particular room one day a week.

In the room, we played various programs from the center. Some were followed by a discussion and some were not, depending on the topic. Of course, it was always mentioned that this program and others like it were available at the center. We were careful to pick programs that were of broad interest and entertaining as well. We announced the schedule and room by means of fliers posted in the cafeteria. The idea was a great success, not only for publicizing the center but also for the development of the people who took part. It helped us acquire new ideas for center programs.

Center Program Booklet. House newspapers, fliers, and brown bag seminars are also useful tools for continuing center publicity, as is the publication of a center program booklet. This booklet can be as simple as a list by title of available programs. On the other hand, it might include a synopsis of each program, its intended audience, and its objectives.

That last item can be very useful. It's surprising how many people come to a center by management decree, or due to word-of-mouth publicity, without knowing what the program they are requesting really teaches. Send your booklet to all managers, department heads, and so on, and maybe a few special copies to your best center customers.

If you do opt for a more complex book, keep the binding

simple. A strong, growing center will be adding programs often, and revisions will be necessary. Quarterly revisions, or in some cases revisions every other month, are a good idea. They keep your listing current and provide continuing shots of publicity. I always like to spotlight a few of the newest or most popular programs on the first pages of every issue. This gives first-time readers ideas on what they may want to look for when they get into the listing itself.

There is a lot to think about in operating a learning center and many decisions to make long before your doors ever open. I've tried to touch on the most common aspects, but each center will have its own needs. The key, as usual, is to plan in advance. Running a center is never as simple as it seems, and some early thought will save you a lot of headaches later.

Evaluating a Center

The last aspect of operating a learning center—one that is often overlooked until it's too late—is evaluation. No matter how good your center is, sooner or later someone is going to ask the most important question, "Is it worth it?" If you wait until this question is asked to find the answer, you've already lost some credibility. You need to develop a plan to evaluate your center and its programs as part of your normal operations. As in a distributed SDL, there are two factors to consider. For this type of implementation, we'll term them *package evaluation* and *center evaluation*.

Package Evaluation

Package evaluation in a learning center is much like package evaluation in a distributed implementation. You need to consider package effectiveness as your main evaluation measure. One of the important indicators you look for in package effectiveness is transfer of knowledge and skills to the job.

Evaluating Job Transfer as an Indicator of Package Effectiveness. This was a much easier process to evaluate in a distributed system, since the supervisors were usually well aware of what the packages taught. Often they functioned as site implementors or evaluators. Thus, they could easily tell you if the knowledge and skills presented in the packages were transferred to the job.

In a learning center implementation, evaluation of job transfer is not as easy. The packages are not done on the job. The supervisors, unless they go through them personally, have little idea what they contain. So evaluating transfer is not as simple as just asking the supervisors. You or your facilitators will need to go out to the job site and check transfer for yourself.

You can accomplish this in several ways, though I prefer to talk directly with both supervisors and trainees. I ask them specific, directed questions concerning what a package covered and if it is being used on the job. Whatever approach you choose to evaluate transfer, remember that in a learning center environment, only the package developer, and perhaps the facilitator, will know enough about the package to be able to ask proper transfer-type evaluation questions.

Evaluating Trainee Learning for Package Effectiveness. On the other hand, direct evaluation of trainee learning, as a measure of package effectiveness, is much easier in a learning center. Your trained facilitator can monitor, correct, and analyze both tests and the completion of performances. This provides you with a much more controlled evaluation situation than you have in a distributed environment.

To achieve this, however, you will need to have facilitator time available. One facilitator, trying to cope with trainee traffic, scheduling, and evaluation of new packages, will have very few hours left to devote to trainee evaluation.

Center Evaluation

Total center evaluation rests on the combination of package effectiveness in trainee learning and transfer, which we've just discussed, and overall efficiency in performing its function.

Center Efficiency. Efficiency considers how much the center is being used and whether this makes it the most cost-effective method of doing what it's doing. We've already mentioned an evaluation mechanism for usage: the sign-in sheet. Many people scoff at this process, calling it a "warm-body evaluation," but it can be useful.

It definitely will provide you with one of the things that is hardest to find in any training evaluation, quantifiable data.

You can use your sign-in sheet strictly as a measure of how many people visit your center, or you can focus it. Items such as how many trainees use a particular program, a particular category of program, or for expansion purposes, a particular machine, can provide useful data if part of the sign-in sheet process.

The focus and complexity of the sign-in process depend on you and your needs. I've used ones as simple as a name and a time-in/time-out column, and as complex as additional columns for programs, type of machine, and learning objectives. They can be at the door of the center, next to each machine, or on each program. I've seen centers where even the sign-in sheet is computerized.

Whatever the mechanism, the purpose is to get data on center usage. You can manipulate this data to show hours of training per trainee, cost per hour of training, or what is and is not being done in your center.

Another instrument for gathering data on center efficiency is the opinionnaire. Opinionnaires have drawbacks, but for a center, they can be useful. Measurements of trainee satisfaction with the training process are acceptable evaluation parameters in most situations. When combined with the evaluation parameters we've already discussed, they can be part of a valid training center evaluation.

Opinionnaires also might be used to detect trainee satisfaction with specific training programs, for center service satisfaction, and to gather data on what new programs may be needed. I consider these purposes as being more valid for an opinionnaire mechanism, but if you need quick data for a center efficiency evaluation, opinionnaires may suffice.

In the final analysis, when you are looking at center efficiency, what you are talking about is a cost-benefit analysis: How many people are we training and for how long, for the dollars we are expending. Throw in package effectiveness and you have a fair evaluation that answers the key question "Should the center continue?" Is it of enough benefit to the organization to continue funding it?

This is a question of continuing budget, which, in the end, is what all evaluation comes down to in a business environment. It is based on how well the center is functioning and what the continuing needs are. It should consider how much can be spent for new equipment, replacement equipment, new programs, machine maintenance, salaries, and if you want to get down to the real basics, operations expenses like space, electricity, and other overhead items.

Kearsley (1982) simplifies this entire process into three steps: calculate costs, calculate benefits, and compare the results.

A good cost-benefit analysis will say to you and to those who must make the final decision, "This center concept is working, it does its job well, and we should put this much more in the way of resources into continuing and expanding it," or "The idea isn't right for us and should be terminated," or "The idea is right but has grown as far as it needs to. It should be continued but not expanded."

Which of these answers your evaluation presents will depend on how well you analyzed your training needs, whether you picked a proper design, the care with which you developed your packages, your choice of the correct implementation strategy, and your ability to evaluate properly. In other words, it depends on your expertise in creating SDL.

Exhibit 11.2. A Checklist for SDL.

Operating a Learning Center

☐ An acceptable location for the learning center has been found.

☐ Adequate furniture has been purchased.
  • Special consideration has been given to chairs.

☐ Storage space is sufficient.

☐ Lighting, HVAC, and interior decoration have been considered.

☐ Electrical needs have been fulfilled.

☐ Hardware requirements have been satisfied.
  • Diversity in media formats has been attempted.

☐ Prepackaged materials have been obtained where possible.

☐ Facilitators have been appointed.
  • Staffing will be continuous.

☐ Hours of operation have been set.
  • Contingencies for shift workers have been developed.

☐ Scheduling policy and procedures have been set.
  • A decision on sign-in sheets has been made.

☐ A card catalogue system or its equivalent has been developed.

☐ The mechanism by which trainees obtain packages is functional.

☐ Center directions have been posted.

☐ Program directions accompany programs where needed.

☐ Directions for using machines have been posted.

☐ A center orientation for new users has been developed.

☐ Center initation publicity has been done.
  • Group initial orientations have been done.
  • The corporate newsletter has been used.
  • A center program booklet has been developed.

☐ Center evaluation mechanisms have been developed.
  • Package effectiveness via job transfer has been considered.
  • Evaluation of trainee learning has been systematized.
  • Center efficiency evaluation through use of sign-in sheets and opinionnaires has been considered.
  • Enough data are available for a center cost-benefit analysis.

12

The Best It Can Be

Evaluating and Improving
Your Self-Directed Learning System

When we discussed trainee evaluation, we mentioned that the other half of evaluation in SDL is concerned with your SDL system as a whole. This system might be one package or many packages that you've separated into classes, courses, or even a year-long curriculum. In Chapter Eleven, we considered how to evaluate your learning center and/or the packages contained in it. This chapter will take the evaluation process one step further by considering how to evaluate your entire SDL system (Figure 12.1).

Since we are talking about a system again, this discussion will be pointed toward a distributed SDL process. However, you will recognize some of the evaluation criteria as having been covered in our learning center discussions. The evaluation methodology as a whole can be used, with minor modifications, for both SDL implementations, and it should be if you wish to fully evaluate your SDL plan.

Theoretical Basis for Self-Directed Learning

While our division of SDL evaluation into the two major areas of trainee evaluation and package or system evaluation would seem to be logical, there is some disagreement about this approach. Kirkpatrick (1977) defends it and describes these procedures as the verification of the results of instruction (validation) and the long-term benefits of training to the organization (evaluation). Romiszowski (1986), on the other hand, feels that such distinctions are not

Figure 12.1. A Model for SDL.

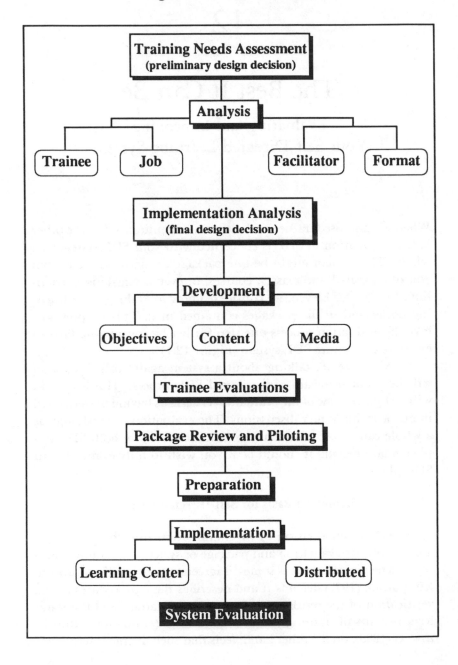

useful, because the real measure is *value* to the organization or the learner. He further refines the concept of value in terms of materials evaluation, technical and instructional validity, student reaction, costs, and a number of other factors. Rowntree (1986) discards the term *evaluation* completely and details the process of formative and summative assessments of, for, and by the trainees. His program evaluation methodology seems to end when the materials reach the trainees. Boud and Falchikov (1989) disagree, considering self-assessment to be little more than grade guessing. Hammond and Collins (1991) specifically note a lack of clarity in the literature concerning assessment and evaluation. They go on to distinguish between evaluation (self, peer, client) and learning validation, which, according to Loacker and Doherty (1984), requires the demonstration of a skill in at least two other settings.

Such varied opinions on even the most basic concepts of SDL evaluation create confusion for any instructional designer who is attempting to evaluate an SDL system or package. For simplicity's sake and to at least establish a starting point, it is a convenient if not a perfect solution to return to our previous notion of dividing SDL evaluation into trainee and system aspects.

SDL System Evaluation

Your system evaluation must be developed to answer one simple question: *Does the SDL system work?* The question is simple, but finding the answer is not. There are many variables that affect this determination. The data you need to collect will depend on your system and the corporate environment in which your training functions.

Self-Directed Learning and Cost-Benefit Analysis

This brings up the issue of cost-benefit analysis—a topic mentioned in the previous chapter in relation to learning centers and continuing budgets. This type of approach is also valid for SDL system evaluation. Romiszowski (1986) refers to it as analysis of value.

As in the learning center discussion, the reason for a cost-benefit analysis is often created by the need your boss or the corporation has to make sure that resources are being invested wisely.

Once again, we are not going to go into CBA and its alter ego ROI (return on investment) in detail. There are good sources for both these concepts in the Suggested Readings. I highly recommend the *Info-line* on CBA for a quick review and Kearsley's book for an in-depth approach.

SDL has no real advantage over other training formats when it comes to the cost part of a cost-benefit analysis. You are not talking about simple comparison of cost-effectiveness in this case, but rather a structured assessment of the actual cost of producing SDL. This cost, as we have already discussed at length in the preceding chapters, depends on your development time and implementation strategy. Both of the previously mentioned resources provide excellent case studies for figuring costs. If you substitute the SDL costs we've isolated for those itemized in the examples, you should arrive at a valid cost figure.

However, SDL does have what I consider to be a distinct advantage in the benefits calculation. Basically, the benefit question is simply a restatement of the primary evaluation question "Does the training work?" This is true because in proper SDL construction, appropriately assessed and analyzed training needs have been met by training that is suitably job-task based and effectively implemented. In other words, if you've done your SDL design, development, and implementation well, you should be confident in saying that if the training works, the resources have been wisely allocated and the company is receiving proper value from the training.

You then only need to compare your costs to this benefit of meeting training needs to complete your cost-benefit analysis. The rest of system evaluation will be concerned with answering the question "Does the SDL work?" so that you can decide if the benefit is real.

Criteria for a Self-Directed Learning System Evaluation

To get this answer, you need to set up an evaluation process that fits your particular SDL system. However, you must be as objective as possible in designing it. Your process and so your data will be skewed if you go into your evaluation with too many preconceived notions of what you think you will find.

The evaluation of training in a business environment is more often than not a matter of opinionnaires and other forms of "feel good" instruments. Occasionally some testing is done to monitor the trainees' progress, but in the majority of training systems, "Did you feel the course was useful?" and "Did the instructor do a good job?" are the main evaluative queries.

In SDL, where there is no instructor to "feel good" about and where the usefulness of a particular set of skills or knowledge may not become apparent for a period of time, this opinionnaire evaluation methodology is not particularly relevant. There is some question as to its relevance for any training design, but its limitations make it decidedly useless for SDL evaluation, except in limited circumstances such as those discussed earlier for learning center evaluation.

To create a useful yet unbiased evaluation process for your SDL system, you must base it on the way the packages were designed. I'll exemplify this concept by taking you through the steps of an evaluation process I developed for a distributed SDL system that was based on the ISD process.

One problem with basing evaluation on ISD is that ISD is not a linear approach, contrary to what many people think. It is more a series of overlapping circles that intersect at various points as you analyze, design, develop, implement, and evaluate what your training and training materials are or should be.

However, in developing this particular methodology, I tried to match each of the five phases of ISD to an evaluation criterion. I ended up with five criteria that I feel cover the spectrum of decisions concerning SDL. And in its simplest form, the purpose of an SDL system evaluation is to evaluate the decisions you made during the other phases of the methodology. The most basic and important of these is "Did I choose the right training intervention?"—or once again, *Does it work?*

I don't always use this methodology in its entirety as presented here. Depending on my implementation strategy and what I think the company wants to or needs to know, I may enhance one criterion and diminish others. With modifications for the implementation strategy, such as those discussed in Chapters Nine and Eleven, I've found this process applicable in most SDL scenarios.

Sufficiency. The first criterion is *sufficiency,* which simply stated asks the question "Is all the information that needs to be out there, out there?" Sufficiency is actually evaluating your analysis phase of the SDL model, particularly your job analysis. There are two levels to sufficiency. The first is the package level, which evaluates the sufficiency of material in each of your packages. The second is the system level, which evaluates the sufficiency of the total amount of material in your system. To illustrate system sufficiency: if you have twelve packages available on twelve different topics but there is one topic that you missed, this evaluation should tell you what that topic is.

General system sufficiency evaluation is most important in a distributed SDL implementation where the packages are normally part of an integrated system. However, it is applicable in a learning center environment as well, particularly if the learning center is fulfilling the role of an assessment and/or management development facility. In this case, it almost takes on the aspect of a needs evaluation.

Key sufficiency question. Sufficiency evaluations can be simple. There is really only one question you need to ask at either level. At the package level, the question should be something like, "Is all the information necessary to master this topic contained in the package?" You ask this for each package. At the system level, as you might suspect, the question is much the same: "Are there any topics (tasks, areas, procedures, and so on) missing from the training system as a whole?" As I said, you probably asked these questions a dozen times during the analysis phase (if you didn't, you should have). What you're doing now is evaluating, from experience, whether or not your assessment was correct.

Who do you ask? You can make the process more formalized—or at least can make it look more formal—by breaking down your questions into smaller parts. However, you will rarely need to ask for information at this level of detail, as long as you ask the right people in the first place. For a package evaluation, the right people are those that have done the package and have been performing the tasks it specifies for a significant period—that is, your trainees. This means a little research to ferret out these people before you ask the question, but that research will make the data you gather more valid. Just a word of caution: when I say research here, I mean real "go and find out for yourself" research. Don't trust supervisors, managers, or anyone else to give you the right people for your evaluation, particularly if you think they might have a stake in the answers you get. For a sufficiency evaluation, I once asked managers to supply the names of five trainees who had completed the package and were doing the tasks it taught as part of their daily work. The answers the trainees gave to my evaluation question were so disparate that I personally visited each one. I found that only about half met my simple criterion. When I asked the managers why, they told me they didn't want it to get back to their bosses that they weren't doing enough training! This information was not the purpose of the evaluation, though it was interesting. I don't want to tell you not to trust anyone other than yourself to find the right evaluation subjects, but . . .

You also can ask your facilitator or implementators for information in a sufficiency evaluation, but only if they are subject matter experts who have gone through the package. What you get from them will probably not be as valid as what you get from the real users. However, it often provides a different perspective.

For a sufficiency system evaluation, the users should not be your first choice. Often they don't have the breadth of knowledge to know what's missing overall. Supervisors, managers, and administrators are the people you need to hear from in this case. Your facilitator/implementors might be able to add something as well.

Methods for evaluating sufficiency. The method for doing a sufficiency evaluation depends on how you designed it. If you are using the one-question approach, personal visits or telephone calls work well. This also gives you a chance to ask follow-up questions if needed and to check on the reliability of your evaluators. If you decide to expand the questions to get more detail, a paper-and-pencil instrument will probably be the way to go. This is a pretty straightforward opinionnaire process.

Exhibit 12.1 illustrates an example of a more-or-less formal data gathering instrument for this criteria. It can be used for managers, site implementors, or trainees.

Exhibit 12.1. SDL Package Questionnaire.

Place an X in the box next to the ones you've completed.	Now that you've completed the packages, tell us if there is any information missing from each SDL that you feel would be helpful to a new employee.
☐ *Orientation*	
☐ *Interstore Transfers*	
☐ *Merchandising*	
☐ *Ordering*	
☐ *Order Receiving*	
☐ *Outside Vendors*	
☐ *Photofinishing*	
☐ *Recalls*	

Usability. The second criterion for an SDL system evaluation is *usability*. The main question for a usability evaluation is "Are the packages as easy to use as possible?" This process is a general look at the overall design of your system and the individual packages.

Who and what do you ask? Since you are investigating how

easy your packages are for the users to use, it seems pretty obvious that you should ask the users. No problem with picking subjects here; anyone who has completed the package will do. What you will ask depends a lot on how you designed your package and what you want to know. There is no singular general question as was the case with the sufficiency criterion. Queries such as "How hard is the package to read?"; "Did you have trouble getting the necessary supplies?"; "Were the exercises difficult to complete?"; and "Did you like the layout of the package?" are all good possibilities. Exhibit 12.2 illustrates a simple checklist that a trainee might complete for gathering data on this criterion.

Currency. The third evaluation criterion is *currency*. An account friend of mine who happened to read parts of this manuscript saw this criteria and said, "Ah, Now you're getting down to the important stuff, the cost!" He was a little off the mark. The question for currency is "Are the materials in your packages up to date, or current?" Needless to say my disappointed accountant friend read no further when he saw the question. Currency entails looking at the material that you wrote during the development of your SDL.

Key currency question. As with sufficiency, this is more-or-less a one-question evaluation: "Is the information up to date?" Though you need to ask it for each package separately, it can easily be handled by the phone call or personal visit method. The important thing here is to again be careful about who you phone or visit. Your users are unlikely to know if the information is up to date unless someone has told them. Even supervisors and managers might not know what changes have been made unless your company is very good at communications.

Who do you ask? The people you want to ask the currency question are those responsible for making changes and informing others of them. This may be administration, or operations, or even accounting (don't tell them it's a currency evaluation). You need to do pre-evaluation planning again, to find out who these decision makers are at the right level.

Those last four words are critical. "At the right level" means people who know what changes might have occurred but are also close enough to the process that they can tell you what those changes mean and how they affect your packages. Every company

Exhibit 12.2. Store Associate Questionnaire.

This survey is designed to give the Training Department an idea of how the self-directed learning packages are working. There are no right or wrong answers to these questions; just tell us how they work in your store.

1.   Are the packages easy to read?   Yes ☐   No ☐

2.   Are the instructions in the SDL packages clear and easy to follow?   Yes ☐   No ☐

3.   Were the activities and practice exercises "doable" in your store?   Yes ☐   No ☐

4.   Did the activities and practice exercises help you perform the actual task?   Yes ☐   No ☐

5.   Did the objectives give you a clear picture of what you were to know and be able to do at the end of the package?   Yes ☐   No ☐

6.   On the average, how long does it take you complete an SDL? _____

7.   Are you usually able to complete an SDL from start to finish without interruptions?   Yes ☐   No ☐

8.   How often does the Store Manager check on your progress when you're completing an SDL?

   _____

9.   Where do you usually go to complete the SDL? _____

   _____

10.   When you finish an SDL, does the Store Manager watch you perform the procedure before you're expected to do it on your own?   Yes ☐   No ☐

---

has these individuals. You seldom find them at the top of the organization chart; often they are not even in managerial positions. However, they are the ones responsible for making changes happen, so they will be able to tell you if your material is current. They also can be useful for helping revise your material, but that's a topic for the next section. At any rate, when you find the right people, ask them the question. Your currency evaluation begins here.

Compliance. The fourth criterion is *compliance.* Your concern here is to find out if your packages are being employed the way you expected them to be—in other words, whether they are being implemented according to plan.

Who and what to ask. The questions you ask for a compliance evaluation will depend on which implementation strategy you are using. However, who you ask the questions of should be about the same for both—normally the users and the facilitators or implementors.

Questions for the user should be related to those you asked them for the usability criteria. However, direct the questions now toward the system as a whole. You're looking for information on whether they were able to obtain the packages, whether they were given the time to use them, whether they were able to do the activities adequately, and so on. In simple terms, are they able to use the SDL packages as they were told to use them, or are there mechanical obstacles to this process?

Since there will be several factors that you'll want to check, depending on your system and particularly on your implementation format, the most logical approach will be a written questionnaire of some type. Give it to any user who has been engaged in your system for a long enough period to make his or her comments valid.

The other individuals that can give you data in a compliance evaluation are your facilitators or implementors. Though you'll frame your questions differently, they'll have much the same general purpose as the central question asked of the trainees: "Are the SDL packages being implemented as planned?" In a learning center approach, this may turn out to be a simple usage ratio, unless you have a special assessment center or some other similar system in your center. For distributed implementation, this takes on much greater significance, a discussion of which can be found in the section on evaluating distributed SDL system in Chapter Nine.

Exhibit 12.3 illustrates a compliance questionnaire used to gather data from site implementors in a distributed SDL implementation.

Effectiveness. The final system evaluation criterion is *effectiveness.* Effectiveness evaluation involves posing the following question: "Have the trainees mastered the objectives of the package?" In other words, have they learned what your analysis indi-

Exhibit 12.3. Store Manager Questionnaire.

This survey is designed to give the Training Department an idea of how the self-directed learning packages are working. There are no right or wrong answers to these questions; just tell us how they work in your store.

1. Look again at the list of SDL topics and tell us if there are any additional topics that should become an SDL.

    _____

    _____

    _____

2. What is the average length of time it takes an employee to complete an SDL package?

    _____

    _____

3. Do your employees complete an SDL from start to finish without interruptions?

    _____

    _____

4. Do your employees complete all activities and practice exercises contained in the SDLs?

    _____

    _____

5. How often do you check on employees while they are completing SDLs?

    _____

    _____

6. Where do you have employees go to complete an SDL?

    _____

    _____

7. Do you provide at least one opportunity for guided practice to each employee when they complete an SDL?

    _____

    _____

Exhibit 12.4. SDL Observation Checklist.

	Employee Is ABLE To	*Employee Is UNABLE To*

Ordering

1. Define the words "Order Point." ☐ ☐

   Answer: Order Point is the inventory level at which replenishment is needed.

2. List the steps to follow in preparing your section for ordering. ☐ ☐

   Answer: (1) Put away the previous week's order. (2) Check stockroom for overstock. (3) Check your section and straighten and face the merchandise. (4) Bring the overstock from the stockroom out to the shelves. (5) Check off-shelf displays.

3. Describe the purpose of the Store To Order Ad Product Listing. ☐ ☐

   Answer: Eleven weeks prior to an ad, your store receives a Store To Order Ad Product Listing that details all of the products that are going to be featured in an upcoming ad and the quantities that your store will either receive automatically or should order from outside vendors.

4. List the reasons you would need to override the Order Point System. ☐ ☐

   Answer: (1) You have several rainchecks to fill. (2) A customer requests a large quantity of a product. (3) You need more than normal quantities for an ad.

Photofinishing

1. State the three options for film processing at _____ . ☐ ☐

   Answer: 4″ Super Prints, Express Prints, Second Set Free

2. What is the purpose of the photofinishing invoice? ☐ ☐

   Answer: It lists returned orders by customer account number.

Exhibit 12.4. SDL Observation Checklist, Cont'd.

	Employee Is ABLE To	Employee Is UNABLE To
3. If a customer's order appears to be late, what three things should you do? *Answer: (1) Check to see if the film processing envelope has been misfiled. (2) Check the Log Book to see when the order was picked up. (3) Check the Log Book to see if the order was returned.*	☐	☐
4. Who is responsible for stocking the photo supply tubs? *Answer: Your photofinishing account representative.*	☐	☐
5. When completed photo orders are returned to your store by the film processor, where and how are they filed? *Answer: Completed orders are filed in the film box under the checkout counter in alphabetical order.*	☐	☐

cated they needed to learn? The best indicators of effectiveness are the user evaluations discussed in Chapter Five.

With this criterion, the two aspects of the evaluation process come together. The tools used to evaluate trainee effectiveness are used as part of the evaluation of process effectiveness. If you're content with the accuracy of your user evaluation methods, simple compilation of statistics will provide most of what you need to do for an effectiveness evaluation. How many mastered the material and how many did not is the main indicator. Systems where mastery is imperative may require a deeper look into the reasons behind your statistics, but you may already have this information if you evaluated the other four criteria properly.

In large distributed systems, there may be some question about the accuracy of the user evaluations, particularly the performance-based aspects. In these cases, a spot check of mastery is in order. This might take any form, from a formalized competency

An SDL Simulation

To evaluate your package, you decide that you need to consider sufficiency, usability, compliance, and effectiveness. You've already been getting some data during your impromptu site visits, but now you formalize the visits and make their evaluative purpose known. In discussions with trainees, you ask if there were other time management concepts they felt were important, or if there were areas that needed to be expanded on in the package. You also ask if they had difficulty using the package. In discussions with the supervisors, you ask for the same information from their perspective and ask the important question of whether they feel the package is effective in making better time managers out of the trainees. Finally, you gather statistics on how many trainees used the package and how many mastered the material, based on both the final test and the performances. You summarize your findings in a short report to management, suggesting that the data show SDL to be an effective and efficient training method and that you feel more packages—possibly an entire system of management SDL—are in order for your company.

test, to a questionnaire, to random meetings with users to check their knowledge and skills in specific subject areas. How deeply you want to get involved in this, or how statistically significant you want to make these random checks, will depend on how much you trust the basic user evaluation data. In a distributed system I developed, where we had no real control over the user evaluations, we felt it necessary to design a checklist. The staff and field trainers used this tool to randomly perfect spot checks of user mastery. Two examples can be found in Exhibit 12.4.

These system evaluation criteria, their basic questions, and their relations to ISD are summarized in Table 12.1.

Table 12.1. Evaluation System for Self-Directed Learning.

ISD phase	What's being evaluated?	What do we want to know?	Who can tell us?	How can they tell us?
Analysis	Sufficiency	Is all the information there?	1. Store managers who have gone through the SDLs. 2. Associates who have gone through SDLs and are regularly performing those tasks.	Paper and pencil Phone call Store visit
		Are there any SDL topics missing?	1. Store managers 2. District managers 3. Store operations	Paper and pencil Phone call Store visit
Design	Usability	Are the packages as easy to use as possible?	Store associates	Paper and pencil
Development	Currency	Is the information up to date?	Store operations	Phone call Meeting
Implementation	Compliance	Are the packages being used as expected?	1. Store associates 2. Store managers	Paper and pencil Observation
Evaluation	Effectiveness	Have the trainees mastered the objectives?	1. Store managers 2. Store associates	SDL Completion Record Observation by regional trainers Spot checks

In the Final Analysis

With the completion of your effectiveness study, you should now be able to answer the question that began this system evaluation, "Does the SDL system work?"—or in instructional design terms, "Did I make the right training design decision?"

I tried once to rank the five criteria, in order to shortcut obtaining this answer. I started with the thought that if the trainee didn't master the material (effectiveness), the answer to the question was no. Then I realized that if the material was not all there (sufficiency) or was not up to date (currency), it didn't matter what the trainees mastered. Usability and compliance are just as important, particularly if you are looking at the instructional design aspect of the question. The simple fact is, to perform a good system evaluation of SDL, you must consider—even if only informally—all five of the criteria. Only then can you say with certainty, "It works!"

Revision as an Aspect of Evaluation

One of the primary outcomes of evaluation is revision. In most organizations things change, often quite rapidly. You need to revise your SDL packages in a timely manner to keep up with the changes. We've discussed the importance of considering revision, particularly when choosing and formatting your media, so you already have a fair idea of its significance.

In the preceding evaluation methodology, the currency criterion is the one you might feel most closely relates to the idea of revision. However, on closer reflection, you will see the data from any of the evaluation criteria may create the need for revision. This is because there are two types of revisions normally performed for SDL packages: planned and as-needed.

As-Needed Revisions

As-needed revisions are what most people think of first when you bring up the subject of revision, and currency is the main reason why. One day you're sitting there wading through your in-basket and you notice that the systems department has bought a new mainframe. Now you will need to enter ALT C instead of ALT D to get into it. Big deal, you think. Then you remember that you have twelve packages in the field, all of which say to begin with ALT D. You have an as-needed revision.

You can't stop the process of as-needed revisions; in most situations, you won't even be able to control it. The best you can do is to keep in close contact with those people who may create a change that will necessitate an as-needed revision. This way, at least you can get a jump on it when it happens.

Planned Revisions

A more serious problem occurs when you need a revision and don't know about it. In our example, what would have happened if you weren't on the systems department's mailing list or if you missed the significance of the change to your SDL materials? *Planned revisions* are necessary to deal with this type of occurrence. If you're using an evaluation system like the one discussed in the last section, your mechanism for planned revision is already in place. It is based on the data obtained through the five evaluation criteria. A planned revision might occur if any one of the five criteria justify it, though currency is again the most likely reason.

A good rule of thumb for planning revisions is that there is no good rule of thumb for planning revisions. It depends totally on the material you're dealing with and the environment you're in. I've worked in a company where the changes that occurred in policy and procedure dictated a planned revision every six months for those packages that related to them. In the same company, we had some basic management SDL packages that were scheduled for revision every two years. Technical subjects need planned revisions more often, basic topics, less. Companies that are fast growing, or in crisis, will demand shorter revision cycles. Stable companies can use longer ones.

You need to decide what is best for each of your programs, then set a schedule and, most important, abide by the schedule. If you're in the middle of something big and a package comes up on the revision schedule, it's easy to say, "Well, that material hasn't changed, so let's just skip it until the next time." Don't!

The purpose of planned revisions is to find out if anything

has happened that you don't know about. If nothing did, that's fine, and your revision becomes simply a review with no changes made. But if something did change, and your SDL program doesn't reflect it now, it won't for another year. You've decreased its effectiveness and its usefulness in the eyes of those who matter most, your trainees. I've said it before, but it's of critical importance, so I'll reiterate it: *There is no one out there to make up for mistakes in your program, and so each package has to be as flawless as possible.* And part of keeping it as flawless as possible is a planned revision schedule that you follow religiously.

Sources of Revised Information

Once a revision has been indicated, there are two procedures you need to follow. The first is to get the correct information for the revision, and the second is to get your revised packages back out to the training sites. You can get revision information from your evaluation system or, particularly in an as-needed mode, through a variety of other sources such as memos, meetings, and so on.

Your best sources for correct revision information are your customers—that is, the people who initiated the writing of your SDL packages in the first place. Again, it is critical that you ask the right customers. As we discussed in the evaluation process, look for the people who know what is going on in their area. Open lines of communication with them. If you can, work out a relationship in which they feel a responsibility for the information in your SDL package. When a planned revision occurs, send them the package for their comments. If possible, start grooming them from the beginning as the subject matter experts who help you do the analysis and primary reviews. In return, they'll let you know if something changes that demands an as-needed revision. Over time, they'll develop a feeling of ownership of the material, which is exactly what you want.

Other sources of information include your facilitators, site implementors, and field trainers. If you don't use them as part of your evaluation system, be sure to keep in touch with them concerning revisions. Since these people continuously work with the subject matter, they'll have firsthand knowledge of areas that are out of date or that now contain erroneous information. They should be feeding you this information on a continual basis.

Who Should Perform a Revision?

There is some controversy as to who is best suited to actually perform a revision. One school of thought maintains that the original designer is the only one close enough to the material to do a revision efficiently. The other proposes that if you are going to revise, you should try to get some fresh ideas into your package. Thus, the original designer is the last person you'd want to use.

As usual, I think the answer is somewhere in between. Who does a revision depends on why the revision is being done. If it's simply a matter of currency, the original designer will be most efficient at adding, subtracting, or changing material. However, if usability or effectiveness is the problem, you might want to try a somewhat different approach from a new person.

A lot also depends on the abilities of your training group, the time they have, and the time you can afford in general to do revisions. There is no question that the original designer will do a revision more efficiently. Whether it will be more effective or not is the call of the person in charge. The key is to consider the alternatives and needs before assigning revision work. Too often the original designer is the choice by default; sometimes this person is not the best choice at all.

Controlling Revisions

When the content has been revised, the procedure for getting your package back to the training sites becomes paramount. Stories of SDL programs that have become ineffective because someone is using the wrong revision are legion. I've had it happen more than once myself. Consider using some type of revision tracking mechanism. For example, each of your programs should have a very visible revision number on it, preferably on the front or back cover of the print piece. Don't develop fancy codes or cryptic numbers. This process isn't for your use as much as for the people who are using your packages. "Revision 1" or the abbreviated form "Rev. 2," and possibly a date, will be more than adequate.

Now you need a way to inform your users of which revision is most current. In a learning center approach, your facilitator should find it easy to keep up on revisions. Even if you have several learning centers, this should not be much of a problem, since you will have a facilitator for each. However, it's still wise to periodically put out a revision list that details the current revision for each program.

If you are using a distributed approach, where you have programs at on-the-job training sites in various locations, such a list becomes mandatory. The period between lists should be short; I'd suggest three to six months as a limit. You also will need a person at the training site to be your checker. To formalize the process a bit, you can have the checker sign off on your revision list and return it to you. If you want to get even more formal, you can have the out-of-date packages returned to you. I encountered one system in which the procedure was for the coversheet from the print portion of the out-of-date package to be returned.

In the nuclear industry, correct revisions are so critical to the training process that some facilities have a department whose only job is to keep revisions up to date in the files and check to make sure there are no invalid copies in the plant. I'm not suggesting that you go quite that far. However, if you are going to put the time and energy into doing revisions properly, be sure you work out a mechanism to ensure that the correct revisions to your SDL packages are being used.

Other Revision Considerations

We've discussed the importance of planning media formats for efficient revision, so I won't go into this area again in detail. Don't forget to consider the difficulty of revising video, keeping print costs low in often-revised programs by holding down colors, and binding print materials in ways that relate to how often they will be revised as you make your design and development decisions.

Another revision argument, concerning whether to revise pieces or only whole packages, again depends on your preferences

Exhibit 12.5. Project Overview.

PROJECT OVERVIEW

Project Title: *Store Operations Self-Directed Learning System*

ISD Phase	Time Frame	Tools Developed/Results Achieved
ANALYSIS Conducted Organization Training Needs Assessment	4 months	Developed, assembled, packaged, and distributed the *Operating Policies and Procedures Manual*
Investigated Appropriate Instructional Delivery Systems	2 weeks	Chose self-directed learning as the instructional delivery system.
Conducted a Topic and a Job Analysis	6 weeks	Defined topics for the self-directed learning system.
DESIGN Designed the Store Operations Self-Directed Learning System • Trained Regional Trainers to become subject matter experts.	4 months 1 week	Conducted training workshop for Regional Trainers. Developed an implemented SDL package on *Writing Behavioral Objectives.*
• Designed content review process for initial drafts.	1 week	Developed and implemented the *Subject Matter Review Checklist.*
DEVELOPMENT Developed the 10 self-directed learning packages.	6 months	Assembled, packaged and distributed SDLs to 2,000 locations.
Designed the record-keeping system.	1 week	Developed and implemented the *SDL Completion Record.*
Designed the review and revision system.	2 weeks	Developed and implemented an annual SDL review schedule.
IMPLEMENTATION Prepared the Organization for the Implementation of the Store Operations Self-Directed Learning System	1 month	Introduced the concept of self-directed learning to the organization from upper management through store level by defining everyone's role in the implementation process with the following interventions.
• Introduced the concept of self-directed learning and prepared district management for implementation.	1 week	Developed and implemented the *District Manager Fact Sheet.*
• Introduced the concept of self-directed learning and prepared store management for implementation.	2 weeks	Developed and implemented the *SDL Package on Self-Directed Learning* for store managers. Developed and implemented the *SDL Implementation Checklist.*
• Introduce the concept of self-directed learning to all new hires.	Ongoing	Developed an SDL titled *Your Training and Orientation,* which is part of the New Hire Orientation Kit.
EVALUATION Designed a Formative Evaluation Process of the Store Operations Self-Directed Learning System • Evaluated sufficiency of SDL content and the accuracy of original topic and job analysis.	4 months	Developed and implemented the *SDL Evaluation Model* based on the ISD approach to training. Developed and implemented questionnaires for Store Managers, Store Associates, and District Managers.
• Evaluated usability of the SDL packages and the appropriateness of our selection of self-directed learning as our methodology.		Developed and implemented questionnaires for Store Managers, Store Associates, and District Managers.
• Evaluated compliance of the SDL packages and reviewed the implementation process.		Developed and implemented questionnaires for Store Managers, Store Associates, and District Managers.
• Evaluated the currency of the SDL packages and assessed our development process.		Held meetings with Store Operations personnel to review and revise materials. Conducted training class for Regional Trainers on how to review SDLs.
• Evaluated the effectiveness of the SDL packages and our training system through a formative evaluation process.		Developed an *Observation Checklist* for each SDL to determine if trainees had mastered the objectives. The direct observations were conducted in store, by our Regional Trainers.

and the particular needs of your system. However, this decision also affects processes like binding and media choices and development, so be sure that you consider all the ramifications before you decide.

In anticipation of revisions, you need to keep intact masters of all materials stored where no one can use them or take them accidentally. I've found that you also should be diligent in keeping a revision copy of everything handy. That way, when anyone thinks of something or finds out something that needs to go into the next revision, it can be recorded where the revisor can find it.

This is true not only for printed materials, but also for video scripts and storyboards, slide-tape programs, and computer materials as well. In a large SDL system, I'd suggest a file drawer that has revision copies of everything that you have in current use. I used such a system when I had a staff of four designers working on thirty different SDL packages, and it functioned quite well. Even when one of my designers left, we had all her thoughts on how to revise her materials where we could find them.

SDL is a training design, one that works best where it works best. If this statement once sounded facetious to you, it shouldn't any longer. You should now be able to assess whether the reason for which you were considering using SDL back when you picked up this book was a valid one. And if it was, you now know how to develop and implement SDL properly to produce the most cost-efficient and effective training program for your organization. To help you plan this process, Exhibit 12.5 gives you an overview of how one SDL project I was involved with was set up and the amount of time involved.

There is but one step left for you now as creator of SDL, and I wish you good luck as you put everything you've learned to use. If your training situation warrants, *do it*.

Exhibit 12.6. A Checklist for SDL.

System Evaluation and Revision

☐   Your system evaluation is based on how you designed your SDL.

☐   You can gather the right data to do a cost-benefit analysis if necessary.

☐   Your evaluation methodology considers how adequate your SDL materials are on both a package and a system level.
 •   You are asking the right questions of the right people.

☐   Your evaluation methodology considers how usable your materials are.
 •   You are asking the right questions of the right people.

☐   Your evaluation methodology ensures that your SDL is current.
 •   You are asking the right questions of the right people.
 •   You have considered the question of timing.

☐   You are checking on program compliance.
 •   You are asking and observing.

☐   You have evaluation measures in place that will give you data on package and system effectiveness.

☐   Using all your evaluative data, you are able to answer the question, "Does my SDL system work?"

☐   Using your evaluation reports, your company is able to answer the question, "Are we allocating our resources for training wisely?"

☐   You have developed a mechanism for analyzing your evaluation data to decide if you require as-needed revisions.

☐   You have a procedure in effect for doing planned revisions.

☐   You have implemented revision control procedures.

Glossary

Affective domain. The domain of human learning that involves emotion as well as interests, attitudes, and values.

Audiotape. One of the media that can support SDL. It is used less often than it should be.

Authoring language. The type of authoring system in which you must type commands to describe how you want your lesson to work.

Authoring system. A software program that enables you to create computer-based training lessons. Authoring systems can be languages or menu-driven systems.

Behavioral (performance) objective. A statement of the new capability the learner should possess at the completion of instruction. A formal, well-stated objective names the intended audience, then specifies (1) the performance or capability to be learned, (2) the conditions under which the performance is to be demonstrated, and (3) the criterion or standard of acceptable performance.

Branching. Allows the sequence of frames in a lesson to be changed during the lesson itself. Branching can occur because of the performance of the users (they get three questions wrong), or because the users decide to see something (they press a function key to see a glossary).

Chunking.   The process of dividing a portion of training material into smaller, easier-to-deal-with pieces.

Cognitive dissonance.   The incompatibility of a written or spoken message with the visuals that were developed to enhance the message.

Cognitive domain.   The domain of human learning involving intellectual skills, such as assimilation of information or knowledge.

Computer-based training (CBT).   A media design in which the computer is the method for disseminating the training material.

Criterion.   As part of a performance objective, the standard by which acceptable performance will be judged; may include a time limit, accuracy tolerance, proportion of correct responses required, and/or qualitative standards.

Criterion-referenced evaluation.   An evaluation methodology in which each question or performance is written from and can be related back to an objective in the learning process.

Digital scanner.   A machine that digitizes paper graphics or print materials and transfers the images into a computer for manipulation or inclusion in learning programs and other output.

Digital video interactive (DVI).   A media design characteristic in which a digital disk is added to the computer to expand its ability to use video, graphics, and sound as part of the training presentation.

Distributed implementation.   A self-directed learning implementation strategy in which there is no designated learning center. The packages are sent to the trainees' job locations and usually facilitated by a supervisor or other line individual.

Download.   Information is sent from a mainframe computer to a computer terminal. Some authoring systems store the CBT lesson on a mainframe and send information down to the terminal so that the users can take the lesson.

Education. Instruction that emphasizes far-transfer learning objectives; traditionally, knowledge-based instruction that is not tied to a specific job, as opposed to training.

Effectiveness. A measure of whether a procedure or action achieves its purpose.

Efficiency. A measure of the timeliness and affordability of an action.

Electronic mail (E-mail). A means of sending text messages to individuals or groups of individuals using a computer network. The sender inputs a message to the computer via a terminal, and the receiver also uses a terminal to read and respond to messages.

Environment analysis. The context of any instructional system, both where the instruction will occur and how the instructional materials will be used. In SDL, this includes format and implementation analysis.

Evaluation. The process of delineating, obtaining, and providing useful information for judging decision alternatives; the basis and methods by which data are collected and analyzed to revise and improve the overall operation of a training program or system.

Facsimile (fax). The communications process in which graphics and text documents are scanned, transmitted via a telephone line, and reconstructed by a receiver.

Filmstrip. A medium based on 35mm film. It displays a series of still frames one at a time. You can coordinate audio with the film. This medium is disappearing.

HVAC. Acronym for "heating, ventilation, and air conditioning systems."

Hypertext (and Hypermedia). Originally coined to describe vast databases of interconnected documents that can be browsed by moving from one document to another along meaningful links. Now used for any flexibly linked set of text (or other media) segments organized for easy, user-directed browsing. It involves nonlinear text. Imagine a computer screen with a word in bold. You click on the word and it "zooms in" to greater detail. Hypertext allows you to zoom in and zoom out of subjects and make connections between topics. Hypertext programs are useful for instruction and for information access.

Individualized instruction. A learning design in which each trainee works on materials without regard to what other trainees in the same class or facility are doing. Sometimes the learning is prescriptive; often it is self-paced.

Instructional design. The activity of planning and designing for instruction. Also, a discipline associated with the activity.

Instructional Systems Design (ISD). A formalized process for producing training materials that requires the steps of analysis, design, development, implementation, and evaluation.

Interactive video. Video images for instruction that can be controlled through the use of a computer by the learner. Video is supplied by either videocassette or videodisc.

Job aid. A device that an employee uses to perform reliably. May be simple or complex and is usually employed to increase the likelihood of highly skilled performance. Sometimes the employee may depend completely on the job aid for correct performance. The person needs less training to perform reliably. The best known example of a job aid is the pilot's checklist.

Job analysis. A process of arriving at a description of all the performance elements (tasks) that make up a job. Analysis is done by questionnaires, observations of performance, and interviews with incumbents and supervisors. May also be called *task analysis* or *skills analysis. Job analysis* usually designates the complete set of duties a person performs on the job, while task and skills analysis are subsets of the complete job analysis.

Learning center.   A designated facility, usually staffed by one or more facilitators, where trainees go to view self-directed learning packages.

Learning organization.   A company that teaches its employees the critical thinking process for understanding what they do and why they do it.

Lesson plan.   An outline of important points of a lesson arranged in the order in which they are to be presented, including (1) activities of the student and instructor, (2) specific points to be made, and (3) resources to be used and when and how to use them. The lesson plan should be detailed enough so that instructors with similar backgrounds can conduct the same course with a minimum of preparation.

Mainframe.   A large computer that usually has hundreds or thousands of computer terminals plugged into it. Information can be stored centrally and retrieved at any terminal.

Mastery learning.   A design characteristic in which the trainee is expected to achieve a preset level of mastery for the material to be learned. This mastery level is usually measured through a criterion-referenced evaluation.

Media.   All forms and channels used in the transmission of information; commonly refers to audiovisual materials.

Module.   A unit of instruction. An SDL package may be made up of a number of modules.

Multimedia.   Use of two or more instructional media together. Technically, examples should include slide-tape. This term has come to represent optical disk technology, usually encompassing digital audio and at times digital video.

Needs assessment. The collection of "real-world" data from groups and individuals involved in a specific training situation in order to determine if a training problem exists and, if so, its nature and degree of severity. It is a methodical process to delineate the problem as it really is and to determine if training would resolve it.

Objective. An intent communicated by a statement describing a proposed change in the learners—a statement of what the learners are to be like when they have successfully completed a learning experience.

Prescriptive learning. A learning design in which each learner is measured against a set group of skills and then assigned work based on this measurement. The learning may be individualized and/or self-paced.

Programmed instruction. A step-by-step way of learning a given topic. In recent years, it has become computer-based instruction.

Psychomotor skills domain. The category of human learning that involves manual and other physical action skills.

Return on Investment (ROI). A model that compares the ratio of outcomes to costs for a training approach.

Self-directed learning (SDL). A training design in which the trainees master packages of predetermined material, at their own pace, without the aid of an instructor.

Self-paced. A design characteristic where the learner works at his or her own speed to complete the learning assignment.

Student-centered learning. A design characteristic where objectives are written from the learner's point of view and activities are developed to relate more to the learner than the instructor.

Subject matter expert. An individual with specialist knowledge of a particular subject who is used to help analyze, write, or evaluate the training material for that topic.

Systems approach. A complex plan or strategy that logically accounts for goals, behavior, implementation strategies, and resources in an orderly fashion, for the purpose of eliminating or reducing problems associated with the training of learners.

Task. A set of skills performed to accomplish a specific objective; may also refer to a subset of a job.

Task analysis. The study of a job or task in order to determine its component parts, including knowledge and skills.

Training. Instruction that emphasizes job-specific, near-transfer learning objectives; traditionally skills-based instruction, as opposed to education.

VHS. Originally the Video Home System format for recording on a 1/2-in. videocassette. It is not compatible with the Beta 1/2-in. format.

Videodisc player. A video playback device that retrieves information from a prerecorded flat disc through the use of a laser stylus. Full-motion video segments or still frames can be retrieved in random order. It is often coupled with a computer for interactive instruction.

References

American Society for Training and Development. *How to Conduct a Cost-Benefit Analysis. Info-Line* Report No. 007. Alexandria, Va.: American Society for Training and Development, 1990.

Anderson, R., and Reynolds, A. *Selecting and Developing Media for Instruction.* (3rd ed.) New York: Van Nostrand Reinhold, 1992.

Boud, D., and Falchikov, N. "Quantitative Studies of Student Self-Assessment in Higher Education: A Critical Analysis of Findings." *Higher Education,* 1989, *18,* 529–549.

Dewey, F. J. *Experience and Education.* New York: Collier, 1938.

Even, M. J. "Adapting Cognitive Style Theory in Practice." *Lifelong Learning: The Adult Years,* 1982, *5*(5), 14–17.

Gagne, R., Briggs, L., and Wagner, W. *Principles of Instructional Design.* (3rd ed.) Troy, Mo.: Holt, Reinhart & Winston, 1988.

Hammond, M., and Collins, R. *Self-Directed Learning: Critical Practice.* New York: Nichols/GP, 1991.

Hiemstra, R., and Sisco, B. *Individualizing Instruction: Making Learning Personal, Empowering, and Successful.* San Francisco: Jossey-Bass, 1990.

Kearsley, G. *Costs, Benefits, and Productivity in Training Systems.* Reading, Mass.: Addison-Wesley, 1982.

Kirkpatrick, D. "Evaluation of Training Programs: Evidence vs. Proof." *Training and Development Journal,* 1977.

Knowles, M. K. *Self-Directed Learning.* Chicago: Follett, 1975.

Knowles, M. K. *The Modern Practice of Adult Education.* (Rev. ed.) New York: Cambridge University Press, 1980.

Leed, K. B., and Leed, J. R. *Building for Adult Learning.* Cincinnati, Ohio: LDA Publishing, 1987.

Loacker, G., and Doherty, A. "Self-Directed Undergraduate Study."

In M. S. Knowles and Associates, *Andragogy in Action: Applying Modern Principles of Adult Learning*. San Francisco: Jossey-Bass, 1984.

Long, H. "Changing Concepts of Self-Direction in Learning." In H. Long and Associates, *Advances in Research and Practice in Self-Directed Learning*. Norman: University of Oklahoma Press, 1990.

Mager, R. *Preparing Instructional Objectives*. (2nd ed.) Belmont, Calif.: Lake, 1984.

Mentzer, D. "The Effect of Response Mode upon the Achievement and Retention of Student-Nurses Taught Life-Science by Audio-Tutorial Instruction." Ann Arbor, Mich.: University Microfilms International, 1974.

Penland, P. "Self-Initiated Learning." *Adult Education*, 1979, *29*, 170–179.

Romiszowski, A. J. *Developing Auto-Instructional Materials*. London: Kogan Page, 1986.

Rowntree, D. *Teaching Through Self-Instruction*. London: Kogan Page, 1986.

Snow, R. E. "Aptitude, Learner Control, and Adaptive Instruction." *Educational Psychologist*, 1980, *15*, 151–158.

Suggested Readings

History of Self-Directed Learning

Bloom, B. S. "Learning for Mastery." *University of California Evaluation Comment*, 1968, *1*, 1–11.

Dewey, F. J. *Experience and Education*. New York: Collier, 1938.

Feeney, E. J. "Beat the High Cost of Training Through LCI." *Training and Development Journal*, 1981, *35*, 41–43.

Knowles, M. K. *Self-Directed Learning*. Chicago: Follett, 1975.

Knowles, M. K. "How Do You Get People to Be Self-Directed Learners?" *Training and Development Journal*, 1980a, *34*, 96–99.

Knowles, M. K. *The Modern Practice of Adult Education*. (Rev. ed.) New York: Cambridge University Press, 1980b.

Lumsdaine, A., and Glaser, R. *Teaching Machines and Program Learning: A Source Book*. Washington, D.C.: National Education Association, 1960.

Mentzer, D. "The Effect of Response Mode upon the Achievement and Retention of Student-Nurses Taught Life-Science by Audio-Tutorial Instruction." Ann Arbor, Mich.: University Microfilms International, 1974.

Postelthwait, S., Novak, J., and Murray, H. *The Audio-Tutorial Approach to Learning*. (3rd ed.) Minneapolis, Minn.: Burgess, 1972.

Stolovich, H. *Audiovisual Training Modules*. Englewood Cliffs, N.J.: Educational Technology Publications, 1978.

Williams, M. *Self-Guided Learning: What the Literature Says to Designers*. Washington, D.C.: National Society for Performance and Instruction, 1990.

Current Theories of Self-Directed Learning

Boud, D., and Falchikov, N. "Quantitative Studies of Student Self-Assessment in Higher Education: A Critical Analysis of Findings." *Higher Education,* 1989, *18,* 529–549.

Bynum, M., and Rosenblatt, N. "Self-Study: Boon or Bust?" *Training,* Nov. 1984, pp. 61–64.

Cox, J. H. "A New Look at Learner-Controlled Instruction." *Training and Development Journal,* 1982, *36,* 90–94.

Even, M. J. "Adapting Cognitive Style Theory in Practice." *Lifelong Learning: The Adult Years,* 1982, *5*(5), 14–17.

Hammond, M., and Collins, R. *Self-Directed Learning: Critical Practice.* New York: Nichols/GP, 1991.

Loacker, G., and Doherty, A. "Self-Directed Undergraduate Study." In M. S. Knowles and Associates, *Andragogy in Action: Applying Modern Principles of Adult Learning.* San Francisco: Jossey-Bass, 1984.

Long, H. "Truth Unguessed and Yet to Be Discovered." In H. Long and Associates, *Self-Directed Learning: Emerging Theory and Practice.* Norman: University of Oklahoma Press, 1989.

Long, H. "Changing Concepts of Self-Direction in Learning." In H. Long and Associates, *Advances in Research and Practice in Self-Directed Learning.* Norman: University of Oklahoma Press, 1990.

Penland, P. "Self-Initiated Learning." *Adult Education,* 1979, *29,* 170–179.

Riesman, D. *The Lonely Crowd: A Study of Changing American Culture.* New Haven, Conn.: Yale University Press, 1950.

Romiszowski, A. J. *Developing Auto-Instructional Materials.* London: Kogan Page, 1986.

Rowntree, D. Teaching Through Self-Instruction. London: Kogan Page, 1986.

Russell, J. D. *Modular Instruction: A Guide to the Design, Selection, Utilization, and Evaluation of Modular Materials.* Minneapolis, Minn.: Burgess, 1974.

Snow, R. E. "Aptitude, Learner Control, and Adaptive Instruction." *Educational Psychologist,* 1980, *15,* 151–158.

Young, D. "An Exploratory Study of the Relationship Between

Organizational Climate and Self-Directed Learning Among Organizational Managers." Unpublished doctoral dissertation, University of Missouri, 1986.

Current Practice in Self-Directed Learning

Hiemstra, R., and Sisco, B. *Individualizing Instruction: Making Learning Personal, Empowering, and Successful.* San Francisco: Jossey-Bass, 1990.

Honold, L. "The Power of Learning at Johnsonville Foods." *Training*, Apr. 1991, pp. 55–58.

Lusterman, S. Trends in Corporate Education and Training. New York: Conference Board, 1985.

Piskurich, G. "Individualized Media Instruction: A Dream Come True?" *Training and Development Journal*, 1983, *37*, 68–69.

Piskurich, G. "A Partially Centralized and Partially Decentralized Training System in a Health Care Setting." Ann Arbor, Mich.: University Microfilms International, 1985.

Piskurich, G. "Ensure Quality and Quality Training Through Self-Directed Learning." *Training and Development Journal*, 1991, *45*, 37–38.

Romiszowski, A. J., and DeHaas, J. "Computer-Mediated Communication for Instruction: Using E-Mail as a Seminar." *Educational Technology*, Oct. 1989.

Steinberg, E. R. *Teaching Computers to Teach.* Hillsdale, N.J.: Erlbaum, 1984.

Needs Assessment

Bucalo, J. "An Operational Approach to Training Needs Analysis." *Training and Development Journal*, 1984, *38*(12), 80–84.

Flagg, B. N. *Formative Evaluation for Educational Technologies.* Hillsdale, N.J.: Erlbaum, 1990.

Germany, P., and Von Bergen, C. "How to Determine the Training Needs of Your Supervisors—When They're Spread Across the Map." In L. Baird and others (eds.), *The Training and Development Sourcebook.* Amherst, Mass.: Human Resource Development Press, 1983.

Huff, J. O. "How to Determine What Course Design Will Be Most Effective." *Journal of Educational Technology Systems,* 1984–85, *13*(3), 227–232.

Lawson, T. E. *Formative Instructional Product Evaluation: Instruments and Strategies.* Englewood Cliffs, N.J.: Educational Technology Publications, 1973.

Rossett, A. *Training Needs Assessment.* Englewood Cliffs, N.J.: Educational Technology Publications, 1987.

Scott, D., and Deadrick, D. "The Nominal Group Technique: Applications for Training Needs Assessment." In L. Baird and others (eds.), *The Training and Development Sourcebook.* Amherst, Mass.: Human Resource Development Press, 1983.

Whitten, J. L., Bentley, L. D., and Barlow, V. M. *Systems Analysis and Design Models.* (2nd ed.) Homewood, Ill.: Irwin, 1989.

Zemke, R., and Kramlinger, T. *Figuring Things Out: A Trainer's Guide to Needs and Task Analysis.* Reading, Mass.: Addison-Wesley, 1982.

Job and Task Analysis

"Be a Better Job Analyst." *Info-Line,* American Society for Training and Development, 1989, "Be a Better Task Analyst." *Info-Line.* American Society for Training and Development, 1985.

Companion, M., and Teichner, W. *Application of Task Theory to Task Analysis.* Washington, D.C.: Air Force Office of Scientific Research, 1977.

Fine, S. A. "Functional Job Analysis: An Approach to a Technology for Manpower Planning." *Personnel Journal,* Nov. 1974, pp. 813–818.

Flanagan, J. C. "The Critical Incident Technique." *Psychological Bulletin,* July, 1954, pp. 327–358.

Harless, J. "Guide to Front End Analysis." Newman, Ga.: Harless Performance Guild, 1979.

Jonassen, D. H. "Performance Analysis." *Performance and Instruction,* 1989, *28*(4), 15–23.

McCormick, E. *Job Analysis: Methods and Applications.* New York: AMACOM, 1979.

Mager, R. F., and Pipe, P. *Analyzing Performance Problems.* (2nd ed.) Belmont, Calif.: Lake, 1984.

Mallory, W. "A Task-Analytic Approach to Specifying Technical Training Needs." *Training and Development Journal,* 1982, *36*(9), 66-73.

Utt, C. "Flow Process Charts: How They Help Determine Employee Training Needs." *Training,* Jan. 1982, pp. 21-22.

Zemke, R., and Kramlinger, T. *Figuring Things Out: A Trainer's Guide to Needs and Task Analysis.* Reading, Mass.: Addison-Wesley, 1982.

Instructional Systems Design (ISD)

Anderson, G. H., and Goodson, L. A. "A Comparative Analysis of Models of Instructional Design." *Journal of Instructional Development,* 1980, *3*(4), 2-16.

Banathy, B. H. *Instructional Systems.* Palo Alto, Calif.: Fearon, 1968.

Gagne, R., Briggs, L., and Wagner, W. *Principles of Instructional Design.* (3rd ed.) Troy, Mo.: Holt, Reinhart & Winston, 1988.

Grodvalh, E. C., and Lange, R. R. "Does Anyone Really Use Instructional Systems Design?" *Educational Technology,* 1989, *29*(11), 34-37.

Institute of Nuclear Power Operations. *Principles of Training System Design.* Atlanta, Ga.: Institute of Nuclear Power Operations, 1985.

Merrill, M. D., Li, Z., and Jones, M. K. "Limitations of First Generation Instructional Design." *Educational Technology,* 1990, *30*(1), 7-11.

Nervig, N. N. "Instructional Systems Development: A Reconstructed ISD Model." *Educational Technology,* 1990, *30*, 40-46.

Reigeluth, C. M. (ed.). *Instructional Design Theories and Models: An Overview of Their Current Status.* Hillsdale, N.J.: Erlbaum, 1983.

Rosenberg, M. J. "The ABCs of ISD (Instructional Systems Design)." *Training and Development Journal,* Sept. 1982, pp. 44-50.

Rossett, A. "What Your Professor Never Told You About the Mundane Practice of Instructional Design." *TechTrends*, 1987, *32*(1), 10–13.

Snelbecker, G. E. "Is Instructional Theory Alive and Well?" In C. M. Reigeluth (ed.), *Instructional Design Theories and Models: An Overview of Their Current Status*. Hillsdale, N.J.: Erlbaum, 1983.

Wilson, B. G., and Jonassen, D. H. "Automated Instructional Systems Design: A Review of Prototype Systems." *Journal of Artificial Intelligence in Education*, 1990–91, *2*(2), 17–30.

Objectives

Broadwell, M. "I Don't Teach Behavioral Objectives Anymore." *Training*, July 1988, pp. 33–34.

Carnarius, S. "A New Approach to Designing Training Programs." *Training and Development Journal*, 1981, *35*(2), 40–44.

Gronlund, N. *Stating Behavioral Objectives for Classroom Instruction*. London: Macmillan, 1970.

Heines, J. "Writing Objectives with Style." *Training*, July 1980, pp. 31–32.

Limon, L. "Speed Learning by Presenting Objectives in Teachable Parts." *Training*, Apr. 1980, pp. 29–30.

Mager, R. F. *Preparing Instructional Objectives*. (2nd ed.) Belmont, Calif.: Lake, 1984.

Martin, B. L., and Briggs, L. J. *The Affective and Cognitive Domains: Integration for Instruction and Research*. Englewood Cliffs, N.J.: Educational Technology Publications, 1986.

Stein, D. "Designing Performance-Oriented Training Programs." *Training and Development Journal*, 1981, *35*, 12–16.

Stepich, D. A., and Newby, T. J. "Teaching Concepts." *Performance and Instruction*, 1989, *28*(8), 47–48.

Stepich, D. A., and Newby, T. J. "Teaching Psychomotor Skills." *Performance and Instruction*, 1990a, *29*(4), 47–48.

Stepich, D. A., and Newby, T. J. "Teaching Verbal Information." *Performance and Instruction*, 1990b, *29*(2), 44–45.

Media

General Media

Allen, S. *A Manager's Guide to Audiovisuals*. New York: McGraw-Hill, 1979.

"Audio, Film, Video: Choose the Right Medium." *Info-Line*, American Society for Training and Development, Sept. 1985 (entire issue).

Brown, J., Lewis, R., and Harcleroad, F. *AV Instruction: Technology, Media, and Methods*. (6th ed.) New York: McGraw-Hill, 1982.

Heinich, R., Molenda, M., and Russell, J. *Instructional Media and the New Technologies of Instruction*. (3rd ed.) New York: Macmillan, 1989.

International Communications Industry Association. *The Equipment Directory of Audio-Visual, Computer, and Video Products*. (36th ed.) Fairfax, Va.: International Communications Industry Association, 1990.

Kemp, J., and Smellie, D. *Planning and Producing Audiovisual Materials*. (6th ed.) New York: HarperCollins, 1989.

Piskurich, G. (ed.). *Selected Readings on Instructional Technology*. Alexandria, Va.: American Society for Training and Development, 1987.

Reiser, R., and Gagne, M. *Selecting Media for Instruction*. Englewood Cliffs, N.J.: Educational Technology Publications, 1983.

Romiszowski, A. *The Selection and Use of Instructional Media*. New York: Nichols, 1987.

Sullivan, S., and Baker, B. *A Handbook of Operating Information and Simplified Maintenance Instructions for Commonly Used Audio-Visual Equipment*. (Rev. ed.) Huntsville, Tex.: KBS, 1982.

Print Materials

Adult Learning Satellite Service. *Edit by Design*. Six video programs, 60 min. each, PBS. Adult Learning Satellite Service, 1991.

BFA. *Art Elements: An Introduction.* 16mm film, 18 min. BFA, 1981.

BFA. *The Alphabet in Art.* 16mm film, 13 min. BFA, 1969.

British Broadcasting Corporation (BBC). *Communication Skills.* 16mm film, 25 min. London: BBC, 1983.

Burbank, L., and Pett, D. "Designing Printed Instructional Materials." *Performance and Instruction,* 1986, *25,* 5–9.

Davies, D. *The Telling Image: The Changing Balance Between Pictures and Words in a Technological Age.* New York: Oxford University Press, 1990.

Eastman Kodak Co. *Effective Visual Presentations.* Slide-tape program no. V10-10. Rochester, N.Y.: Eastman Kodak Co., 1980.

Eastman Kodak Co. *Legibility: Artwork to Screen.* Pamphlet no. S-24. Rochester, N.Y.: Eastman Kodak Co., 1981.

Hartley, J. *Designing Instructional Text.* (2nd ed.) London: Kogan Page, 1985.

Indiana University Audiovisual Center. *Designing Visuals That Communicate Series.* Four slide-tape programs. Bloomington: Indiana University Audiovisual Center, 1988.

Indiana University Audiovisual Center. *Lettering for Instructional Materials Series.* Five slide-tape programs. Bloomington: Indiana University Audiovisual Center, 1988.

Jonassen, D. H. (ed.). *The Technology of Text.* Englewood Cliffs, N.J.: Educational Technology Publications, 1985.

Tufte, E. R. *Envisioning Information.* Cheshire, Conn.: Graphics Press, 1990.

Slide-Tape Materials

Association for Educational Communications and Technology (ACET). *Producing Slide and Tape Presentations.* Washington, D.C.: AECT, 1980.

Clark, J. "Filmstrips: Versatility and Visual Impact." *Media and Methods,* Jan.–Feb. 1988, pp. 20–21.

Eastman Kodak Co. *Planning and Producing Slide Programs.* Pamphlet no. S-30. Rochester, N.Y.: Eastman Kodak Co., 1981a.

Eastman Kodak Co. *Slides with a Purpose.* Pamphlet no. V1-15. Rochester, N.Y.: Eastman Kodak Co., 1981b.

Farace, J. "10 Steps to Better Slide Shows." *Training*, July 1984, pp. 52–57.

Hendricson, W. A. "Beginner's Guide to Storyboarding." *Biomedical Communications*, Dec. 1983, pp. 25–29.

Professional Photographers of America. *Photomethods for the Complete Visual Communicator*. Des Plaines, Ill.: Professional Photographers of America, n.d.

Smith, J. "New and Tested Ways to Use Slides for Effective Training." *Training/HRD*, May 1982, pp. 41–49.

Smith, J. "Becoming Your Own Audio Producer." *Training/HRD*, July 1982, pp. 14–18.

Smith, J. "A Trainer's Picture Primer." *Training*, May 1983, pp. 60–64.

Scripting and Narrating

Bunch, J. "Designing Audio for Effective Listening." *Training and Development Journal*, 1982, *36*, 31–40.

Frye, R. *The Script Shop: Instructional Scriptwriter's Course*. Glenview, Ill.: Learning Shop, 1981.

Jacobs, A. "No Scriptwriting." *Training and Development Journal*, 1984, *38*, 69–70.

McCanna, M. "The Basic Techniques of Scriptwriting." *Biomedical Communications*, Oct. 1984, pp. 18–20.

Matrazzo, D. *The Corporate Scriptwriting Book*. Philadelphia: Media Concept Press, 1980.

Van Nostrand, W. *The Scriptwriter's Handbook*. White Plains, N.Y.: Knowledge Industry Publications, 1989.

Wilson, M. "Scripting for Instructional Television." *Technical Horizons in Education Journal*, May 1982, pp. 80–82.

Video

Carlberg, S. "Are Your Training Videos Real, or Really Bad?" *Training and Development Journal*, 1985, *39*, 62–63.

Cartwright, S. *Secrets of Successful Video Training*. White Plains, N.Y.: Knowledge Industry Publications, 1990.

Gayeski, D. *Corporate and Instructional Video Design and Production.* Englewood Cliffs, N.J.: Prentice Hall, 1983.

MCO. *Preparation of Artwork for Videotape Production.* 16mm film, 15 min. MCO, 1977.

Millerson, G. *Video Production Handbook.* Stoneham, Mass.: Focal, 1986.

Sambul, N. (ed.). *The Handbook of Private Television.* New York: McGraw-Hill, 1982.

Schleger, P. "Don't Sing the First Time Video Blues." *Training and Development Journal,* 1983, *37,* 59–61.

Smith, W. *Basic Video.* Fairfax, Va.: Development Associates, 1982.

Utz, P. *The Video User's Handbook.* Englewood Cliffs, N.J.: Prentice Hall, 1982.

The Video Register. White Plains, N.Y.: Knowledge Industry Publications, 1991.

Willard, T. "The Payoffs and Pitfalls of Video-Based Training." *Training and Development Journal,* 1984, *38,* 67–69.

Technology-Based Media

Computer-Based Training (CBT)

Alessi, S., and Trollip, S. *Computer-Based Instruction: Methods and Development.* Englewood Cliffs, N.J.: Prentice Hall, 1985.

Association for the Development of Computer-Based Instructional Systems (ACDIS). *Journal of Computer-Based Instruction.* (Quarterly.) ADCIS, 409 Miller Hall, Western Washington University, Bellingham, WA 98225.

CBT Authoring System Guide. Boston: Weingarten Publications, n.d.

CBT Horizons. (Monthly.) Weingarten Publications, Inc., 38 Chauncey St., Boston, MA 02111.

Computer Pictures for Creators and Producers of Graphics and Multimedia. White Plains, N.Y.: Montage Publishing, n.d.

Gery, G. *Making CBT Happen.* Boston: Weingarten Publications, 1987.

Gillespie, L., and Buck, J. *CBT Starter Kit.* Reston, V.A.: Longman-Crown, 1984.

Heines, J. *Screen Designs for Computer-Assisted Instruction.* Bedford, Mass.: Digital Press, 1984.

The International Directory of Performance Support Authoring Systems. Northboro, Mass.: Barry Raybould & Associates, n.d.

Kearsley, G. "Authoring Systems in Computer Based Education." *Communications of ACM,* 1982, *25*(7), 95–103.

Kearsley, G. *Training for Tomorrow: Distributed Learning Through Computer and Communications Technology.* Reading, Mass.: Addison-Wesley, 1985.

Reynolds, A. "A Computer-Based Learning Glossary for Human Resource Development Professionals." In *Computer-Based Training Today: A Guide to Research, Specialized Terms, and Publications in the Field.* Arlington, Va.: American Society for Training and Development, 1987.

Winblad, A. L., Edwards, S. D., and King, D. R. *Object-Oriented Software.* Reading, Mass.: Addison-Wesley, 1990.

HyperCard and Hypertext

Bevilacqua, A. "Hypertext: Behind the Hype." *American Libraries,* Feb. 1989, pp. 158–162.

DeVoto, J. *Techniques for Stack Development: Tricks of the Hyper-Talk Masters.* Indianapolis, Ind.: Hayden Books, 1989.

Goodman, D. *The Two Faces of HyperCard: The Information Age Classroom: Using the Computer as a Tool.* Irvine, Calif.: Franklin, Beedle, and Associates, 1988.

Goodman, D. *HyperCard 2.0.* New York: Bantam Books, 1991.

Haavind, R. "The Smart Tool for Information Overload." *Technology Review,* 1990, pp. 43–50.

Horn, R. *Mapping Hypertext.* Lexington, Mass.: Lexington Institute, 1989.

Jonassen, D. H. "Hypertext as Instructional Design." *Educational Technology Research and Development,* 1991, *39*, 83–92.

Kitze, C. "The Real Standards Issues (Do I Hear ISO-9661?)." *CD-ROM End User,* 1991, *2*(8/9), 22–24.

Wagner, R. "Hypermedia in Apple Computer, Inc.: The Apple II Guide." San Francisco: Author, 1990.

Interactive Video

Barr, S. "Optical Disc: The Press Is On." *Corporate Video Decisions,* Feb. 1990, pp. 40–47.
DeBloois, M. (ed.). *Videodisc/Microcomputer Courseware Design.* Englewood Cliffs, N.J.: Prentice Hall, 1982.
Gayeski, D. *Interactive Toolkit.* Ithaca, N.Y.: OmniCom Associates, 1987.
Gayeski, D., and Williams, D. V. "In Your Own Backyard." *Corporate Television,* Sept. 1987, pp. 39–43.
Gayeski, D., and Williams, D. V. "Videodisc and the "Teflon" Factor: Does It Stick?" *Videodisc Monitor,* June 1989, pp. 22–26.
Haynes, G. *Opening Minds: The Evolution of Videodiscs and Interactive Learning.* Dubuque, Iowa: Kendall/Hunt, 1989.
Miller, R. *Compatibility of Interactive Videodisc Systems.* Falls Church, Va.: Future Systems, 1987.
Reeves, T. C. "Research and Evaluation Models for the Study of Interactive Video." *Journal of Computer-Based Instruction, 13*(4), 102–106.
Reeves, T. C. "Redirecting Evaluation of Interactive Video: The Case for Complexity." *Studies in Education Evaluation,* 1990, *16,* 115–131.
Reeves, T. C. "Ten Commandments for the Evaluation of Interactive Multimedia in Higher Education." *Journal of Computing in Higher Education,* 1991, (2), 84–113.
Schwier, R. *Interactive Video.* Englewood Cliffs, N.J.: Educational Technology Publications, 1987.

Multimedia

CBT Directions Magazine. Weingarten Publications, Inc., 38 Chauncey St., Boston, MA 02111.
Gayeski, D. M. "The Desktop Trainer." *Training,* July 1989, pp. 34–37.
Geest, D. *CD-I: A Designer's Overview.* New York: McGraw-Hill, 1988.
Locatis, C., Charuhas, J., and Banvard, R. "Hypervideo." *Educational Technology: Research and Development,* 1990, *38,* 41–49.

Consultants

AV Market Place 1992—The Complete Business Directory of Audio, Audiovisual, Computer Systems, Film, Video, Programming. New York: Bowker, 1992.

Axline, L. "Hiring a Consultant? First Do Your Homework." *Personnel,* Nov.-Dec. 1981, pp. 39-43.

Bell, C., and Nadler, L. *The Client Consultant Handbook.* Houston: Gulf, 1979.

Berardo, D. "Consult Yourself Before Seeking a Consultant." *Computerworld,* Mar. 1982, p. 39.

Carson, C. "Use Consultants to Expand Your Staff and Resources." *Association Management,* June 1980, pp. 87-89.

Cothran, R. "Build or Buy?" *Training,* May 1987, pp. 83-85.

"Find the Right Consultant." *Info-Line,* American Society for Training and Development, 1986 (entire issue).

Gorovitz, E. "Consultants: The Buyer's Point of View." *Training and Development Journal,* 1983, *37,* 67-68.

"Make or Buy, How to Decide." *Info-Line,* American Society for Training and Development, 1988 (entire issue).

Nadler, L. *Developing Human Resources.* Houston, Tex.: Gulf, 1970.

Tartell, R. "What to Look for When You Buy Training." *Training and Development Journal,* 1987, *41,* 28-30.

Trainee Evaluation

Criterion-Referenced Test Questions

Berk, R. *Criterion-Referenced Measurement: The State of the Art.* Baltimore, Md.: Johns Hopkins University Press, 1980.

Berk, R. *A Guide to Criterion-Referenced Test Construction.* Baltimore, Md.: Johns Hopkins University Press, 1984.

Haertel, E. "Construct Validity and Criterion-Referenced Testing." *Review of Educational Research,* 1985, 23-46.

Shrock, S. A. *Criterion-Referenced Test Development: Technical and Legal Guidelines for Corporate Training.* Reading, Mass.: Addison-Wesley, 1989.

Swezey, R. *Individual Performance Assessment: An Approach to Criterion-Referenced Test Development*. Reston, Va.: Reston Publishing, 1981.

Test Question Development

Ahmann, J. *Multiple Choice Questions: A Close Look*. Princeton, N.J.: Educational Testing Service, 1963.

Brody, W. "A New Approach to Oral Testing." *Educational and Psychological Measurement, 7*.

Denova, C. *Test Construction for Training Evaluation*. New York: Van Nostrand Reinhold, 1979.

Ebel, R. "Can Teachers Write Good True-False Test Items?" *Journal of Educational Measurement*, Spring 1975.

Follman, J. "Relationship Between Objective Test Formats." *Educational Review*, February 1974.

Gronlund, N. E. *Constructing Achievement Tests*. (4th ed.) Englewood Cliffs, N.J.: Prentice Hall, 1988.

Hughes, H. "The Use of Complex Alternatives in Multiple Choice Items." *Educational and Psychological Measurement, 25*.

Performance Evaluation

Deming, B. S. *Evaluating Job-Related Training: A Guide for Training the Trainer*. Englewood Cliffs, N.J.: Prentice Hall, 1982.

"Measuring Attitudinal and Behavioral Change." *Info-Line*, American Society for Training and Development, 1991 (entire issue).

Morris, L. L., Fitz-Gibbon, C. T., and Lindheim, E. *How to Measure Performance and Use Tests*. Newbury Park, Calif.: Sage, 1987.

Robinson, D., and Robinson, J. "Breaking Barriers to Skill Transfer." *Training and Development Journal*, 1985, *39*, 82–83.

Siro, E. "Performance Tests and Objective Evaluation." *Industrial Arts and Vocational Education, 32*.

Learners and SDL

Gordon, J. "Learning How to Learn." *Training*, May 1990, pp. 51–62.

Howard, M. *Modeling a Training and Development System and Employee Motivation to Learn.* Norman: University of Oklahoma Press, 1985.

Knowles, M. *The Adult Learner: A Neglected Species.* Houston, Tex.: Gulf, 1978.

Knowles, M. *The Modern Practice of Adult Education: From Pedagogy to Andragogy.* Chicago: Follett, 1980.

Resnick, L. B. "Learning in School and Out." *Educational Researcher,* 1987, 13-20.

Ross, S. M., and Morrison, G. R. "Adapting Instruction to Learner Performance and Background Variables." In D. H. Jonassen (ed.), *Instructional Designs for Microcomputer Courseware.* Hillsdale, N.J.: Erlbaum, n.d.

Schank, R. C., and Jona, M. Y. "Empowering the Student: New Perspectives on the Design of Teaching Systems." *Journal of the Learning Sciences,* 1991, *1*(1), 7-35.

Developing and Operating Learning Facilities

Birren, F. *Light, Color, and Environment.* (Rev. ed.) New York: Von Nostrand Reinhold, 1982.

Eastman Kodak Co. *Index to Kodak Information.* Pamphlet no. L-5. Rochester, N.Y.: Eastman Kodak Co., 1991.

Finkel, C. "Six Common Errors in Facilities Design." *Training and Development Journal,* 1981, *35,* 6-7.

Finkel, C. "Where Learning Happens." *Training and Development Journal,* 1984, *38,* 32-36.

Gwynne, S. K. (ed.). *Guide for Planning Educational Facilities.* Columbus, Ohio: Council of Educational Facility Planners, International, 1976.

Hauf, H. D., Koppes, W. F., Green, A. C., and Gassman, M. C. "New Spaces for Learning. 'How to Create a Good Learning Environment.'" *Info-Line,* American Society for Training and Development, June 1985 (entire issue).

"How to Design Training Rooms." *Info-Line,* American Society for Training and Development, Dec. 1989 (entire issue).

King, W. (ed.). "Designing Facilities for New Technologies." *Media Management Journal,* 1986, *6* (entire issue 1).

Leed, K. B., and Leed, J. R. *Building for Adult Learning.* Cincinnati, Ohio: LDA Publishing, 1987.

Lightolier, Inc. "Incandescent Downlighting." Lightolier, Inc., 1981.

Reynolds, A. "The Computer-Based Learning Center." In W. R. Tracey (ed.), *Human Resource Management and Development Handbook.* New York: American Management Association, 1984.

Schmid, W. *Media Center Management: A Practical Guide.* New York: Hasting House, 1980.

Tuck, J. W. *Individualized Learning in the Information Age.* College Park: Center for Productivity and Quality of Working Life, University of Maryland, 1986.

Tuck, J. W. "Professional Development Through Learning-Centers." *Training and Development Journal,* 1988, *42,* 76–79.

Carrel Producers

Synsor Corporation. Woodinville, WA 98072 1-800-426-0193

Winsted Corporation, Minneapolis, MN 55438 1-800-447-2257

Program Evaluation

Brinkerhoff, R. O. (ed.). *Evaluating Training Programs in Business and Industry.* San Francisco: Jossey-Bass, 1989.

Caffarella, R. S. (R. Shelly). *Program Development and Evaluation Resource Book for Trainers.* New York: Wiley, 1988.

Grider, D. T., Capps, C. J., and Toombs, L. A. "Evaluating Evaluations." *Training and Development Journal,* 1988, *42*(11), 11–12.

Hawthorne, E. M. *Evaluating Employee Training Programs: A Research-Based Guide for Human Resources Managers.* New York: Quorum Books, 1987.

Kirkpatrick, D. L. "Techniques for Evaluating Training Programs." *Training and Development Journal,* 1959.

Kirkpatrick, D. L. "Evaluation of Training Programs: Evidence vs. Proof." *Training and Development Journal, 31,* 1977.

Merwin, S. J. *Effective Evaluation Strategies and Techniques: A*

Key to Successful Training. San Diego, Calif.: University Associates, 1986.

Phillips, J. J. *Handbook of Training Evaluation and Measurement Methods.* Houston, Tex.: Gulf, 1983.

Sanders, N. M. "Evaluation of Training by Trainers." In R. O. Brinkerhoff (ed.), *Evaluating Training Programs in Business and Industry.* San Francisco: Jossey-Bass, 1989.

Cost-Benefit Analysis and Return on Investment

American Society for Training and Development. "How to Conduct a Cost-Benefit Analysis." *Info-Line,* report no. 007, American Society for Training and Development, 1990 (entire issue).

Cascio, V. *Costing Human Resources: The Financial Impact of Behavior in Organizations.* New York: Van Nostrand Reinhold, 1982.

"Chargeback for Computer-Based Training." *Data Training.* Boston: Weingarten Publications, 1984.

Horrigan, J. "The Effects of Training on Turnover: A Cost Justification Model." *Training and Development Journal,* 1979, 3–7.

Kearsley, G. *Costs, Benefits, and Productivity in Training Systems.* Reading, Mass.: Addison-Wesley, 1982.

Kearsley, G. "Analyzing the Costs and Benefits of Training, Parts I–V." *Performance and Instruction Journal,* 1986, *25*(2, 3, 4, 5, 6).

Levin, H. *Cost-Effectiveness: A Primer.* Newbury Park, Calif.: Sage, 1983.

Sikorski, M., Niemiec, R., and Walberg, R. "The Bottom Line for Education and Training." *Performance Improvement Quarterly,* 1989, *2*(4), 42–50.

Spencer, L. *Calculating Human Resource Costs and Benefits.* New York: Wiley, 1986.

Swanson, R. A., and Gradous, D. B. *Forecasting Financial Benefits of Human Resource Development.* San Francisco: Jossey-Bass, 1988.

Thompson, M. *Benefit-Cost Analysis for Program Evaluation.* Newbury Park, Calif.: Sage, 1980.

Transfer of Training

Georgenson, D. "The Problem of Transfer Calls for Partnership." *Training and Development Journal*, 1982, *36*(10), 75–78.

Kelly, K. "A Primer on Transfer of Training." *Training and Development Journal*, 1982, *36*(11), 102–106.

McNamara, J. "Why Aren't They Doing What We Trained Them To Do?" In L. Baird (ed.), *The Training and Development Sourcebook*. Amherst, MA: Human Resource Development Press, 1983.

Robinson, D., and Robinson, J. "Breaking Barriers to Skill Transfer." *Training and Development Journal*, 1985, *39*(1), 82–83.

Professional Organizations

Some of these organizations may have a local chapter near you and a special interest group (SIG) that matches your needs.

American Society for Training and Development (ASTD), 1630 Duke Street, Alexandria, VA 22313 (703)683-8100

Association for Educational Communications and Technology (AECT), 1126 16th Street, NW, Washington, DC 20036 (202)466-4780

Association for the Development of Computer-Based Instructional Systems (ADCIS), Miller Hall, Room 409, Western Washington University, Bellingham, WA 98225 (206)676-2860

National Society for Performance and Instruction (NSPI), 1126 16th Street, NW, Suite 214, Washington, DC 20036 (202)861-0777

Society for Applied Learning Technology (SALT), 50 Culpepper Street, Warrenton, VA 22186 (703)347-0055

Index